INDEX ON CENSORSHIP

VOLUME 31 • NO 3 • JULY 2002 • ISSUE 204

WEBSITE NEWS UPDATED WEEKLY
WWW.INDEXONCENSORSHIP.ORG • CONTACT@INDEXONCENSORSHIP.ORG
TEL: 020 7278 2313 • FAX: 020 7278 1878

This issue of *Index* is published in collaboration with the Axial Writing research project (award no. L214252030), University of Wales, Swansea, under the Transnational Communities research programme of the Economic and Social Research Council (www.transcomm.ox.ac.uk)

CONTENTS

NO READMIITANCE

TALKING DIASPORAS

ONCE UPON A TIME, DIASPORIC LITERATURE WAS POLITICAL LITERATURE, OUR INTEREST IN IT FOCUSED, AS JOSEPH BRODSKY SAID, BY 'THE RISE OF TYRANNIES' AND OUR ENGAGEMENT IN THE COLD WAR. TODAY, THE COLLAPSE OF OLD POLITICAL CERTAINTIES HAS FUNDAMENTALLY ALTERED THE DEBATE OVER IMMIGRATION AND THE SIGNIFICANCE OF IMMIGRANT LITERATURE

Arrival of the SS Empire Windrush *from the West Indies in 1964. Credit: courtesy* Evening Standard

DIASPORA DIALOGUE

TOM CHEESMAN & MARIE GILLESPIE

Diaspora connotes the pain and loss of mass exile. The etymology, 'scattered seed', suggests immutable ties of history and heredity reaching back to a mythic place and time of origin.

In recent years, diaspora has acquired broader and more positive resonances, become a marketing term even. Bollywood movies target diaspora South Asians with scenes set in London or New York, and storylines that fetch westernised youth back to their spiritual home. 'Diaspora' is the title of this summer's Music Village Festival in London, featuring visiting and local musicians, and this year, London Arts Board ran a 'Diaspora City' writing competition.

In cultural studies, scholars like Stuart Hall and Paul Gilroy (*The Black Atlantic*) established the transnational African diaspora as a crucible of modern aesthetics and social thought. In migration studies, the diaspora concept has enabled researchers to jettison the binary model of 'sending and receiving countries', and the 'race relations' paradigm of migrants as 'guestworkers'. Recent research emphasises the triple connection of migrant populations to place of origin, place of settlement and larger diaspora: 'routes become more crucial than roots'.

The widening currency of the term diaspora is a symptom of globalisation. Globalising processes challenge nation states both from above – in the shape of supra-state organisations and transnational corporations – and from below, in the shape of grass-roots movements and networks, often taking diaspora forms. The events of 11 September were evidence of the security threat posed by transnational politico-religious networks. But the growing economic, political and socio-cultural significance of diasporas has long been clear. The global Chinese diaspora is the world's third-biggest economic entity; migrant workers' remittances to families back home, as well as in the form of local investment, dwarf official western aid budgets.

Nowadays, migrants can far more easily sustain close contact with kin and others back home and elsewhere thanks to improved communications and cheaper transport. Growing numbers participate in two or more societies at once, have multiple loyalties and citizenship rights. Axial writers – those who 'divide their time' between Karachi and Leicester, London and Bombay, or LA and Singapore – are highly visible examples of a new class of creative cosmopolitans (see Kamila Shamsie, p86). But, of course, their privileges are rare. Most ethnically based diaspora groups are severely disadvantaged, now more than ever in some contexts. Diasporas of wealthy graduates have little in common with diasporas of domestic workers, child sex workers, or asylum seekers.

'Diaspora' is used in a bewildering variety of ways, but three overlapping usages dominate recent research. Diaspora as social formation refers to the cross-border networks that migrants maintain: business, political, religious and philanthropic organisations, as well as informal networks. Diaspora consciousness identifies forms of the 'double consciousness' of WE DuBois, the sense of being neither 'home' nor 'away' anywhere, scarred by shared histories of genocide, slavery, colonialism and exploitation. Diaspora culture is created at the confluence of different traditions of thought and creativity, in narratives of plural and fluid identity, whether in hip hop or bhangra, Vikram Seth or Zadie Smith, or Meera Syal and Andrew Lloyd Webber's musical *Bombay Dreams*.

Globalisation foments fears of cultural homogenisation while 'diaspora chic', with its neatly packaged difference at arm's length, reassures metropolitan cosmopolitans. This is multiculturalism for global cultural tourists, an intercontinental aesthetic underpinned by consumerist ethics and neo-liberal politics. Commodified exoticism – ethnic otherness in cuisine, fashion, music, film and literature – effectively silences less easily consumable voices.

Britain's arts establishment mostly fails to recognise diaspora writers and artists living and working here. Their public consists of scattered fellow expats and, if political conditions allow, an audience 'back home'. Getting published can be difficult both 'home' and 'away'. For those whose vehicle is not English, finding a translator is still harder. The proportion of books published in English which are translations has fallen below 3 per cent, with scandalously few from non-European languages. Despite some small publishers' efforts, in a London where over 200 languages are spoken by schoolchildren, the literary world seems largely oblivious to local and global diversity. A thin line divides ignorance from censorship.

This volume juxtaposes voices from newer and older diasporas, ranging from well-established writers with homes and jobs in two continents, to writers uprooted, traumatised and destitute in London. Writers from post-communist Europe come into dialogue with South Asian, African, Chinese and Kurdish writers. Celebrated cosmopolitans vie for the reader's attention with previously unheard voices. Who is a political refugee, who an economic migrant, who was born into a diaspora? For a society dependent on migration – as all now are – diaspora writers of all kinds have much to say. ❑

Tom Cheesman *and* ***Marie Gillespie*** *directed the Axial Writing research project (award no. L214252030). He is senior lecturer in German at the University of Wales, Swansea; she is senior lecturer in sociology at the Open University*

POLITICS INTO ECONOMICS DON'T GO

AKASH KAPUR

Amid all the rhetoric over cultural homogeneity and collapsing welfare systems, it's easy to forget that the debate on immigration was once driven by geopolitical considerations. Today, the West's attitude to immigration is insular, expressed as a provincial fear of the outside world; but for much of the late twentieth century the politics of immigration was a window on to that world, a sign of the West's inextricable – if often misguided – engagement with lives and events beyond its borders. Refugees from behind the Iron Curtain were fleeing a tyranny that threatened us all. Immigrants from the former colonies, while received less enthusiastically, were none the less reminders of a common history, of imperial entanglements that were not so easily disentangled.

Perhaps inevitably, the literature produced by these immigrants was invested with an often obsfuscatory symbolism. A generation of writers who had little in common other than their non-westernness were conflated under the rubric of post-coloniality; authors as varied as Salman Rushdie, Derek Walcott and Chinua Achebe were grouped together, their wildly varying uses of the English language reduced to the slogan of 'empire writing back'. Writers from the communist world likewise became tokens of freedom and democracy. When, in 1980, the Polish poet Czeslaw Milosz was awarded the Nobel Prize, art was demoted to *témoignage*, Milosz's historical chronicling garnering at least as much attention as his metaphysical poetry.

Diasporic literature was political literature; in 1987, Joseph Brodsky, also a Nobel laureate and also an often reluctant ambassador for warring Cold War ideologies, made explicit the equation, telling an audience in Vienna that 'the current interest in the literature of exiles has to do, of course, with the rise of tyrannies.'

Today, Brodsky's remark seems positively quaint. The collapse of old political certainties has fundamentally altered the debate over immigration and, with it, the significance of immigrant literature. Abdulrazak Gurnah, himself an emigrant to England in the 1960s, captured some of this shifting landscape in his last book, *By the Sea*, a novel of multiple journeys and exiles. Latif Mahmud, one of Gurnah's narrators, follows a previously common trajectory, escaping on a communist scholarship from Africa to East Germany some time during the Cold War; he then jumps ship and escapes to England, where he is welcomed by a government eager to score propaganda points, sharing coffee and sandwiches with the harbour policeman who finds him. Decades later, Omar Saleh, Gurnah's primary narrator, flees imprisonment and torture in the same country as Mahmud, but receives an altogether less friendly reception in England: berated and humiliated by an immigration officer at Gatwick, he is locked up in an immigrant detention centre, enacting the sad prison-to-prison trajectory that has become the plight of so many refugees to the West today.

The irony of Saleh's reception is that he, much more so than Mahmud, who is clothed and fed by the East Germans, fits the bill of a political refugee. Now, however, the distant rumblings of African political upheaval no longer carry much significance in the West. Immigrants like Saleh are escaping local, not global, tyranny; the only thing they represent to the West is danger, a threat to cosy post-Cold-War prosperity. 'This asylum business . . . is really just looking for jobs and prosperity in Europe,' says the immigration officer, in disgust. 'There is nothing moral in it, just greed.' It's a self-righteous line we read every day in the tabloids, and it suggests the extent to which the political narratives of immigration have been replaced by economic narratives. It no longer really matters whether a refugee is friend or foe; ideological considerations are bit players in the drama of asylum, and today what really matters is whether an outsider is rich or poor, whether he will top up the state's coffers, or sponge off it. (Sometimes, of course, these economic considerations masquerade as cultural concerns. But it's telling that, in their attempts to solve the 'problem of immigration', European governments have been moving towards a North American system, in which doors are opened to immigrants with certain skills and income levels.)

Predictably, the new narratives of immigration have attached themselves to diasporic writing, filtering what the West reads, and how it reads it. Immigrant writers today tell us very little about politics or 'tyrannies'; they are emblems, rather, of a new economic order and, in particular, of a new cosmopolitan class that has emerged triumphant from that order. The rise of South Asian writing – probably the most flourishing and readily identifiable diasporic school of writing to have emerged post-1989 – is a prime example. Insofar as South Asian writers today do indeed constitute a diaspora, they do so not because they are exiles, banished from their homes, but because they possess the financial means and cultural vocabulary to have two homes. VS Naipaul has written that RK Narayan worked in a vacuum, without the comfort of history or literary tradition; much the same could be said of Naipaul's early struggle to find his voice, but one would be hard-pressed to say it of today's post-colonial authors, who confidently occupy a terrain charted by the rise of global capitalism and culture. Culture brokers rather than culturally marginal, they display none of the tortured relationship to home evident in the works of such writers as Naipaul and Walcott; nor is one likely to find the poignant sense of estrangement, of writing in a foreign language for a foreign audience, that populated the writings of disinherited communists such as Milosz and Brodsky.

The problem with the predominance of cosmopolitan diasporic writing does not lie in the familiar charge of inauthenticity: cultural heterogeneity is an undeniable post-colonial (and, indeed, western) reality, and multicultural literature is giving voice to a very real condition of our times. The problem, rather, is in the absence of that other diasporic voice, in the silencing of the men and women who arrive in Europe not safely buckled into their seats, but clinging frozen to the undercarriage of aeroplanes and trains, or suffocated in the backs of lorries and vans. If immigrants are today a window on to global economics rather than global politics, then the literature of immigration is a window only on to the sunny side of the new economic order – a happy (and, for the West, self-congratulatory) literature of Video Nights in Kathmandu and Global Souls that comforts with its false promises of converging living standards and common culture.

This silencing of the diasporic underclass may be unavoidable: literature is, after all, a luxury. Perhaps, too, an alternative literature may develop over time: immigrant populations take years, even decades, to form new communities and communal voices. But if such voices do develop, what story will they tell the West? As anthropologists know very well, all ethnography is a form of autobiography, the fascination of the genre lying as much in what it tells us about the other as it does about ourselves. In a marketplace where diasporic literature is still read (and certainly promoted) primarily as ethnography, it's not very clear what light tales of immigrant hardship can shed on the West's knowledge of itself. Cosmopolitan writers – and their so-called chutnified literatures – speak to the West of a world it understands, and of values it shares. The current interest in diasporic literature, we might say some 15 years after Brodsky, has to do with the (perceived) end of tyranny and the (once again perceived) rise of global democratic capitalism. This provinciality in reading tastes has much in common, of course, with the general insularity of western immigration policy – except that while the latter is motivated by fear (by the imperative of keeping out what Robert Kaplan has notoriously called 'the coming anarchy'), the former is motivated by an impulse far more banal: boredom, a lack of interest in anything that is not about ourselves.

It's possible that the events of 11 September may change some of this. Certainly the war on terrorism has reintroduced into our political lexicon the all-encompassing – and brutally simplifying – narrative previously provided by the Cold War. Literature from the Islamic world will never be read in the same way. Nor, post-Afghanistan, can those distant broken states ever seem quite so remote and tangential to the West again. It may be that out of this enforced banishment from insularity a more global (which is to say representative) diasporic literature will develop. But until then, the literature of emigrants continues to be a literature about ourselves, the diasporas we know only the diasporas we want to know. ❑

Akash Kapur *is contributing editor at* Transitions *magazine and Squadron Fellow in media law at Cardoso Law School, New York. He has written extensively in the press in the USA and the UK*

EUROPE: BEFORE AND AFTER IDEOLOGY

Polish Club in Sheffield: young members watching an entertainment. Credit: Tim Smith

THE MAIDEN AND THE PRIEST & OTHER POEMS

GYÔZÔ HATÁR

THE MAIDEN AND THE PRIEST

they walk like this in their untended place
the maiden and the priest for quite a while
two down-and-outs exchanging an embrace
and lissom-dead uniting in a smile

they only know the unsubstantial view
of walk-on-the-wall spirits – that dimension
where they are left alone the precious two
they're fond of staying in pseudo-pretension

of barely-being and greyness eternal
of being tuned to one wavelength of mood
of never picking up a book or journal
and studying a silent attitude

what's not rust-eaten is the prey of weeds
gamekeepers don't go wolfing in a rush
no pack no drive no view-halloo succeeds
but nature is in heat all cruel and lush

they live in a cocoon – their room's a mess –
they hold each other in a long embrace
the maiden and the priest as they caress
regard the other as their exit place

THE ÉMIGRÉ

last night it was internment prison cells
tomorrow brings expulsion somewhere else
I envy those who are obliged to stay!
it's not the old stork with the swaddling band
it's not the house the street and not the land:
it is the planet where I went astray

the other tramps will make their journey back
why was I made a white-pigmented black
whose smile and smell are strange and different
could I have risen from another source
where is the sea to end my river's course
the last song of a lost itinerant?

LET DOWN

why the moans the blues
and why the heavy sigh
my beloved muse
has left me high and dry

sorry old has-been
it is now dogrel time
let your poem lean
on the Zimmer-frame of rhyme ❑

Gyôzô Határ *was born in Hungary and came to the UK in 1956.* The Right to Sanity: A Victor Határ Reader *was published in 1994 (Corvina, Budapest)*

Translated by Peter Zollman

END OF HISTORY

EVALD FLISAR

The thing was not like anything that any of us had ever seen. Above all, it had no flat surface upon which we might rest it. From out of the central mass, which had neither a recognisable shape nor an evident function, there protruded on all sides, without order or symmetry, all kinds of steel, aluminium-like, and even wooden outgrowths. With some imagination, it was possible to discern among them the cubistically displaced shapes of a spade, a pick, a hoe, perhaps a sickle or a scythe, perhaps a rake and several other kinds of implements, although they were just the beginnings or ends of what they might have been. In between, in various conjunctions with other parts, it was possible to recognise the links of a chain, half of a cog-wheel, a toilet bowl, the distorted mechanism of a wall-clock, two weights and the blackened handle of a kitchen pan.

If all these extensions or fragments of something had at least been bound together by wire! Or welded into a whole! Then the whole thing could have been passed off as the fanciful imagining of a modernistic sculptor, and, by being shifted over to the domain of art, where all is possible and permitted, deprived of the aggressive point of inconceivable concreteness, before which we had clustered round like frail children.

Uncle Vinko, with a visible effort, collected himself and announced that we were going to dump this abortive joke by a drunken village blacksmith into a ditch, bury it and forget all about it. Peter was resolutely opposed to this: the thing might be an integral component of a spaceship, which had crash-landed somewhere nearby! And anyway, one should first of all examine any unknown thing, give it a name and a purpose, so that it should not at some later time surge up from our subconscious in the form of a neurosis. Vinko, however, stubbornly persisted in having his way. I think he would have hauled the thing away by himself, if mama had not turned up at that moment, having returned from her afternoon marathon (the morning run had been called off because of the showers). She came to a stop, examined the implement from all possible angles, pressing here, tugging there, and shaking it from left to right. Finally, with a voice all quivering with agitation, she ordered me to go and call father. Within five minutes, the whole family had gathered around the finding, including even Vladimir's wife, who had just then returned from one of her rendezvous.

We were all waiting to hear what father would say. For a long time he said nothing at all. When finally he did open his lips, he did not express a decisive opinion, but instead merely asked us what we thought of the thing.

Elizabeta said that before us was a '*machine infernale*', which under the cloak of darkness had been forged together by evil spirits in order to bring into our family conflict and confusion, and to drive us away, since it was more than evident that in this place we would find neither peace nor happiness. 'Nonsense,' mother burst out, 'we'll start talking about spirits only once the last – and that truly the last – attempt at rational explanation has failed.' However, since she herself was not able to find one, she fell into an embarrassed silence.

It very soon became evident that, in seeking for an answer to the conundrum that lay before us, we were not searching through the memorial archives of appropriate knowledge, but instead chiefly competing in imaginings. In this, the one who showed up best was Vladimir's wife, who attributed the origin of the object to a collision between a sports car and a tractor which was transporting agricultural implements: under the powerful impact, and following the explosion of fuel, it had all been scrunched together and agglutinated into something about which we were now needlessly giving ourselves grey hairs and wasting time which could be spent on pleasanter occupations (in her case, private calls in town, to one of which she promptly set off).

Vladimir announced that for him, as a scientific materialist, there were no secrets in this world to the bottom of which one could not come by the dialectical historical approach. All that was needed was to look into the past, to question the former owner and his predecessors, for the thing had not fallen from the sky, it had derived from somewhere, somebody had left it there or placed it there, somebody was involved, somebody was guilty. And it was necessary to determine who that was, for freedom is possible only when – for one and all alike, and even for insignificant trifles – the guilt has been justly apportioned.

Aunt Mara brought her easel and began painting the unknown object. She said that the thing had certainly fallen from the sky, although this did not seem to her essentially to matter. Everything on this earth was first of all an artistic challenge, then for a long time nothing, and only thereafter everything else.

'And you?' father turned towards me. Since I didn't want to create the impression that it was all the same to me, I hastily added the thought that – considering the wire and lead seals and clockworks in the centre – the thing was undoubtedly a bomb, after the detonation of which something had short-circuited, with the result that it had not *ex*ploded but *im*ploded, and collapsed inwards upon itself.

Peter said that the idea did not seem to him wholly stupid, although the cog mechanism at the centre was not that of a clock but of a shortwave radio. He fetched three batteries, thrust them one after the other into the little container at the centre of the mechanism, and the strange creature spluttered and began to emit a programme on which a man's voice in an unknown language – quite likely closest to Arabic – was screeching out some announcement or explanation.

With sagging hands and eyes we stood around the diabolical creature, listening to this voice which came from God-knows-where, perhaps from outer space, perhaps from the inner being of the object itself, or from our defeated imagination which, under the weight of the event, had agglutinated – just like the object before us – into a mass of uncertainty and unease. It had begun to rain; we draped the object in a canvas cover and went off to our rooms.

The renovation of the house had begun to flag; finally, it came to a halt. Peter began to neglect his studies, and in the end he chose not to take his final exams, and put them off for a year. The unknown object was lying in the middle of the orchard, in full view of all. It calmly withstood the heat, the downpours, the kicking and tugging, chemical analyses, photographic sessions, and above all the public interest, for our house had in a short time become a tourist attraction, both for domestic and for foreign visitors. One American had offered father a quarter of a million dollars for the mysterious object. Father replied that he could have it for free – if he could first tell him what the object was, where it had come from, and what use it had. In the end, the attention of inquisitive visitors and journalists began to stifle us; around the house and the orchard we built a high wall with a sturdy lock set into iron gates. From then on, mama ran around the house, doing about two hundred circuits a day. Every few minutes, her shadow would flash past all our windows – except for those of father, who had his room on the first floor.

Although father would not have noticed her anyway, even if she had flapped on wings past his window. He was up to his neck in his studies of machine engineering, chemistry, agronomy, physics and similar sciences. Some of the books he had borrowed from Peter, while others he had picked up from libraries and bookshops, and brought them home in the van. He was becoming ever more desiccated; his eyes glowed as if from within, slowly but surely, he was being consumed by a hellish flame. Cousin Vladimir's method likewise did not bear fruit: although he had actually compiled an account of the history of the house and its former owners, not even the last of these, from whom we had purchased the house, was able to recall ever having seen that object in the shed. He himself had also dumped some outworn stuff into the shack, but most of the things had been there since time immemorial.

After a few months, the search for an answer was being carried on only by father and Peter; the rest of us had grown weary of it, and gradually went back to our old habits and occupations. The secret had become troublesome, even somewhat laughable, particularly when late at night we could observe through the windows how father and Peter, in the midst of the orchard, were measuring by torchlight the distances and angles between the parts of the implement, and noting it all down; and then when from the rooms above us we had to listen till the early hours of the morning to their noisy debating and quarrelling. One day, mama, in front of everyone, begged father to give up this behaviour which was leading nowhere but into ruin; to do so, if not for his own sake then on account of his son, a student who had been a star at the university, yet was now on the point of becoming deranged. 'I beg you,' she said, 'I beg both of you in the name of the family – stop!'

Peter said nothing. Father, however, for the first time in a long while, addressed the family much in the way he had liked to do at the times before the mysterious object appeared. He said that the family had not been visited by misfortune, as some of us thought. Quite the opposite. Everything in this world had its sense and its answer: no thing, whether created by God or by man, was without a source. And if we set God aside, we are still left with evolution, the quantum theory and the theory of chaos: these theories, too, do not allow for the possibility that anything could have come from nowhere, could have found itself somewhere without reason, and without use to anyone.

'Let's look the truth in the eyes: we are a family which, under the stress of civilisation, has taken the wrong road and, in fear of the ultimate derailment, has returned to the countryside to seek out its roots. And in them fresh blood, energy for the new life-drive. Although it is more than evident that trust in flight is an illusion. Whatever direction you choose, everywhere you come up against the sphinx, which will not let you go ahead. Frequently, the sphinx itself is a conundrum which you must resolve if you do not want to be stuck to the place, or to flee back to from where you have already fled. In our family we have always been fleeing: from poverty to the town, from town poverty to America, from the foreign world back home, from disillusionment into alcohol, from alcohol into therapy, from the exertions of the healthy life into mysticism, and from there back towards faith in the omnipotence of Reason. Over the past three hundred years nobody in our family has even dared to confront that great, central obstacle on the way, the Conundrum, which can be neither bypassed nor overleapt. Now has come the moment of decision for us as well. Are we to flee, or are we to grapple with the challenge which lies before us?'

With these words, father turned away and went off to his room; he had not even touched the food on his plate. Wordlessly, mother began to wail. Heavy tears softly dropped on to the pieces of cauliflower which she had absently placed in her mouth. Peter attempted to add something more, perhaps to explain what father had left unsaid, or had not explained understandably enough; or so it seemed to me, for his eyes rested on each of us as though he were seeking encouragement and the assurance that we would understand the words which he intended to utter – but which, after facing our lacklustre eyes, he simply could not get out of him.

Father and Peter began inviting 'experts' into the house. They drank a fair amount of wine, and uttered a great many words. One of them, using Peter's computer, devised a special program to analyse the shapes and relations between the parts of the implement. It was he himself who was most surprised by the result: following each attempt, there appeared to him on the screen the message 'object of unknown origin', as we had already known. Shortly afterwards, a farmer from some village at the other end of the country wrote to father to say that this was not a mysterious implement – as might have been judged from the photograph in the paper – but nothing more or less than a plough. Without even waiting for a reply, the farmer three days later pitched up at the doorstep, excusing himself by saying that the matter would give him no peace: if we had a field somewhere that needed ploughing he would quickly show us that sound farmer's common sense could solve any mystery.

The field and the ox he borrowed from the closest neighbour, who also helped us to heave the implement over the hill and down, and to attach the ox-yoke to the two extrusions, one of which was reminiscent of part of a spade and the other of a chain link. Then, with his left hand, the farmer seized the extrusion which resembled a hoe, and with his right hand the handle of the kitchen pan, turned the implement over in such a way that the wavy blade was pressed against the ground, cracked the whip, and the ox pulled and the blade furrowed. Behind the implement there remained deep, beautifully even furrows. 'Plough,' the farmer repeated, after he had ploughed the field to the end. However, the radio at the centre of the plough was still, even during the ploughing, emitting the shortwave programme which had not changed since we first heard it: a male voice, ever the same, was somewhat gruffly and didactically announcing, preaching or expounding something. Father asked the farmer if the radio didn't disturb him while ploughing. The farmer replied that he would have preferred some lively folk-dance tune, and then – embarrassed and none too satisfied with himself – took his leave. ❏

Stane Jagodic, Pasion*: 'Christ nailed to the cross of human technology'*

***Evald Flisar** is a Slovenian writer who first came to London in 1975 and has been commuting between Slovenia and England ever since. He has travelled in over 80 countries, mostly in the third world, and is the author of some highly praised travel books,* The Sorcerer's Apprentice*, six other novels and a number of plays for radio and theatre.* Tomorrow*, initially broadcast as a radio play by* BBC Radio Three*, has been described as 'a brilliant absurdist comedy showing the birth of the postmodern society'*

Translated by Alan McConnell-Duff

INSTEAD OF A CV

PREDRAG FINCI

Dear Sir/Madam

I was born somewhere sometimes and am still alive and kicking. Only 20 I was when I left my parents' home, found small room in mahala and dreamed never to leave my home town. Then, it all happened . . . I am partly dyslectic and my glasses don't help me a lot, probably because they were made in my communist homeland and with them I can see only the bright future. Yes, I was born under the red, red star. And wandering a lot. Compared to my mother-in-law I was lucky. She hardly ever travelled, but her house was in Austria-Hungary, Kingdom of Yugoslavia, Independent State of Croatia, Socialistic Republic of Yugoslavia, Serb Republic and now settled in Bosnia. After the war had broken out I received an invitation from a London university – more a sign of solidarity than academic honour – to be their guest (fellow) for one semester, but I had a feeling that I was going to stay in the UK for much, much longer. I used to travel to many countries; I did not buy much so I had no reason to fear the customs. But then I felt a bit uneasy: a smuggler who is smuggling himself. After a while I started looking for a job. In a local Jobcentre they didn't need philosophers, except those of pizza-delivery orientation. I was also thinking – because of Voltaire and Wittgenstein from different reasons – to turn to gardening or to become a night porter, but it surely wasn't my vocation. So, I ended up at a university once again. C'est la vie. I didn't like school, languages especially. All my life I spent in different schools as a pupil, student, assistant, lecturer, professor. I never was eager to travel but I travelled a lot and learned several languages (I speak my Bonglish fluently now). I never liked a so-called 'warm current' in philosophy and I became one of the sort. Now I sometimes work with the army, surely because I am a pacifist. Temporary I was in different countries, temporary a refugee, temporary a visiting fellow at universities. Temporary, temporary, temporary . . . Luckily enough, life is temporary too. Or so I hope. References: two people whom I talk about more often than anyone else, although in permanent dispute with them, are Plato and Nietzsche, but they can't provide me with any letter of recommendation. At least, not for the time being. Monsieur Descartes is not of relevance in this matter, for my dictum is: 'I am not, therefore I think.' As you certainly know, philosophising is a lonely job. My loneliness is a combination of my individualism and the influence of cheap westerns. As an essayist of successfully unpublished books, a private in a philosophical army with inclination to desertion, a poet of a long, unwritten poem which is hidden in my essays, a writer who sometimes believes that he would end his days in one of his texts (although aware of the fact that the last text wouldn't be written by me but by my doctor), all my adult life I was interested in three questions only (of Being, Aesthetics and God), questions I am thinking of not only on my Philosophishe Weg from my flat to Tesco's but which came to me even in my dreams, and now, after 30 years of reflection I finally understood those questions. And I hope against hope to find an answer, risking not to get any, but why stop now when I am losing in the game in which there is no winner or loser . . .

Sincerely yours
Finci from Finchley

PS As I already mentioned in so many words, of all my other interests film is possibly the greatest. Some of my favourites, like *The Third Man*, I saw more than 100 times and watched it even during turbulent time, when I dreamed to wake up by a cuckoo clock, rather than by the cannonades of ever-promised-and-never-to-materialise Renaissance. The other day I saw Hitchcock's *Vertigo* again. I saw the film for the first time more than 30 years ago, and afterwards, I was pondering on reincarnation for nights on end ('Do you believe that someone from the past, someone dead, can take possessions of a living being?'), thought about obsessive love and its unavoidable fate ('It's too late'), about real and imaginary, about double image of love embodied in one person. Under my eyelids crept a necrophiliac appearance of Judy (Kim Novak), my eyes opened in fear from the dark hiatus of the grave towards which the betrayed idealist Scotty Ferguson (James Stewart) was plunging. Several years later, *Vertigo* again. Again I was bewildered. *Vertigo* is basically a true metaphysical film, because the principal character is the picture of long-time tragically gone Carlotta, the picture of the person that Madelaine (again Kim Novak) is 'identifying' with, so the main character in the film is the phantom of

the past, the reality of the person who exists in her absence. When I watched the film the other day I did not think of Kim Novak, but of Jimmy Stewart, about the film's ending: the betrayed idealist overcame the fear of heights, was staring down the abyss into which his love had just fell; he was staggering on the edge but he was not going to throw himself into it, and he could not go back either . . . Or, how about Spielberg. Which of his film quotes do I prefer now? One of the Ukrainian Jewish émigré mouse who sings on his way to the US 'No cats in America', or the other one, 'ET phone Home'? My home? I clearly remember my first lesson of English. I still see it (present simple) or am seeing it (continuous). And it is only Monday today. ❑

Predrag Finci is a member of Bosnian PEN, the author of six books and was a professor of aesthetics in Sarajevo (Bosnia-Herzegovina). He has lived in the UK since 1993. Since 1999 he has been working on his new project at University College London

Background: James Stewart in Hitchcock's Vertigo.
Credit: BFI / Universal Pictures

TAKE A MAN LIKE ME

MIRZA FEHIMOVIC

THE TWO of them were having a fight, and I didn't want to get involved. I left the room and went out.

There was no one in the street. The wind that had got up in the night was still blowing. Then I saw him. As I was turning into the park the man propped up his back against the rear support of the bench and looked in my direction. Yes, I think he did that . . .

Early mornings in December are often damp and misty; hard to make out someone's features from a distance. But this was a clear, windy morning, no mist at all. And yet I can hardly say I saw him clearly. It was still dark. Maybe too dark for a walk. In spite of that I . . . Not that I'd seen the man before, I mean. Not that I recognised him as someone I already knew. I just realised who he was, even though he wasn't wrapped up in a blanket. A refugee he was. A refugee, in short.

That's what I was about to tell my wife later on our way to Hendon Central tube station. She was talking all the way to the station and wouldn't let me get a word in. I tried to interrupt three times, but my wife talked nineteen to the dozen and then, all of a sudden, hushed. Then she started to cry on our way to Hendon Central tube station.

My wife complained about Hasan. The moment I left the room she was having a row with Sara. I asked her not to weep. Benjamin gets upset easily whenever he sees his mother crying. Benjamin is six. And Hasan, I thought, shouldn't be dragged into it. He had nothing to do with whatever Sara and my wife quarrelled about. Sara is Hasan's wife. And my wife kept on mentioning him unjustly. Perhaps she knew it wasn't fair. That's why, I think, she started crying. But my suppositions can't always be right, can they?

I watched her weeping. I mean, she was crying bitterly and still walking fast, even getting ahead of me for a moment. Benjamin was doing his best to keep up with her. I easily drew level with them since my strides are much longer. My wife's a good walker, but not a match for me in that department. In my imagination I'd never associate her with infantry. Only with the tank crew. She's energetic, but rather short, and it's common knowledge that the short ones fit more easily into the small body of a tank. They cannot keep up the pace while marching, but have tremendous advantages in other respects.

Now I'm not saying my wife's not feminine enough. Far from it. One cannot possibly come across a soldier in a belted raincoat weeping on a huge tank as she holds her son's hand, her hair slightly dishevelled. No, one can't . . .

And generally, my wife's very feminine indeed. And her manners are always ladylike, as they say in English. It's just that she's a real fighter and her build suggests she'd be happier in some kind of armoured vehicle than in an infantry rank.

SO THERE he was, sitting on that rickety old bench. The bench, to be honest, was not rickety at all. Just old and shabby. Perhaps he was rickety, though it didn't show. Perhaps my English is rickety, and it does show. The bench was in good condition though covered with large patches of lichen and moss. If moss means the green soft cover we usually find on wet surfaces.

He was sitting there, but I imagined him running. That's what I told my wife. She remained silent, just trying to make both Benjamin and herself warm and comfortable. When I say Benjamin I mean Benyamin; that's how we pronounce the name.

As if getting ready for a long trip, he snuggled up to his mother and quickly drowsed off. I thought my wife felt like doing the same. I glanced at her. She didn't look back at me. I knew she didn't like the Underground.

The man was there, sitting, but I imagined him running, running faster than a greyhound. If by reading this you can conceive of that world-famous breed, the dog of fascinating stamina and endurance that can run at any speed you can think of. If I should use stamina and endurance one after the other. If I should end the sentence with a preposition. If by writing all this I'm not boring the pants off you.

Now how can anyone tell a war refugee from the rest without having talked to him or asked to see his documents?

Before I went out I glanced in the mirror. I saw a familiar figure wearing very familiar clothes. And the man on the bench looked exactly like myself. That's what I said to my wife. My wife's name is Marta. Marta is Martha in Bosnian. With a long, rising stress on the first syllable.

The closer I got the more he reminded me of myself. And the clothes: they were different from mine, though he, too, looked more or less like a hero from a children's TV programme. A yellowish, army-style jacket almost worn through at the elbows, blue jeans and bright red shoes. Although very colourful in such an attire, he'd already assumed the peculiar look that misfits usually have; those that didn't change their clothes. I think Marta would have butted in with this remark had she felt like saying anything.

Though he was sitting there motionless, probably for ages, the man gave the puzzling impression of someone always on the move. As if covered with fine dust that was to stay there for ever. Was that a way of coping with the surroundings? What do you mean, a way? What dust and surroundings?! The colours of his clothes didn't match any of the colours I was able to see around. Or maybe they did? I don't know. He was of my breed, I felt, and I was of his, and that's what I told Marta on the train to East Croydon.

I PROCEEDED with my walk and when I had almost reached the bench I was sure. We were two of a kind. Though he looked as if he'd already done something I had yet to do.

'So what are you up to?'

That was what he asked in my mother tongue. As if he'd known me for ages. It didn't take me by surprise, though. He gave a smile, too. If by the word smile the English mean slightly tearing your lips apart so that your teeth show.

From the start we talked like two old mates – well, long-standing friends? acquaintances maybe? That's what I pointed out to my wife while we were getting off at East Croydon station. It was raining at the time. She just took the umbrella from her bag and started off down the platform without so much as clearing her throat. Benjamin was stringing along behind her and I paused for a moment, wondering if Marta was angry with me for some reason. She wasn't. She was still quarrelling silently with Sara. Sara didn't get along with Sonja, her daughter. And Sonja had run away from home again. It could be that Marta took Sonja's side.

The man put aside whatever he was holding under his arm and stretched his arms as if ready to go.

'So what are you up to?' he repeated.

'I'm going to register with the Home Office,' I said as if the question came from someone I knew.

The wind was calming down, it seemed, and a pleasant silence was taking over. But there was no change in the heavily overcast sky. It was grey and low. In spite of which you could make out a children's playground in the distance, a tennis court next to it and an expanse further away that was once, I think, a cricket pitch. The park was completely deserted; a vast, gloomy space intersected by paths leading in various directions.

'Have you done that already? The Home Office, I mean.'

'Yep. Social Security too,' he said after some time. 'But charity begins . . .' he paused, waiting for me, I guess, to fill in the blank. 'At the Home Office,' he sighed.

It seems strange I didn't try to avoid the conversation, shy away completely from questions such as: Why should a refugee be so ready to talk? A civil war means one's enemies can only be one's own people, speaking one's language. You would meet them on a battlefield as well as abroad; and, above all, gradually, suddenly even, you would become suspicious of all the blokes you might run into.

I had one more look at him. He was well built, fit to carry all sorts of things I myself wouldn't be able to. Fleetingly, I thought of my brother. I mentioned it to Marta. She said we ought to write to him. There was no war in the States and we had his address . . .

Anyway, he was like my brother: tall, muscular, stalwart . . . I tried to imagine him carrying a bazooka. It worked!

Then I tried to think of him fighting in the open field and he performed convincingly enough.

Then I tried to picture him jumping out from behind a bush, attacking and withdrawing; he fitted the role of a guerrilla perfectly.

But you didn't have to imagine him carrying a bazooka or anything of the sort. Come to think of it, he himself was terrifying enough, and I don't think anybody would want to face him in a fight.

And then, I thought . . . Yes, I thought his face was too sad for a guerrilla's, wasn't it? And his colourful clothes matched his face even less than the surroundings, didn't they? And if there was anything that proved he was a refugee rather than a guerrilla-fighter-lost-his-way it was the sadness and loneliness that hung about him. So I tried to draw Marta's attention to it while waiting in one of the rooms at the Home Office. She wasn't listening.

It started to drizzle. The man took whatever he'd put aside on the bench, stuck it into his pocket and continued to gaze at the trees in the distance. He didn't feel like talking and I didn't feel like making a move. He looked downhearted, as if he'd given up on everything.

Then, from the distance and accompanied by two young Dalmatians, a smartly dressed man popped up. The dogs were running around, their spotted coats the most cheerful sight in the entire park.

They ran over to us and sniffed at the bench, wagging their tails. The man on the bench started to play with one of the dogs. The other one returned to his master.

'An awful day,' muttered the gentleman passing us by briskly. 'Just miserable.'

I was in two minds whether to respond or not. What could I possibly have to say, and in English at that?

'Have you just said a day, my dear?' My acquaintance didn't hesitate, eyeing me as if seeking my approval. The man was already too far away to answer. Not that he'd have bothered anyway. Not that my acquaintance needed his answer.

'A century! A century, if you don't mind,' continued the man on the bench as he rose to his feet, and I realised what it was that distinguished him from my humble self.

Yes, he was built like my brother and, to be honest, just like myself. He was tall, broad-shouldered: it was obvious we were from the same stock. He had Slav features. He, too, was almost bald. He was a refugee. But he was fluent in English and everybody except me could see that even from a distance. ❑

***Mirza Fehimovic** comes from Sarajevo, Bosnia-Herzegovina, where he was a freelance journalist and translator. He taught Serbo-Croat in the University of Delhi for three years and has published collections of poetry and fiction. This excerpt is from his novel* Seventeen lady-teachers and a professor

THE FLYING BOSNIAN

MIROSLAV JANCIC

Some people say
Life consists of departures;
Experiences differ
Particularly if one returns
To the first world,
To his former life
As I, the Flying Bosnian, do.

Yes, one can really live more times
Without getting bored
The only risk is becoming a nuisance;
I was dying now and then
In Sarajevo as well as abroad
Yet nobody around cared
My sacrifices were of no importance
It wasn't much fun either.

I don't know what to say
About the return, yet;
It seems I'm not a nuisance –
Hardly anybody knows me any more
Nor have I recognised anybody so far –
We shall see. ❑

Miroslav Jancic *is a Bosnian writer who published in Serbo-Croat, a language of former Yugoslavia that no longer exists. He fled the war in that state for London where he suffered an 'attack of poetry' that resulted in* The Flying Bosnian: Poems from Limbo, *from which this poem is taken*

A DRAMA

VALBONA ISMAILI-LUTA

NEVER fight against life,
DO NOT let the horses get lost on the paths,
REMEMBER the dogs barking like mad
and *sofra* laid without bread.
DO NOT open the doors to the wounds
LISTEN!
THE BLOOD will flood
A WHOLE DRAMA on a small stage. ❑

sofra: dinner table

***Valbona Ismaili-Luta** is an Albanian from Kosovo and came to the UK in 1993. She is a freelance reporter for Radio France Inter and writes for the Kosovar women's monthly magazine* Teuta

IN MEMORY OF MY MOTHER

RUDOLF MARKU

Without a word of warning to anyone
My mother died.

She did not want to bother anyone,
The world had enough problems and worries of its own,
She wandered off, so to speak, on tiptoe.

And since then, I have been more caring of old people,
I give them my seat on the train, on the bus,
Sometimes I feel like taking them into my arms like children.

Even when I don't know them, I talk to them, smile idiotically.
In winter I am afraid they will catch a chill or a cough.
I always avoid the obituaries.

I have no desire to read of her age
Now that I know how to decipher the wrinkles
And to fathom the magic of greying hair.

I have the impression that some day
A letter from afar will fall into my hands
'How are you doing? How are the others?'

Without leaving her address
She continues to wander on tiptoe
Amidst the din of the world, its pain and lamentation. ❑

Rudolf Marku is an Albanian who came to the UK in the 1990s

Translated by Robert Elsie

THE END OF THE ICE AGE

DIMITAR GIGOV

One morning the people of Freezing Valley were awakened by something unusual. When they left their caves they felt a warm breeze blowing from the west instead of the usual freezing wind blowing from the north-east.

The sun, which was usually concealed behind impenetrable leaden-grey clouds, appeared from behind the ridge of the Great Ice Mountain, on which the ice had already started to melt in its rays. On Little Ice Mountain, which the sun had not yet reached, the ice was melting more slowly.

The chiefs and the shamans were terrified by this. They were talking heatedly and aiming curses at both the east and the west – but this only heated up the atmosphere still further. They sensed that the end of the Ice Age was also the end of their own Age, and what could be more terrible than that?

'Beware of the warm wind,' they shouted, 'it brings diseases!'

'Don't stay in the sun, it is radioactive!'

'Get back into the caves! There is an ozone hole above us!'

Most people began to have misgivings.

At one point a terrible crash was heard and the Ice Bridge linking the Great to the Little Ice Mountain collapsed. The thick columns of ice, which spelt the words 'eternal and indestructible', could no longer support the huge weight of the bridge, proving that nothing in this world is eternal and indestructible.

What happened to the chiefs, the shamans and their minions? Some hid in their luxury cave galleries to wait for the coming of the new Ice Age. Others began to tell incriminating stories about each other. Others again mingled with the crowd, telling those around them that it was they who had started the process of thawing and melting.

All this was a long time ago. Freezing Valley has not frozen over again for many years. But that doesn't mean it has become Utopia Valley. Contrary to all logic, it has become Desert Valley, where people die from all kinds of sickness, from starvation, from abject misery.

Despite the disinformation given out by the chiefs and shamans, everybody from the West already knew that the climate of Freezing Valley had completely changed. But this is only half the truth. Nobody wants to discover whether it is possible to live in a desert. And anyway, who is interested in the fate of this forgotten place, which is known already as 'Former Freezing Valley'? ❑

***Dimitar Gigov** is from Bulgaria. He came to the UK in the 1990s*

FOOTBALL CRAZY

GYORGI

When you are forced to leave your own country you know only too well that, if you apply for asylum in an embassy, you will not only be refused, you will create more difficulties for yourself. The information about your application for asylum will very quickly reach the authorities. They will then decide what to do with you: whether to let you stay free and eventually leave the country, or to detain you. It is possible an 'accident' could occur to you or a member of your family if you don't stop your application for asylum.

You have to try to create a convincing reason to be granted a visa for travelling abroad. That reason can be, for example, accompanying the national football team to see it play in the European championship final. Some time later, you find yourself at Dover, queuing in front of the immigration desk with other members of your football tourist group. Their pressure does not let you feel free to demonstrate your intention to seek asylum, because there are at least two secret service collaborators among the group.

So, in the presence of the secret service, you lie to the immigration officials about your reasons for entering the country. But you do not imagine how fatal this may become for your new future. The immigration officer may forget to warn you that if you give false reasons for entering the country you could be treated as an illegal entrant and be liable to be detained (despite bringing with you genuine documents and a clean criminal record).

This story would be funny if it wasn't sad and true. Nobody warns you when you first arrive in the country that if you don't apply immediately for asylum you could become an illegal entrant. Is this democratic? I'm deeply doubtful. ❑

Gyorgi *came to the UK from Bulgaria. He wrote this in 1997. It first appeared in* Karibu, *the journal of the WEA London Looking Glass Writers project*

THE ISLAND

LILIYA SAZANAVIETS

People had lived on the island a long time. A very long time. None of the old folk could remember who and when had first set foot there and started to live there permanently. The inhabitants had never seen other people, from other places. No boats ever came here. And forget computers: there was no radio, newspapers or television. Yet the people were happy; they liked things as they were.

True, they knew that somewhere there was another, much bigger island where, tradition had it, the people were far more intelligent. So, periodically, a few, carefully selected members of their own society were sent over to the big island for education. How the chosen ones reached the other island and how they returned, no one ever knew; but these were the people who would later become their island's leaders.

The years passed and the islanders lived peacefully enough. Until the birth of the boy: Tsimon. Up to the age of ten or so, he was just like any other child, but then he started 'disappearing'. Early each morning he would go deep into the interior of the island, returning only late. The interior, where a dreaming forest grew, was forbidden. Why? No one knew and no one tried to find out. When the leaders of the island said that something was forbidden – well, that was that! Enough said!

But here was this boy disobeying the law. The first time he came back from the interior, the people gathered round him. They wanted to hear what he had to say about it, but he told them nothing. The elders of the island breathed a sigh of relief; and Tsimon continued to visit the interior daily until he came of age. At first people laughed at him, but later they ceased to notice. Only his mother would often weep, because the neighbours considered him not quite right in the head.

On the day he came of age, Tsimon collected all the people in the main square of the settlement. From under his arm he pulled out a package, unrolled the cloth wrapping and began to take something out. When the people saw what Tsimon was putting on the cloth, a shudder ran through the crowd. The cloth had concealed human bones.

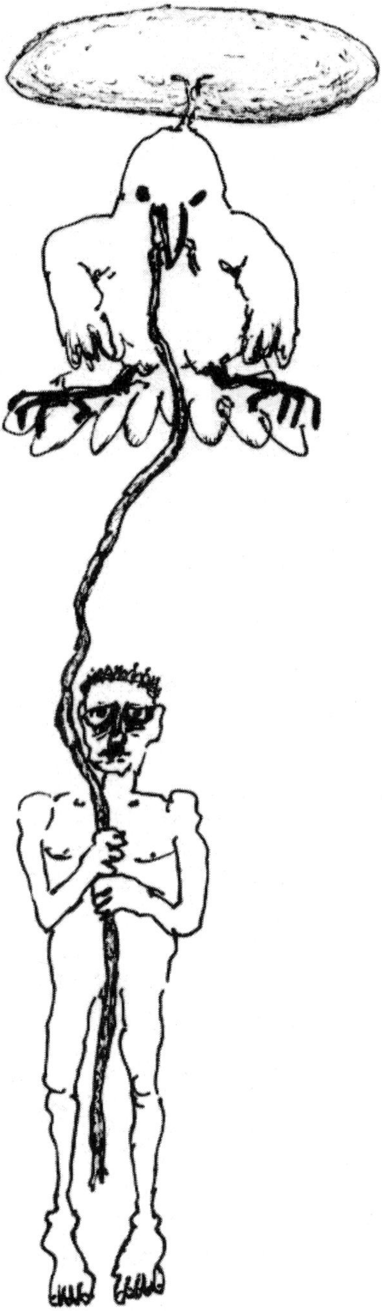

He began to speak:

'I dug up these bones in the depth of the forest. There is a whole mass of them. In there,' – he gestured towards the forest – 'is a huge clearing that contains a gigantic cemetery. Thousands of people are buried there. They did not die naturally; they were killed. "Why were they killed?" you will ask. Because they did not want to be slaves. I have found a box in which there is a mass of papers, written in some language like our own but different. For the last few years I have been reading my way – with some difficulty – through these papers, until I realised that the language in which they are written is *our own true language.*

'Once upon a time,' Tsimon continued, 'people lived on this island who did not speak the way we do now. But, in time, as people began to visit from that other island, they poked fun at our islanders. And so, hating the mockery, our people decided to adopt the language of the big island.

'Not everyone agreed and some spoke out against it. It is they who were killed – most brutally and by their fellow citizens. The people from the other island stood by and watched. It was then that our people moved out from the interior and settled on the coast, where we live now. They intended to hide the evidence of their crime by fostering the legend of the "forbidden forest". For hundreds of years their ruse worked, but now I have found the place. Come!' Tsimon turned to the forest and set off.

Behind him there was a moment of deathly silence, and then a babble of voices:

'It's all nonsense!'

'Not true!'

'He wants to lead us all to our deaths!'

'He wants to put us at odds with the people of the big island.'

'Beat him, the fool!'

The first stone struck the boy on the shoulder. Tsimon tried to protect his head with his arms, but the stones fell on him like hail.

Suddenly, the islanders heard a noise overhead. There in the sky hovered a strange, enormous bird, with something rotating noisily on its head.

Ropes began to descend from the bird's skull. With cries of terror the islanders scattered. They had never seen a helicopter. Only Tsimon remained on the square as the ropes swayed gently down to him. Tsimon grabbed the ropes and was gathered up into the skull; he had no fear of the bird. A man in the skull helped the boy clamber inside.

'What's all the hullabaloo?' the man asked Tsimon.

'Not really a hullabaloo,' Tsimon replied sadly. 'My people simply did not believe me.'

The man nodded sympathetically.

'Too bad they didn't believe you. But never mind. If they don't believe now, they will later. That's for sure!'

The helicopter gathered speed. The islanders, who had rushed back on to the square, looked no larger than insects. Soon they were quite invisible. And in a twinkling the island itself became only a tiny dot in the boundless sea. ❑

***Liliya Sazanaviets** left Belarus for Lithuania in the mid 1990s and came to the UK in 2001. She was secretary to the Speaker of the last fully legitimate parliament, dissolved by President Alaksandr Lukashenka in December 1995*

Translated by Vera Rich

Opposite: Credit: Vladimir Seledtsov, a Belarusan artist living in London and Minsk

ROCK FOR UKRAINE

TARAS ZHYTYNSKYJ

So far now, so far do I wander,
Right up to heaven I fare,
I see a fair country, far country,
What beauty is there.

(*Refrain*) And having seen that beauty,
I carry this with me,
Wherever I go, I always hear
The cranes softly calling,
And having seen that beauty
I carry this with me
Eternal yearning for that quiet land
Above the sea, beneath a mournful heaven.

And there the folk swill vodka, the lads booze
By bucketsful, not drams.
And such are their hangovers that in short
They couldn't give a damn. (*Refrain*)

An old man at the roadside begs for bread,
For pence entreats.
And here they come those kiddy-thieves, each one
With long crime-sheet. (*Refrain*)

And people run away from there
To other lands, far far afield; winds blow
And bear them off into a strange country,
And they carry all with them.
Eternal yearning for that quiet land
Above the sea, beneath a mournful heaven. ❑

Taras Zhytynskyj *was born in Kazakhstan, the son of political deportees from Ukraine, and came to the UK from Ukraine in 1995 seeking asylum. He combines his bread-and-butter job as a chef with a part-time career as singer and entertainer, mainly for the Ukrainian diaspora in the UK*

Translated by Vera Rich

TO POETRY

NEGAR

It's not just words I wish could fly down
from a tough but miraculous pen
but my veins would quiver
and the head would spin from the lines.
But the scream of feelings, deafening heaven
should tear from the immortal heights
to stretch for another span,
somewhere beyond the sunlight.
I want the lines to beat like a heart,
like time in someone's chest
to pace themselves into memory,
that there should be nowhere to go away from them.
That from the noise of mute paradise,
from its ruins and plains
I was full when hungry
remembering the winged Marinas.
I want the sweet stillness of the deadly sea-bed
to burst with waves in front of the eyes,
higher than hats, higher than flat roofs,
to kiss the clouds.
What did it cost them to pluck stars from the heavens
and lay them on strangers' laps
that is my holy Devil should be making mischief,
seducing the shades of the earth,
not for heroic deeds, not for disaster
just to be turned inside out
and in the deep, cherished delirium
to remember my name – the Pretender.
I want the smooth, white paper,
awaiting the coloured inks
to learn to sob from happiness
and be drunk on tears like beer,
poems like a chill over your skin,
like a caress, a blade, to enter the Blood itself!
You cannot run away from this pain,
but sweetness will make you try again and again . . . ❑

***Negar** was born in Azerbaijan, at that time a part of the USSR. She came to the UK in 2001. 'To Poetry' is from her second book* Two Suns *to be published in 2003 (and see also* Index 1/02*). Translated by Richard McKane*

ROMANY TALES

VALDEMAR KALININ

AND A ROMANI SET OFF . . .

Once upon a time, many thousands of years ago, all sorts of people lived in the Garden of Eden. It was the most beautiful garden. Do you know what I mean by Paradise? It's a sophisticated sort of place where truthful people lived in great comfort. They worked hard and had plenty of everything.

Now, one day, believing his people were ready for it, God decided to give them all their own countries and scatter them to the four corners of the earth. He announced a day on which they should present themselves before him to claim their title deeds bearing God's own seal. But since, as you know, God lives in inaccessible light, it was his Angels who dealt with people.

On the appointed day the weather was exceptionally lovely, the morning was warm and the birds were singing. Ah, if only we knew what those birds looked like and the sound of their song . . .

Anyway, the Romani man was so soundly asleep he overslept his appointment. One can only imagine the profound sleep induced by that Garden, shadowed as it must have been by sweetly scented flowers and lulled by the quiet murmuring of distant streams. Suddenly, he was abruptly woken by the sound of joyful singing nearby; indeed, it was only when some Gadzo tripped over him that he sat up.

'Why are you all so happy?' he asked.

'Because I was given my land and I am going to cultivate it. Hurry up, Rom! Otherwise you might be given barren land!' and he hurried on his way.

The Rom set off to Paradise Palace. On his way, he met different Gadze neighbours who told him the good news of their newly inherited land. The Rom realised that by the time he reached the Palace, there'd be nothing left for him, so decided it would be better not to ask. When he arrived at the Palace, everyone was busy discussing the technicalities of settling the lands and dividing up the countries with the Angels. The Senior Angel asked the Rom what he wanted.

'Nothing special,' said the Rom. 'I just want to thank God and his Angels for this wonderful life in the Garden of Eden.'

'But what country would you like?' asked the Angel.

'I'm happy to stay here,' said the Rom. 'Let me once again express my gratitude on behalf of all these people. However, there is one small thing: maybe you would let me visit my neighbours from time to time in their new countries?'

'Because you are the only one who has asked God for nothing, you are given the right to wander the face of the earth, to visit all its countries and stay there as long as you like,' replied the Angel.

The Romani thanked the Angel and set off on a long journey across the countries of his neighbours. And that is why he continues to roam to this day.

DEAD FRIENDS

There is no greater pleasure in life for a Rom than horse trading. He will swap and deal at the drop of a hat. Now, pay attention while I tell you what happened to a Rom in Belarus.

A Rom returning home from the horse fair decides to stop overnight with his Gadzo friend. However, on approaching his friend's house, he realises that his friend has died and is lying in his coffin with mourners in attendance.

The Rom is mortally afraid. But night is coming on fast and he has nowhere else to spend the night. He decides to make the best of it and stay till morning.

Gradually the mourners depart, leaving the dead man's wife and children who are soon asleep.

In the dead of night, the friend rises from his coffin and sidles up to the Rom intent on a little horse trading. The Rom's heart sinks with fear.

'You're dead, I'm alive. What kind of deal could we possibly do? You are bound to the earth while I am still beneath sky.'

But the dead friend won't leave the Rom alone. He starts selling everything he has.

'Faster! Faster!' says the friend. And the Rom sells everything: his best horse, sheep, harness, even the clothes he stands up in.

Appleby Horse Fair, 1950s: established in 1685, now the last great Gypsy gathering place in the UK. Credit: Barry Law

Just as he is beginning to wonder what's left to sell, he hears the first cock crow. The Rom looks down at what he has left to deal with. He starts to strip. Then just as they start off once more, he understands:

'If I don't carry on till dawn, I'm done for!' He resumes selling feverishly until he stands naked except for his pants. The roosters crow a second time and the Rom determines to run for his life. Yet, he holds on. Then as dawn lights the sky, the dead friend says:

'I may be dead, but you're a marvel – you're still alive. You've won your time, you will live and stay blessed.'

Then the dead friend dashes to his coffin before the staring eyes of the half-crazed Rom.

Now you see what horse trading can lead to! ❑

***Valdemar Kalinin** is from Belarus where he started his collection of oral Romani tales in 1972. He came to the UK in 1995, at the invitation of the UK Department of Education, to work with Romani children. He says: 'My translation of the Bible into Baltic Romani is my most challenging achievement.'*

SECRET JOURNEY

IRENA MARYNIAK

As a West London teenager, I lived in a place that wasn't quite on the map. Czeslaw Milosz once called it an 'ideal space'. I was surrounded by people, nourished by reminiscences preserved and ritually revived in religious ceremonies, national festivals and, more privately, in the taste – bland, oleaginous, sweet or occasionally very sour – of that last bastion of ethnicity: food. My identity had been created for me by stories of dispersal and loss, and by linguistic shapes that came not out of the world I could touch but out of people's heads and feelings.

The diaspora, with its ways, was a source of intense pleasure and annoyance. It offered a ready-made context – intellectually constricting but emotionally enriching – and a life-role demarcated from temporal necessities such as exams or elocution lessons. Weekends were accounted for. I was at Polish school on Saturday mornings and Polish Girl Scouts in the afternoons. In the evening I went to Polish dances. On Sunday there was Mass, an hour of Polish folk dancing, then visits to Polish relatives.

Since the 1940s, the Poles have formed one of Britain's biggest, most self-sufficient and introverted minorities. About 160,000 people, many of whom appear fully assimilated by day, come home in the evenings to a Slavic tongue, an ingrained set of family values buoyed up by Catholicism and their own intimate culture. The community is bound by a history of two centuries of oppression, migration or exile, and by often suppressed memories of Nazi prison camps, the army, and the odyssey so many made during World War II to Britain via Siberia, the Middle East, India and Africa.

In September 1939, Poland was attacked from both sides: Nazi Germany from the west and Soviet Russia from the east. Within weeks the country was carved up, with spectacularly brutal regimes in both occupation zones. The Polish government escaped and was interned in Romania. It subsequently mandated its powers to Polish leaders in France who moved to London after the Nazi occupation of Paris.

The war years in Poland are well documented. They saw a campaign of Nazi terror in which all educated people were designated to be slaughtered. Events in the eastern, Soviet sector are less widely known. Polish leaders were arrested, property was confiscated and, in winter 1940, over 1.5

million Poles were deported to the Soviet interior. People from all backgrounds were dispatched by cattle train to collective farms or camps in the Urals, near the Arctic Circle, the Soviet far east and Central Asia. An estimated 380,000 of the deportees were children.

By the time Hitler invaded the Soviet Union in June 1941, more than a third of Poles deported to Soviet labour camps were dead. Complicated negotiations between Stalin and the Polish government in exile in London resulted in an 'amnesty' for the survivors and an agreement to form a Polish army in the Soviet Union, under the leadership of General Wladyslaw Anders, to help fight the Nazis. But news of liberation travelled slowly to the camps. Around 160,500 people eventually found their way to assembly points; many were misdirected or died and over 880,000 were left behind.

In March 1942, the 'Anders Army' was permitted to evacuate to Iran. The troops were moved to British-controlled Palestine for schooling; members of their families were sent to camps in British India and East Africa.

In 1945, following the Yalta conference, Poland was shifted 150km to the west and handed over to the Soviet sphere of influence. Deportees from cities such as Lwow (moved to Soviet Ukraine) and Wilno (moved to Soviet Lithuania) found themselves stateless. The British government withdrew its recognition of the government in exile and encouraged all Poles to go home. Since most had already experienced Stalin's prison and labour camps and the machinations of the NKVD, much of the persuasion fell on deaf ears.

One year on, British policy was amended and Polish troops were shipped in from Italy, Germany and the Middle East. Their dependants and other civilians from camps in Africa and India followed. A brief period in the Polish Resettlement Corps along with a leaflet from the Ministry of Labour offering advice on saying 'sorry', queuing and not kissing a woman's hand, were expected to set them up for British life.

For more than a generation, as people fought to keep their heads above water, most communicated only tentatively with the country they still imagined to be home. The rise of Solidarity dramatically strengthened the connection and, just weeks after Lech Walesa's election victory in 1991, president-in-exile Ryszard Kaczorowski made the symbolic trip to Warsaw to return the presidential insignia held in Britain since the arrival of the Polish government in 1940.

In the 1990s, a steady stream of people arrived in Britain on short-term visas to learn English, and in the hope that they might strike lucky and make enough money to set themselves up either in Britain or back home. ***IM***

VOICES OF THE DIASPORA

EXPULSION

There were five of them and they came at 3 am: two NKVD men with red bands, two Soviet fighters and an officer. They made my father and me stand against the wall and read out the expulsion order. Everyone was weeping. They searched the house and then the lieutenant said to my mother: 'Collect anything you can.' He started loading the sledge himself. It was minus 30 and we took the pigs my father had slaughtered in bags. The officer got some Ukrainians to help. He was young, very humane. He told the fighters to help my mother. The NKVD men just stood there playing with their pistols. We knew them: they were Jewish kids from Slutsk. 'You thought you had all the power. Well, now it's our turn,' they said. They put us on a sledge and took us to Nesvizh where they read out a decree from the Supreme Soviet that we would be deported to another region of the Soviet Union on the grounds that we were a 'dangerous element'. They resettled us in the Siberian forest, beyond Arkhangelsk. 'Here you shall live and here you shall die.' That was what they said.

Against a background of mass arrests by the USSR, a Soviet sympathiser addresses Polish peasants. Credit: Imperial War Museum

Slave labour camp near the Russian Arctic Circle where over 100,000, many of them Poles, died. Credit: David King

They didn't say anything, just took us to the school where the deportees were being collected and then to the cattle train. Once you were inside they bolted the doors so you couldn't get out. There were bunks high up and people slept on them side by side, or on the floor. There was a small round stove with a chimney, and a hole in the floor to the side. We hung a blanket there for privacy. One man cut his throat at the second stop. They took him out at the third. At the last stop in Lwow a woman in the next carriage threw her baby out through the barred window. People were weeping and wailing. I don't how long we were on that train . . . They called these trains *solominki* (straws). There was wagon after wagon and when the train came to a bend the last carriage was barely visible. Then they put us all on sledges and took us down a frozen river and I saw the sun set over the forest. They brought us to a village in the Urals and sent us to live with Russian families. We were all from eastern Poland; quite a few were from our village. I'm still in touch with one who now lives in Slough (near London).

I'd been a student at the Trade Institute in Bialystok and in July 1941 we were sent to work in Soviet state companies. On the seventeenth I was summoned to see the director of the Institute and he reminded me that a few weeks earlier I'd been offered a secondment to Moscow or Leningrad. The condition was that I must join the Komsomol. This I couldn't do. As we were talking, five NKVD soldiers came in and it turned out that I was under arrest. I was held in an underground cell until September and then transferred to a prison in Minsk where an investigation took place. I was tried with five other scouts. Four of us were sentenced to death and the two youngest boys got ten years in prison. Then we were transferred to a prison cell where we were to await execution. It was 1 February, well below zero, and the windows were just above ground level with no glass. There was nothing to sit on. We spent the night running round the cell. I still had the document which listed the allegations against me because they'd forgotten to take it away, so I put it on the concrete floor for insulation and we took turns lying on it. That night it was just the four of us, but later they had up to 40 prisoners at a time there. Some were taken out to be shot quickly – those who'd been accused of spying, for example. On 10 May, I was summoned to see the prison commandant. He told me that the Supreme Court in Moscow had commuted my sentence to ten years' hard labour.

Summer 1940: Polish deportees cutting timber in the Siberian forest.
Credit: National Museums of Scotland

WANDERING THE FACE OF THE EARTH

There were about 5,000 of us and nothing there when we arrived so we cut down these massive fir trees, tied them into blocks and built wooden barracks. Then we sectioned them off with blankets and each family had its own space of about ten square metres. We picked roots for soup. I bartered my watch for a bag of potatoes and planted them. We had four bags by the winter and carrots a foot long. The land was post-glacial and had never been cultivated. It smelt like Finland.

Some Russians kept an eye on us but it was a formality. Where were we supposed to go? There was forest all around and a wide-flowing river. A young teacher tried to escape 30km to Solvychegodsk. She left Kharitonovo at night. The next day they found her boots about 5km away. Her legs were still inside: the wolves had got her.

Map showing routes taken from Soviet labour camps to the UK after the 'amnesty' of 1941

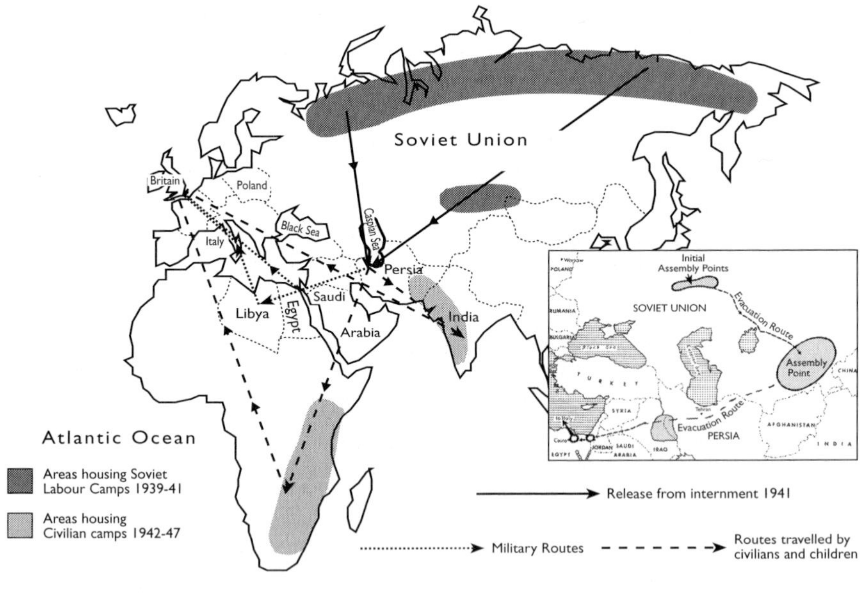

About 2,000 people would die in a single winter. There was graveyard after graveyard. We walked in these graveyards picking berries. There was nothing else. My grandfather is buried in the forest. He was fully conscious as he was dying and said, 'The earth will take me no matter where I am.' Then he turned his head away. He had always prayed for an easy death. In winter we melted the snow for water. It was high as a wardrobe and there was a path cut through it with walls of snow either side and only the sky above.

General Sikorski and General Wladyslaw Anders inspect the newly formed Polish Army. Credit: Imperial War Museum

When the Russo–German war broke out [1941] there was panic, but then the Sikorski–Maiskii Pact was signed and we were told that we were free to leave Komi. My father arranged for us to go to Kuybyshev. When we got there it was no longer possible to get in: the Germans were on the outskirts of Moscow and the Russian government had moved its embassies there. We were redirected to Kitab on the Afghan border but they didn't want us there either. There were food shortages and no work on the cotton harvest. They had a row, piled us on to the train again and sent us back. As we approached Tashkent, we blocked the main rails and they had to unload us: 60 carriages, about 3,000 people. Some were already dead so they buried them by the railway track. They didn't know what to do with us, so they sent us to work on state farms.

Polish workers were taken as labour to the cotton-growing areas of Kazakhstan, as here, and Uzbekistan. Credit: Sikorski Museum

I don't know how long we were in the Urals. When Stalin and Sikorski made their agreement you had to pay for your own transport. We sold what we could: our landlady only wanted bedding, earrings and necklaces. She helped us get to the nearest town where a single wagon on rails took us away. We went on to Uzbekistan and Kirgizstan, and I slept in a manger.

In Uzbekistan my mother worked in a bank. She cleaned floors and a Russian with a gun followed her. My father worked nights in a laboratory and sprayed the bogs in daytime. Those who really suffered were the people who had businesses before the war, Jewish people mostly. You'd see them all bloated with hunger. They didn't know how to deal with it. Many of them died.

My father decided to try to find the Polish army and we had to cross a river that was high. I'm terrified of rivers to this day. We crossed on foot, holding hands, the four of us, and the water tore at our bodies and nearly carried us away. Then we picked up a transport to Pahlevi. First, they put us in the 'dirty camp' where all our clothes were burned and our hair was cut and we were put under a shower. My mother got typhoid there and had to stay behind. My father, my sister and I were taken to Tehran. He joined the army and we were left on our own.

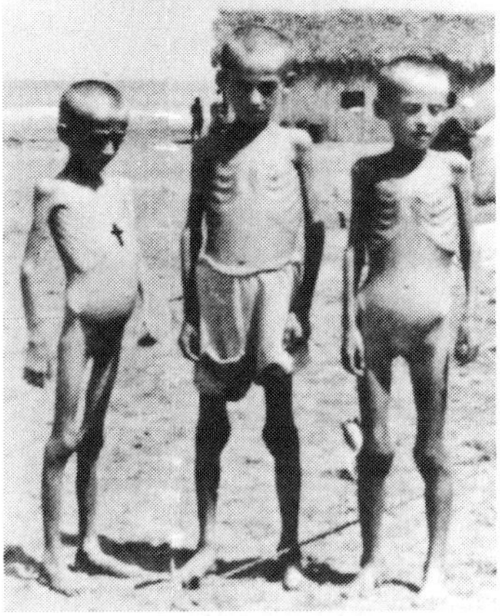

Children on their way to reception camps in the Middle East after their escape from the USSR. Credit: Sikorski Museum

Then I was in Karachi. There were hundreds of other people, too. We were on a beach outside the city in tents. The jackals came at night because they wanted something to eat but we didn't have anything either.

Afterwards, we got taken to Rhodesia to these little huts with thatch that crumbled on to your face as you slept. And every night you had to check under the bed for a snake, and under the pillow for a poisonous spider. We were there about six years.

When the amnesty was declared in 1941, it took a long time for people to collect themselves and go south. By the time we got to Yangiyul it was spring and the fruit trees were in blossom. We went by train through Tashkent. I was travelling with my mother because my father had gone to join his staff separately. From Yangiyul, they started the transports out of Russia; Stalin allowed a limited number of civilians to leave, too. But it wasn't long before people stopped gettting permission to leave and many were left behind. We were lucky. We got out to Krasnovodsk and to Pahlevi by boat across the Caspian Sea. In Krasnovodsk there was a special train waiting to take mothers with young children.

All kinds of things happened in Tehran. Thousands gathered there. Many of the children were orphaned. The army took care of everything. And from Tehran, through Baghdad, Palestine and Egypt, we went to Italy. My husband, General Anders, was commander. He was treated like a king. We all survived only thanks to him. He had some kind of special rapport with Stalin who had a soft spot for him. He sensed the energy of a good soldier and my husband spoke Russian very well so they had a common language. That was the difference between Sikorski and Anders. Sikorski didn't

Polish women and children arriving in Tehran from the USSR. Credit: Sikorski Museum

know Russia. He was a gentleman but he had no idea how to get through to them. My husband had them in the palm of his hand. He knew how to time it: when to flatter, compromise, and slam his fist on the table. That was how he kept winning with Stalin, to the extent that he got a horse from him and a car, and Stalin really listened to what he said.

ARRIVAL

My brother met us in Southampton and took us to a flat in Brighton. When we arrived I sat down on the sofa and wept. I couldn't stop. No matter how terrible things had been until then you could always speak your own language. Now I was completely cut off. We had left the British refugee camp too soon. We should have stayed on. You're isolated from people you understand, you don't know any of the customs. You can just about say 'thank you 'and goodbye' and that's it. This was the worst thing of all.

Wherever you went they'd say: 'You bloody foreigner, why don't you go home. Your country needs you. Go build your own country.' And I'd say: 'You sold my country down the river. Where am I supposed to go? I've nowhere to go.' I wasn't going to let it get me down. They never liked anything foreign in Britain. It's a solid country but very conservative. They keep saying things can't be done.

Top: after the war, orphans from camps in India were transported to the UK by the Polish Red Cross. Credit: Bradford Heritage Recording Unit

Above: identity card of Genowesa Sobucka, taken to Germany as a slave labourer and now living in Sheffield, UK. Credit: Bradford Heritage Recording Unit

Edinburgh 1940s: dance organised for Polish officers. Credit: Sikorski Museum

We didn't know what would happen or how long we'd be staying. One of my husband's brothers worked as a tailor, another learned upholstery, a third worked in a Welsh quarry. People tried to pick up skills in order not to be dependent on benefits. We were pretty destitute. Some people went back to Poland which distressed my husband, General Anders, very much. He felt they were doing the wrong thing. Some disappeared. The General thought that if we went home we'd be dispersed, lost to the world. We'd cease to exist as a group. My husband had a chauffeur called Pawluk. He was tormented with worry about his wife and children who were still in Poland and in the end he told my husband that he felt he had to go back. My husband said: 'Do what your conscience dictates but I'm very concerned about what might happen to you.' He was right. They finished him off. Pawluk vanished.

The government in exile was an extension of the pre-war government. When the war ended there were 250,000 Polish soldiers, sailors and airmen in London. The London-based government was recognised by a number of countries including Spain, Portugal, Ireland, China and the Vatican. Not everyone turned their backs on us overnight. We were there to retain what is most important for any national group that wants to survive: sovereignty.

We didn't accept what had happened. I didn't go back to Poland for 50 years. Our predecessors had said they would transfer the presidency to any person freely chosen by the Polish people, and when Lech Walesa was elected we knew that our mission was over.

HOLDING TOGETHER

Wherever Poles found themselves during the World War II, wherever they managed to get out to, they recreated a little piece of Poland – whether it was Iran or Palestine or England. Wherever there was a Polish military presence there was another little Polish state because they were, in a sense, trying to rebuild the country they had lost. And by carrying on doing this they got into a sort of habit, it became a self-perpetuating thing. I think the key to this lies in the patriotic tradition rather than in religion. Since the eighteenth century there was the idea that territory isn't the most important thing, as long as you stick together you can get back into the fight. It had become second nature: you go abroad, you re-form and start again. There was also a tremendous sense of *civisme* which was imbued by the pre-war Polish government – a remarkable achievement in itself.

One of the things that held the Polish colony in England together was their unpopularity in this country in the closing stages of the war and immediately after it. That survived until Solidarity and then decreased. But it never went away completely. There was, of course, a positive view of the Poles as nice guys, good fun, gallant with the ladies, brave, hard-working and all that. But this was overlain by a general feeling that the Poles were inveterate right-wing bigots, natural anti-Semites and political incompetents.

Until the 1840s, the Poles had been extremely popular in England and indeed in Germany. This changed radically in Germany in 1848, when German nationalism asserted itself. A necessary corollary of this was to denigrate the Poles as culturally inferior. There ensued this terrific barrage of German propaganda – that the Poles were immature politically, had no real history, no literature, no culture, nothing worth admiring, with an irresponsible elite who couldn't look after themselves. That got into the English history books – British historians could read about that part of the world in German sources. Then, throughout the latter part of the nineteenth century, there was a status quo that suited all the established powers, including Britain, and the Poles were seen as potentially troublesome people who wanted to upset and change it. Ironically, after 1917, when communism became fashionable, the Poles were seen as people who were anti-communist and unprogressive. In the 1920s, the Poles were one of the few nations whose elites believed in God, in patriotism and in traditional values. It was a cocktail that could not fail to offend *bien-pensant*

Anglo-Saxon and French intellectuals who thought that socialism, if not communism, was a good thing, religion, and certainly a Catholic type of religion, a bad thing, and patriotism – or nationalism as they preferred to call it – something bad that in the past had caused the most evil wars. As far as they were concerned, the Poles were ignorant, Catholic, nationalistic, apparently anti-Semitic, clearly anti-communist and so they were almost more wrong than German or Italian fascists. Such images die hard.

When I was at university in the 1960s, I was labelled a 'Polish White Guard' (whatever that was supposed to mean) and a crypto-fascist reactionary before I'd even opened my mouth. People would say things like: 'Why are you lot always complaining? After all, the Poles have never been any good at ruling themselves and at the moment you're being very well ruled: Poland's quite free, it's got elections and its own parliament, I know you wouldn't like it because you lost all your lands but it's a progressive country.' Occasionally you argued if you thought it was worthwhile, but it was easier just to laugh it off. Easier for me than for people who had been through the war and all that, who'd fought and suffered sometimes unimaginable horrors and hardships, and for whom the cause of Poland was everything – for them it was like adding insult to injury. A lot of people did become paranoid and I think felt that the whole outside world was somehow fundamentally hostile to them and to everything they held dear. They could therefore only really find understanding and sympathy among themselves. In their communities at least they felt safe. ❑

***Adam Zamoyski** is a writer and historian of Polish origin who lives and works in London. He has published several books, including* The Polish Way: A Thousand-Year History of the Poles and their Culture, The Forgotten Few: The Polish Air Force in the Second World War *and* Holy Madness: Patriots, Romantics and Revolutionaries 1776–1871

Interview by IM

THROUGH AUSCHWITZ

In September 1939, I was taken prisoner but managed to escape from the hospital and join the underground resistance. Then I was mistaken for someone else and taken prisoner again. The Gestapo didn't know what I'd been doing in the resistance or I wouldn't have survived. I was taken to Oswiecim [Auschwitz]. The transport arrived in Oswiecim and we were greeted by an SS officer who said: 'This is a German camp. If there are Jews among you, you'll live a week; if there are priests, you'll live a month; the rest of you can expect to survive three months.' That was the beginning. It was a world upside down. Absurd.

We'd work in teams from 4 am or 5 am. One day in July 1943, an order was issued that all prisoners were to stay in their barracks. Nobody was allowed out and food parcels were distributed. It turned out there was a transport of Jews from Hungary coming. The crematoria had just been opened and that day the Germans preferred us not to see what was happening. So we stayed in our barracks and 3,000 Jews went to the gas chambers in Brzezinka [Birkenau] just hundreds of metres away. And there we were with our parcels . . . If we'd engaged in what was happening to all those people, we'd have destroyed ourselves. Nearly everyone compromised. People are quite prepared to be good until they're in trouble. I learned there that the main thing is not to jump to any conclusions.

My wife and I had always promised each other to meet in the West. She was Irish, born in Liverpool. She had survived the Warsaw uprising; I had survived Auschwitz. In American-occupied Germany, I found out by chance that my wife was living in London. I wrote to her. I'd written to her mother before but never got any replies. And so we met in the West. I was an émigré and she was British. I knew I couldn't go home because Poland had been handed over to Soviet rule. As a former officer in the High Command of the Armia Krajowa [Home Army] I wouldn't have survived.

Jozef Garlinski

Buchenwald: thousands of Polish intellectuals were taken here in 1939. Nine hundred prisoners died every day in the winter months. Credit: Imperial War Museum

Bombay: Polish Red Cross orphanage for Polish children evacuated from the USSR.
Credit: Bradford Heritage Recording Unit

All photographs from Keeping the Faith: The Polish Community in Exile *edited by Tim Smith & Michelle Winslow (Bradford Heritage Recording Unit with the University of Sheffield, 2000)*

AND AFTER . . .

I came to Britain three years ago with no English and didn't know where to turn. I stayed with friends for three months and that's when I got to know 'Father Jan'. He was head of a Polish Catholic Order here. He heard that I'd been a journalist in Poland, and offered a formal invitation to extend my stay if I did some editing for the Order's publishing company. I got involved with other projects too: Radio Vatican was coming to interview 'Father Jan' and he wanted it to go well. I wrote his presentation for him.

My documents said the Order would cover all my needs, including accommodation and food. But then I discovered that 'Father Jan' issued invitations to male students from Poland under false pretences. If the students weren't sexually cooperative, he'd throw them out. I complained in public and the Order ended my sponsorship. I went to see the relevant authorities in the Vatican and asked for an investigation but they told me that they wouldn't be examining the case. I'm too unimportant. I mean nothing. Now I'm appealing direct to the Pope and writing a book that tells my story and the stories of other students the priest had invited, who weren't necessarily gay, didn't let themselves be abused and found they were on the streets.

I had come to Britain looking for freedom. No one was putting me in handcuffs or threatening me with prison, but I kept hitting information barriers. In the new Poland, we live by a definition of freedom that's full of ideals and bears no relation to realities. For decades we were caught up in communist structures that kept us enslaved, and for 200 years before we'd been living under partition. We've forgotten what freedom is. In Britain, when I look at newspapers, the media, and the topics they address, I see a range of reference points. In Poland, you talk about freedom either from the point of view of the Church or of the political party in government.

British society makes me feel incognito. I think that in interpersonal terms it's one of the most mature societies in Europe, though perhaps not the most educated. It has glamour, kitsch, folly and immense wisdom. And every aspect of it has a voice.

Leszek

I came to Britain in 1995, spent the first week with a cousin and then went to the 'Wailing Wall' to look for work and accommodation. The 'Wall' is in a Hindu-owned shop, next door to POSK (the Polish Cultural Centre, Hammersmith). I suppose it's called that because people who come might be in distress. They say it's monitored: the police keep it under observation. They closed off the road once and raided the area. Anyway, I went there and found work in a small guesthouse in Acton. Everything worked out fine though I was exploited a bit, I suppose. The landlady must have come during World War II. She was very prejudiced against newcomers and said things like: 'You eat dogs.' I think she must have seen something on TV.

It annoys me when old émigrés talk about 'Poles from Poland'. I suppose they must have been selected by the British when they first came and felt inferior because they were never recognised as English. Now they want someone to push around. But I helped out in church and got a job in the promotions department of a TV channel and that encouraged them to treat me better. They seemed genuinely pleased that I didn't have to wash up like those countesses who came during the war.

The church is important. There's a restaurant in the parish centre and people get to know each other. If they have difficulties with accommodation they come and sleep on chairs there. In Poland, newspapers carry ads offering work with accommodation in Britain. Sometimes people get conned. They arrive, meet the agent at the bus station, pay, then find their guide has vanished. They're alone on the Tube with no idea where to go or what to do. Some find their way to the church. ❏

Jacek

Irena R Anders (Renata Bogdanska), Alina Dadlez, Janina Maczka, Ryszard Kaczorowski *(former president in exile),* ***Ryszard Gabrielczyk, Jozef Garlinski, Leszek*** *and* ***Jacek*** *were interviewed by* ***Irena Maryniak*** *who also translated the interviews*

AFRICA

London 1964: arriving at the Lycée Française, London.
Credit: Eve Arnold / Magnum

EXILE

WOLE SOYINKA

'I BORROW SEASONS OF AN ALIEN LAND
TO STAY THE SEASON OF A MIND'

Having proposed the question '*When* is a nation?' in my collection of essays *The Open Sore of a Continent*, I suppose I should have realised that it was only a matter of time before I would confront myself with one of its potential corollaries: When is exile?

Speculations over that transposition did not, however, commence without some external stimulus. The theme of exile appears to hold great fascination for literary critics, mere artistic consumers, anthologists and festival directors of all artistic genres; and a week or two had hardly passed after my vanishing trick from my homeland before I began to be bombarded with enquires about how exile was affecting my writing: 'Are you still able to write?' 'What does exile mean to your writing?' Ad infinitum. Invitations from literary journals were not slow to follow, then desperate summonses to conferences, seminars, etc., all in the quest of the elusive quarry – both process and product – that bears the invisible stigmata of literature in exile.

Indignant, I refused to cooperate: no, I had not gone into exile, I was merely away from home on a political sabbatical. That, plus a dozen other variants of the Great Evasion in which I lavishly indulged. Among those variants, one could argue that the one that remained in its own zone of subjective impregnability was that of identity. I was not in exile because I did not feel that I was in exile: I feel, therefore I am; I do not, therefore I ain't! I had not remotely begun to sense the beginning of an exile identity. Literary history and sociology are incomplete without colourful, intrigue-filled accounts of (national) colonies of exiles – a familiar enough categorisation for those literary and artistic émigrés who swamped the congenial cafés of Paris both during the Tsarist era and following the Bolshevik Revolution. Richard Wright and James Baldwin remain among the earliest famous writers of the black American émigré colony and, towards the end of the 1950s, I encountered the distinct Guatemalan micro-community, also in Paris. Yet even if, objectively, some equally obstinate critic would refer to me as having swelled the increasing stream of exiled Nigerian writers, professionals and intellectuals, he would be hard put to it, I insisted, to prove that my identity was thereby transformed and could now be described not as African, Nigerian or Yoruba, but as uniquely Exile!

Of course I knew I had gone into exile! You don't plunge into the forest of a thousand demons on a sputtering two-wheeler just for a brief change of environment in a neighbouring country; you go through the airport or use the autoroute. I had, however, closed my mind: I simply set up barriers against the acceptance of the condition of exile.

Going into exile was one thing, I argued, arriving there was another. Who was to tell me that I had indeed arrived in exile? That unique status of going into, but not having arrived at, was a luxury I could bestow on myself with the authority of lines from Lenrie Peters:

> Earth has nowhere to go
> You are at the starting point
> Jumping across worlds
> In condensed time
> After the awkward fall
> We are always at the starting point

Those lines are from his poem 'Parachute Men'; and if ever there was an image that is appropriate and definitive on the liminal but dynamic condition of the exiled writer, the parachutist or free-fall glider is surely a front-runner.

Those interviews, however: magazine editors and literary *conférenciers* are nothing if not persistent, and perhaps it was in an effort to sustain my stubbornness that I began to ask myself the question: *When* is exile? Other tantalising variants follow: *Where* is exile? Is there a state of exile? For surely even an exile must exist in some space physical and mental. Even more optimistically, there is that strong temptation to describe exile as simply a state of mind. Over any state of mind we may arm ourselves with the challenging power of the will and thus negate all debilitating tendencies that threaten the ego from the inescapable fact of exile. Still, the questions persist, prodded into being by a sensation of loss, absence – however temporary – and by whatever strategies are adopted by individuals to counter the interruption in, or distortion of, their routine sense of being.

But sometimes exile is indeed a place, and thus a new-found-land, to borrow the name of that desolate space, a wasteland that, for tropical blood like mine, must have been a naming ceremony of supreme self-consolation. And so, in both physical and other senses, one confronts the question: Is there a moment when, on arriving there, one knows intuitively, and accepts that one has now truly arrived in exile? (For now, we may postpone the complex but real experience of exile as a state of mind that separates present consciousness from originating zone of self-cognisance: in short, exile as a home of alienation.) Arriving in exile as spatial change may happen to one in any numbers of ways, defining each individual's specific quality of exile. If the nature of departure from homeland has been marked by total rejection, by the necessity for a near-total obliteration of memory, then an encounter with an environment that is a complete antithesis of the place of setting out – from topography to emotive and sensory properties – may find the wanderer breathing a sigh of relief: finally, I have arrived in exile. No more sounds, no more sights, textures or smells, no exhalation from any section of humanity that evokes the memory of home. To put it in more familiar words, the wanderer shakes the dust of erstwhile habitation off his feet.

The opposite, of course, may come to pass. Exile may hanker for a sympathetic environment; one that trails an umbilical cord to abandoned roots, as if a handful of earth has been sneaked into the baggage and delivered ahead of the wanderer at his destination. Mentally, the newcomer does the papal rite – kneels down and kisses the ground. There, indeed, a close duplicate of habitation is recognised and adopted, while the self is schooled in a few minor adaptations. Or else schooled to exist in a kind of paradox, a state of tension where the mind simultaneously embraces an anchor in alien territory yet ensures that it stays at one remove from that alien milieu. This requires erecting a creative barrier, sometimes half-hearted but sufficient to distance complete absorption. In such an instance, the writer reflects present reality, but deflects its seductiveness through literary strategies of a markedly different temper from those that define or dominate the space that has given him shelter.

Ben Okri springs to mind as being an embodiment of that temper, always bearing in mind, however, that his novel *The Famished Road*, so deeply embedded in mythic reconstructions from homeland, did have its beginnings in earlier works – short stories – that were published while he was still in Nigeria. Living by choice in England, he peoples his habitation with beings of a world that is reminiscent of the abandoned terrain, even though placed at a heightened remove from that distant reality. Actually, this makes Ben Okri a prime candidate for that whimsical, half-serious definition that I once proposed for the true temperament of the writer or the artist tribe in general: a creature in a permanent state of exile, since his or her real vocation is the eradication of the barriers of reality (for reality, read intimacy, literal recognition). I was then giving voice to my growing suspicion that few creative terrains appear to be more congenial to the writer than such frontiers – the threshold of reality – and the immediate provocation of my re-examination of such a province was the predicament of Salman Rushdie. At that time, I wrote:

> Indeed, I am more than ever persuaded that this is what defines the breed: living the paradox that embraces, even interiorises the barrier, yet insisting that the barrier should not be there. And thus, charging at, manoeuvring past, slithering through, hurling imprecations and shaking the fists at; simply insisting that the frontier be shattered, that the barricades be lifted, that human communication be not controlled, constricted or manipulated. For this activity takes place on all fronts – it is both elemental and social. Political. And this last results not infrequently in the writer himself finding the barricades sharply lifted at a critical moment of contest: the momentum carries him forward and, by the time he has regained balance, he finds himself across the frontier, the barricade neatly, definitively or temporarily lowered behind him. He is compelled to learn a new language of the space beyond the frontiers, the mores, customs, taboos . . . in short, he encounters the new language of the frontiers of exile, its joys and anguish, its challenges. This tension has proved, over the ages, a life-and-death recurrence. The conjunction of both the physical and the elemental frontiers has surely never been more dangerously expressed, at least in this century, than in the drama of Salman Rushdie and the satanic regime of fanaticism. For Rushdie, the physical frontier has contracted, while the elemental remains – within the imperatives of creativity – innately expansive.

Since I wrote that, Salman Rushdie has been joined by Taslima Nazreen who, like Rushdie in his time, failed to recognise the definitive lowering of the barrier at the frontier of exile. What really took her home, I have wondered again and again? I understand that her mother was ill and dying, but I suspect that beneath such filial pull was also that periodic need of all creative people to re-cross the threshold of loss, to recharge the batteries of identity and thus engage in the ritual of the lifting of the creative frontier, an attempt yet again to wage war within the liminal zone, the writer's normal place of habitation that sometimes turns unbearably physical. Those creative frontiers, I cautioned, remain 'territories of hazardous navigation for the voyager, the writer, who remains a suspect émigré in a refugee camp and whose status of semi-exile undergoes quite arbitrary forms of articulation.'

The recognition of frontiers can be overwhelming, and the condition of exile is the daily knowledge, indeed the palpable experiencing, of such frontiers. Some writers are more susceptible to their debilitating effects and succumb: Arthur Nortje, the South African poet for example, or Rabearivello, the Madagascan poet, whose career reminds one forcefully that there is also a condition of internal exile. A mixed-up, identity-confused poet of potential genius, Rabearivello occupied a creative habitation whose true *indigènes* were thousands of miles away in France. He grew gradually into that extreme product of the colonial psychic divide, one leg across the threshold of his spiritual home, France. He applied again and again to be fully admitted and his frustration grew as the prospect became more and more remote. Rabearivello, a product of the movement that come to be known as 'Negritude', occupied a very special creative space, unique to himself and untouched by many of the social concerns that relieved other poets from the danger of alienation and a total retreat into a solipsistic creative existence. His true soulmates were Verlaine, Rimbaud and Baudelaire, with whom he shared, in the words of Ulli Beier, 'a disgust of reality'. I tend to express this differently: Rabearivello's world, the world within which alone he found his being as *indigène* and citizen, was simply the frontier zone of reality, that liminal territory to which we earlier referred, where the writer's passport requires no validation and accepts no restrictions. His craving, however, placed him among those writers who appear doomed to remain on the threshold of identity.

Rabearivello's anguish, assuaged only partially by retreats into a surreal imagination, lay, however, in that paradoxical sense of exile: the weight of a distant cultural longing. It overwhelmed him eventually, leading him to commit a very painful suicide. So did Arthur Nortje, through an overdose of drugs, in a different clime but no less a liminal inhabitant of a deceptively congenial environment. Nortje's poetry is permeated with the visceral protest of a sensibility that tries hard, but cannot reconcile itself with a condition of forced exile. He agonised over an existential impotence that commenced with the very political situation that had resulted in his exile – apartheid – that itself constituted another form of exile, an internal one, not self-induced like Rabearivello's, but imposed by the insanity of the state.

Like other victims of apartheid, the forces that controlled his existence effectively annulled his social being, crammed his self-awareness into a ghetto of internal exile and eventually flung him into a wider field of alienation. Coming to terms with the contradictions of this liberating vista, England, which spelt freedom and self-realisation but which, nevertheless, inserted a real territory of loss, of the dissipation of a once-cohered self – in short, exile – did not come easily to Nortje's poetic sensibilities.

Dambudzo Marechera, the Zimbabwean – *Scrapiron Blues*, etc – by contrast, made no effort to come to terms with exile, except as a violent predator, whose real-life excesses were matched only by his intellectual (but rather sophomoric) voracity. Exile was a provider, but not one that should be treated as a willing partner; it had to be a relationship of forcible extraction, as due to a resentful guest from a resented host, whose resources must be laid bare for eclectic, even undisciplined appropriation. He was a vastly different spirit from Rabearivello, yet they shared one thing in common: a frank acknowledgement of an exterior cultural home whose threshold they never fully crossed. For Rabearivello, however, it was a loving recognition; not so for Marechera, who did savour, at first hand, those foraging fields. But the denizens were mere intellectual acquaintances and his frustration at a tacit exclusion made him more demanding, less selective and proportionately hate-filled and despondent.

If ever there was a writer who wore the banner of exile on his brow it was Marechera. His eclectic, voracious appetite for the spoils of exile – the insistence on an exile persona that feeds on the community of the alienated – is a characteristic, also, of Syl Cheney-Coker of distant Sierra Leone who actively sought kindred spirits from within the continent but also in literary careers from all over the world. This was strictly a younger, passing phrase for Cheney-Coker, but it retains its validity both for its time and for many others. What is significant about that phase is that this younger Cheney-Coker confesses a need to become an exile in order to find his creative persona:

Mother, I want to return to exile to be your poet

The mother is both his biological parent and the land with whom the poet has a tortured relationship, a tension of unrequited love and unfulfilled expectations; in short, the very embodiment of the poet's alienation which however he seeks to overcome with a willed passion of commitment:

my mother prevents my flight into myself
speaking to me through her silence through the beat of her heart
the sword fighting my days the lamp lighting my nights
when my heart sinks deep in the oasis
of its pain! she rejuvenates me calling back the me
that has died tracing the man-child to the poet
but finally, the lament:
without understanding the dictates of my soul

And yet, within the same poem,'The Road to Exile Thinking of Vallejo', is the avowal of both umbilical ties of the mother/motherland that nurtured that same poetic persona, and the ironic, separatist consequences. Nothing exceptional, and certainly not unique to this poet:

It is recorded then: I'll die in exile!
thinking of my Sierra Leone
this country which has made me a poet
this country which has honoured me
with the two knives of my death passed crisscross
through my heart
so that I can say to a bleeding mother:
Mother I am returning into exile to be your poet

What he wants to be, what he declares in accents of anguish in 'On Being a Poet in Sierra Leone', remains elusive: to be the breakfast of the peasants, the hands that help the fishermen bring in their catch, a hand on the plough that tills the fields, even, somewhat disturbingly, the national symbol of life. I say 'disturbingly', but perhaps 'awkwardly' states the case better, since there is something rather presumptuous about any writer striving to become a national symbol. However, the theme remains the same: a territory that separates desire and actuality, even when the tools of desire have been forged within the hearth of actuality.

But actuality itself is dual, both present reality and the envisioned reality. In most instances, alas, that envisioned duplicate, the constantly receding actuality, gradually evolves into a mere vision of possibilities, of potential articulation. And so the poet finds he must also separate himself from that source of inspiration – that also translates as the zone of obligation – in order to embrace it more fully and to serve it more faithfully. Nowhere, I believe, is the pathos of this paradox conveyed more effectively than in his 'Letter to a Tormented Playwright':

remember Amadu how terrible I said it was
that you were in exile and working
in the Telephone Office in touch with all
the languages of the world but with no world
to call your own: how sad you looked that winter
drinking your LFE and reading poetry with me
in the damp chilly English coffee shops

It is a most apposite metaphor, truly evocative – 'in touch with all the languages of the world but with no world to call your own' – a true liminal centre of receptivity that is, however, located on the threshold of desired reality, seeking but never truly grasping a world it can call its own. ❑

Wole Soyinka *has published over 20 works of fiction, poetry, drama and autobiography. He was awarded the Nobel Prize for Literature in 1986. He now lives between Nigeria, the USA and the UK*

From 'Thresholds of Loss and Identity', an unpublished lecture. This excerpt was first published in Creating spaces of Freedom *(Prince Claus Fund, Netherlands/ Saqi Books, London, 2002)*

NOW I KNOW THE WORLD

MAX JIMMY

'Talent,' my former schoolmaster once said in our dusty school hall in faraway Massundu in the Kono district of Sierra Leone, 'creates opportunity for travel.' Some people, he further said, 'have their desire to leave what their ancestors lived and worked for spurred by their passion to know the world'. What he never impressed on our childish minds was that disasters, be they natural or man-made, are a major cause of the mass exodus of people. Sometimes, they culminate in even harsher nightmares. Thinking about it today, I realise he probably had no experience of major calamities, and certainly never considered them a factor in migration.

During my schooldays, the state was governed with moral probity and the rule of law. Then, a decade ago, the Revolutionary United Front (RUF) held the nation hostage in a long war and the world woke to one of the worst human disasters in Africa.

That good old teacher is not to blame for that. There can be no control over the happening of things in today's world. He was himself a victim of the brutality of the rebels who besieged and devastated my country: in 1997, they executed him during one of their many raids on my village. The difference between his days and the harsh realities of today is vast. Had the old man not been given an untimely exit to eternity, he would, no doubt, have expanded his horizons on the causes of migration.

He might have touched on globalisation and how it has turned today's world into one big village, eliminating real and imaginary boundaries among human beings. Sadly, few so far have woken up to the virtues of globalisation. Most of us still cannot understand that we are all one people in one huge environment. It will take a lot more schooling for that to be realised.

Today, as I tap on my computer in faraway Britain, a place different in outlook from my birthplace, the full impact of my gracious teacher's utterance that 'talent creates opportunity for travel' dawns on me.

Memories of news of my winning an award to travel to London in the summer of 2001 are still fresh in my mind. It happened when it was to happen. Several earlier efforts at fleeing war-torn Sierra Leone had come to nothing. I remember one of my friends consoling me after one of my failed

Freetown, Sierra Leone 2000: pupils from the Richard Allen High School plead for peace after the murder of their teacher, Ajak D Yonga. Credit: Robert Knoth / Panos Pictures

attempts to flee the country in 1997. The rebels had just invaded downtown Freetown and were hunting down particular journalists accused of opposing their campaign of terror. 'Your time will come, Max, just rest your faith in God,' I remember my friend Abdul Bangura telling me. His words hardly had any impact on my overstretched mind: I shall probably be a dead man before that happens. Death was a short walk. Marauders were busy unleashing terrible atrocities; civilians like myself were at the receiving end of the viciousness of the RUF 'people's revolution'. It was a moment of desperation and frustration; a face-to-face contact with death. Nine months later, the rebels were to be chased out by an international security unit, ECOMOG. But that was not until an estimated 10,000 lives – according to Sierra Leone's media - had been lost.

What started in the winter of 1991 in the form of an attack on a small army garrison in the village of Bomaru in eastern Kailahun district, on the border with Liberia, was to become a nightmarish inferno that has shocked a disbelieving world. There is no secret about the appalling nature of the RUF barbarity. Sad memories of disembowelled pregnant women and slain children, mutilated limbs and burned-out towns, villages and cities will, for a long time, occupy an uncomfortable place in all our minds. Even though laudable steps have been taken to halt the carnage, the effects of the RUF savagery will for ever linger on . . .

The effect has been catastrophic. Many have been forced to flee or face the wrath of unthinking mediocrities whose only trademark is merciless killings and destruction. Such is the situation that prompted and continues to prompt a massive exodus of people from Sierra Leone. Today I count myself among them.

And how life treats you in a foreign land is a whole other story. To be honest, there is nothing romantic about refugee life. Happiness is rare. In most cases, love is replaced by scorn. There hardly exists any room for comfort. Suspicion and humiliation are commonplace. The consequences are both traumatising and devastating. Experience has taught me that living in another man's land can be harrowing. Missing your country and people becomes an everyday reality.

Some people see refugees as seekers of greener pastures. While this could be the result of cultural and social differences, mainly it is because people remain blind to the fact that refugees are simply people who cannot go back home because of insecurity.

Life in London has been a mixed experience. Whereas some days have been really wonderful with friends and other good-hearted, supportive people, other days have brought me only the sense that life is horrible and useless.

Having witnessed gruesome human rights abuses, the thought of going back home still terrifies me. As I journalist, I exposed the perpetrators of despicable offences and this has left me with deadly enemies. I am their target.

For me, the world has stopped smiling. Gone are the days when mankind was at peace with itself and people treated each other with dignity and affection. In the midst of everything, many today find deprivation and humiliation staring at them like foolish sheep. There can be no certainty about life. It could be sunshine now and thundery showers or a dark cloud at another time.

Do not mistake me for a prophet: I have thrown religion to the wind. Do not tell me about religion any more. It is now more than a year since I went to church. No one has asked me to go to church since I landed on British soil. And I have not had the spiritual inspiration to do so myself. My perception of life as a gift from God has changed. My current host is not a Christian. Society has transformed the one-time crusader of Christianity into nothing but a worldly man. Everything he does is self-centred and rooted in materialism. This discovery has come as a rude shock to me. This is not the friend I knew in my little village in the east where many years ago the Bible was our food. I have found out that my educated friend has lost track of love and compassion. He is today harsh and brash, not the loving and caring person I used to know. All because he is today my host. Who knows what may be tomorrow?

That is what I shall tell my mother when I return home. I shall say: 'Mum, don't mind our friend Christian Goodman. He is the direct opposite of his name. The way he treated me in London was incompatible with what he used to teach us.' And I know my mum will be shocked to hear that; she won't believe her ears.

But let me say this. One of my friend's virtues is that he lives in peace and can continue to build on his material gains. I have realised that peace is the bedrock of development. And that is what I shall insist to my younger brother when we meet back home. To my sister, I shall say: 'Stop your sons and daughters from being at war with each other, for that will only undermine their development aspirations.' Otherwise, when they have made their home uninhabitable, they will be made to pay the price in a faraway place. And they will have no one to blame but themselves. I may have realised this a bit late in the day, but, as they say, ' better late than never'. ❑

Max Jimmy *was born in Sierra Leone, where he worked as a journalist. He came to the UK in 2001 seeking asylum after his life had been threatened as a result of his work*

OUBLIE, OUBLIE CHÉRIE

AMBA BONGO

Oublie ce que tu as véçu
Laisse le vent emporter le souvenir
De cet amour à jamais perdu
Laisse la pluie effacer les traces
De ce malheur épouventable
Qui t'a rendue si vulnérable

Ouvre les yeux et regarde
Observe autour de toi, amie
Ne vois-tu pas que tout a changé?
Le chant de l'oiseau, le rire des enfants.
L'agile écureuil sur cet arbre de feu,
Les vagues de l'océan t'appellent au bonheur.

La vie est si belle, crois-moi
La vie est courte aussi bien sur!
Tu ne pourras plus remonter le temps,
Ni saisir entre tes mains
Ces précieuses minutes écoulées pendant
Lesquelles tu es restée pensive et taciturne.

Tourne vite la page, chérie,
Découvre la beauté d'une existence paisible
Ainsi que la joie des choses les plus simples.
Carpe Diem, le moto de ma vie,
C'est lui qui m'a permis de rire et d'aimer
Sous le soleil ou sous la pluie.

Fais de même, mon amie.
Tu y puiseras une force inouie
Qui te rendra ton sourire détruit,
Qui te fera déplacer des montagnes,
Chanter alleluia sur les toits du monde
Comme tu le faisais si bien jadis. ❑

***Amba Bongo** is from the Democratic Republic of Congo (ex-Zaire) and now lives in London. Her first novel,* Une femme en exil *(Harmatton, Paris), was published in 2000*

SAMADOON

CABDULQAADIR XAAJI CALI

and you will say:
deranged people   a huge hole is screened from you
gulleys and eroded water tracts   obstruct descent
paths set with hidden mines   disturbing the eye
traps scattered for you   intending your misery
as you suddenly topple into them   this is not in your interest
clashing together is success   soothing fat
to satan and his injustice
the professed law of God   and religion states
when a murder is committed   and the blame is clear
it is to be tried in law   blood money and hanging
will settle but before   the accusation is made
the discussion conducted   the acacia watered
for the gifted and wise   he enters – peace-refuser
evil brings things   sweet to his saddle

the gun and the ratatat of its bullets   this is not in your interest
denying the search for truth   this is not in your interest
these good young men of yours dead   this is not in your interest
that women wear again and again the mourning scarf   this is
not in your interest
your cow bears each time a donkey   this is not in your interest
sheep suffer from worms and bloating   this is not in your
interest
cholera kills you one and all   this is not in your interest
the typhoon trawls you down to the ocean   this is not in your
interest
your bodies float away on the floods   go'e this is not in your
interest
dizzyness a world cracking your knees   go'e this is not in your
interest
your loved ones stabbed and stabbed by spears   go'e this is not
in your interest
with strife and sorrow from all sides   stinging you naive person
go'e this is not in your interest

staggering exhausted   you lack the camel's back
skin carrier fell from   all that harms him and died
to Daabbad trained   for the bristly blanket and halter
that you no longer say   he's gone and get up
this is not to your advantage or interest
sharing the fireside   with worries that weaken you

this is not to your advantage or interest
all that i tell you   in my testament and that
which through luck passed you by   and the trials that I
have yet to point out   to you as i say
calm down   go'e this is not in your interest

a sky has dropped rain   for Daylo and the lamb
the times of spring   Awl Daybad Dirirad
have shed showers covering   the whole land
the goodness for the season   of Dayr and there where
the people are spread   the herds are grazed
the communal encampment   the hawd's pastures
the place where all points   to milk full udders
the meadowland views unspoilt   clumps of grass
dihi in fresh growth   the plant life and verdure
the mossy shoots   with roots reaching deep
the branches the duur tree   stretches out
all livestock grazed   on abundant lushness
where encampments old and new   know nothing of parasites
dividing up this whole country   go'e it's not in your interest

poverty prevents   the production of milk
the naked now   are hollow-cheeked
the throat and belly   fail to function
the gullet is grilled
searching in strange lands   dejected in the desert
living with infidels   begging from foreigners
oh naive one   it's not in your interest

the children attend school   for learning's light
let them reap its rewards   is society's unhitching
the hobble of poverty
grinding knowledge into the grave   it's not in your interest

ready only for himself   he who acts solely to his own ends
won't even thread a needle for you   he's yesterday's man
the one from before   who held a whip for you
the man who with the dagger   would disembowel dependants
plunge it into you you remember   the difficulties he brought
he now refutes you   as he sets to peel
the fibres to make   a rope to tie you up
the lying MP   those satanic elders
the subjugators making signs   secretly known to each other
those calling turn from the path   the breakers and brokers
tearing things apart
that they still sport   the turban you respect
wield a leather whip   as you bow down behind
go'e it's not in your interest

those who together milk their camels   Deleb Diiran and Doorran
those who produce the fruits of the farms   in community by
the rivers

the trapper and arrow hunter   of little means
the person beyond borrowing   even one thing
the sailor of seafaring boats   setting the mast
the owner of tall buildings   trading from them
those flowing back to the bush   and the neighbours of the town
one people sharing   creating no problems
to face away from each other   is sulking and resentment
walls separating society   screens blocking them off
delineation of nature   splitting up grazing
closing off this region   enclosing that with strict borders
hobbling folding up   separating in hate of their skin
dispersing them and setting out   individual spaces
leaving everything behind   sending apart
dismantling agreements   each aiming their own way a very
long time
piercing peeling back then putting in   watering each other's
spite and jealousy
bringing people to hate   such that fire is not held for another
making them sleep by the side   of badness unblamed
that they scatter apart you'll say to them   it's not in your interest

the killing happens   the destruction of the lands
creation's burial   refugees' flight from the country
as outlaws pass   among the people long suffering
weak wretches
they enter the shade   of the dead wood

the forest's been destroyed   by scorching sand
rotten brush   dense dead thicket
silvered tree stumps   calls of help help
somebody help the woman   the children the frail
licked by the red hot spears
the tank with lust to launch   at even unpeopled places
the playful gun sight   the hollow-stocked gun
the kalashnikov the bomb   the shortened jeep
the rolling mortars   descending from the sky
napalm peeling stripping   your burnt strip
the anti tank   ricocheting ring
the rpg7   the smaller bazooka
and the ammunition belt at the ready
the aloes with their troubles   and painful injury
standing unmilked   and drinking their fill
ready for destruction   sent by death
and guns and gunpowder of satan   it's not in your interest

show-offs boasting   sidling into a position
to metamorphose   into meat-eating animals
slaughtering people   brings no revulsion to them
seeing the corpse's limbs
searching for fat from the butchered   and eliminating the weak
peeling flesh and skin   from the slayed women
and this blood flood in the river beds   this is not in your interest
feeling no nausea   at the oozing water in the well
the sloppy mud   and this wrongful matter
swallow the worm don't look at the core
come down like wild animals every time
do not refuse the snot and slime
hold things in contempt and eat
dead leaves and innards not good meat
this was the testament then   of Koofil and Doofil
the ones I sent to hell   and whose orders I refused
the lackey dogs
and those of their ilk saying   *here boy*
you countered the contempt   of their fathers with
it will not be tried on me
that they now drag you down from there   go'e it's not in your
interest

Go'e: literally 'the one who is dying', used as an insult
Daabbad, Deleb Diiran and Doorran: proper names of burden camels
Daylo: half-black sheep
Awl Daybad Dirirad: sub-seasons in the Somali system of weather lore
Dayr: main rainy season in Somalia – when the rains are good it is a time of plenty
Duur: herbaceous plant with a long stalk
Koofil and Doofil: play on the name Corfield, commander of the camel corps in British Somaliland ❑

Cabdulqaadir Xaaji Cali Xaaji Axmed *was born in Somalia in 1962. 'Samadoon', excerpted above, was composed and first performed in London in 1995 after he had moved to the UK in 1990. It is a powerful indictment of Somalia's civil war and the destruction of the country at the hands of the previous regime and the various militias. 'Samadoon' originally appeared in* Mother Tongues *edited by Daniel Weissbort and Stephen Watts (King's College London, 2001)*

Translated by Martin Orwin

I SAW

GHALAPOUM ABDOULAYE

I saw
I saw horrible scenes
I saw gruesome spectacles
I saw open graves and human slaughter
I saw, I saw and I saw
I saw them
They burned entire villages
They raped the women
They castrated the men
They chopped off the women's breasts and threw them to their dogs
I saw the horror
I saw how many times man can be nasty
I saw how many times the life of a pig is worth more than the life of a man
I saw
I saw our detractors write to say that the war in Chad is fratricide, North–
South, Muslims–Christians,
NO, NO and NO
The people have no responsibility in this war
They have been used
They have been betrayed
The wars in Chad are imposed by war chieftains who are seeking
Power and imposed by warriors seeking loot
I saw bandits become personalities, businessmen
I saw how people steal from the government's coffers
I saw how they got richer illegally
Chad my poor country
May God protect you
Glory to you ❑

***Ghalapoum Abdoulaye** was born in Chad in 1975 and came to the UK in 2000. He is now at the University of Sunderland in the north of England. This poem courtesy The Medical Foundation for the Victims of Torture*

'KARIBU'

FATHI, ANON

THE UNDERGROUND
LONDON

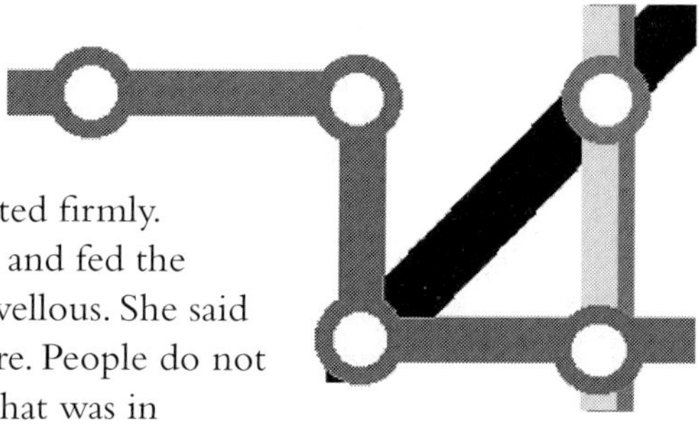

He entered the station where every sign for assistance was erected firmly. He bought a ticket, using a coin, and fed the machine with it. It opened! Marvellous. She said underground was part of Life here. People do not think much about it. No reply. That was in summer time, when people felt free. A crowd of naked legs rushed in, with a boyfriend or a husband. They are all long, beautiful, swinging on high-heel shoes to make them longer and higher. Inside, he heard only non-English speakers chatting, not a single word of a native character. A young woman smoked a cigarette! Some gentleman got down, maybe looking for another place. No one was bothered. No one was looking at other people's eyes. He disembarked and disappeared. ❑

***Fathi** was born in the Sudan and wrote this in 1997*

NO FISHING

It is important to have a day centre where asylum seekers can come to meet other people who speak their language. For some people it is very important because they don't have family in the UK. Some people have stress at home. They need to come to the centre to meet other people.

My friend has been in trouble and had to go into hospital. He was there for two months. I told him he got depressed because he did not come to the day centre. Some people are very sick. They need to talk to someone. I have another friend who has heaps of food in the fridge but cannot eat when he is alone. In some countries, people only eat when they are alone. In some countries, people only eat in a family situation with father, mother, brother or sisters. He cannot eat when he is alone, so he gets very thin.

When he comes to the centre, he feels much better. He can eat when he is with friends.

Sometimes when my friend comes to the centre, they say, 'What have you come for? Do you need advice?' He doesn't need advice, but he does need someone to talk to, otherwise he'll get sick. He does not know what to say. Sometimes he gets a ticket to go upstairs and sometimes he is turned away because people on income support are not entitled to meals.

Many people work in the new centre. The language courses and the training are good, but the atmosphere is different. Few people here help you if you are in trouble. The Karibu centre was smaller and they knew who you were. It was more like a family situation.

Sometimes I come because I have no one to talk to. If you go to the Algerian coffee shop you still have to speak low. We are frightened; you do not know who can overhear you.

When you come here, you can get good advice. Asylum seekers who have been here some time can help you. For a new person it is OK if they come for just one day. They get a good service. Older people think their family is here. When you come here, people know your story. You don't have to go over it again and again. Some people don't like to go over their story because it is painful. Each time you retell it, there is more pain and fear. You don't know what your future will be. One day I had an appointment with a woman who asked me to tell her my story. I made an excuse and left.

At home, I used to go night-fishing every Thursday. When we come here, there's no fishing. I used to go camping by the sea for two months every year. Now I am here, I don't go anywhere. Stay at home; go to job; come back; TV; that's it. ❑

The author*, who wishes to remain anonymous, is from Algeria.*
He wrote this in 1999

This work, including the illustrations, appeared in Karibu *magazine, part of WEA London Looking Glass Writers project for refugees and asylum seekers*

STRIP SEARCH by Martin Rowson
(3) EXILE! — whether its motivation be flight or the yearning to breathe free, throughout HISTORY humans have upped tents to seek richer or safer pastures, leaving HOME to find refuge in a new, renewing yet unfamiliar home. And yet, and yet... the umbilical cord EVER TWANGS, and shallow roots persistently recall those deeper, distant roots, bifurcating into the rich, chthonic earth of the ORIGINAL HOMELAND —— So, what if we make a dream come true and let
EVERYBODY GO HOME??!?
(4)... as mighty ships traverse the World's Oceans, taking home the immigrant populations of AMERICA, AUSTRALIA, SOUTH AFRICA, NORTHERN IRELAND, PITCAIRN ISLAND, etc...
BUT MOM! WHERE THE HELL IS RUTHENIA?
BACK IN MY OLD DAHOMEY HOME!
(7) With the AMERICAN LANDMASS now safe for buffalo to graze, EUROPE, AFRICA & ASIA are heaving — IRELAND sinks under the weight of returning sons & daughters of ERIN, while the Welsh & Cornish exercise their "right to return" to the abandoned estates of the departing ANGLES, SAXONS & JUTES... Ethnic clashes at airports everywhere... CHINESE claim en masse to be a lost tribe of Israel, leading to enormous tailbacks on the Hebron by-pass....
YOU SAID IT, PAL...

(2) At first, of course, the craven jackanapes of FORTRESS EUROPE's Interior Ministries are cock-a-hoop as they empty those DETENTION CENTRES...
BYE BYE! DON'T FORGET TO WRITE!
NO READMITTANCE
(3) But this dream goes much much further... Soon half of Britain's CABINET are back home in crude peat bothies north of the border...
OCH AYE THE NOO!
SHUT UP, GORDON!
(5) And half measures DON'T APPLY, so before they can enjoy the wide & empty prairie that was once Detroit, the NATIVE AMERICANs get back across that landbridge to SIBERIA...
SO WHERE DO WE BUILD THE CASINOS?
(6) Meanwhile, the Israelis return from whence they came. (This entails a short weekend stop in the Bronx, then Kiev, before going back to ISRAEL – oops!)
THE FLIGHT BACK HOME LEAVES IN 20 MINUTES! WE DON'T HAVE TIME TO BUILD SETTLEMENTS ALL OVER UKRAINE!
ANTI-SEMITE!
(8) Until the yearning itch to go home leads the ENTIRE HUMAN RACE to return to Africa's RIFT VALLEY.
ISN'T IT GREAT FOR US ALL FINALLY TO BE HOME?
EXCEPT THAT HALF THE POPULATION OF BRAZIL IS STANDING ON MY FOOT...
(9) Everything thus sorted out, a brief word from our sponsors...
HEY CHICO! PEOPLE SAY I'M MAD BECAUSE I LIVE IN A TENT!
BOSS! YOU'RA NO MAD!
I'M A NOMAD! THAT'S WHY I LIVE IN A TENT!

SOUTH ASIA

Rabindra KD Kaur Singh, 'From Zero to Hero', 2002. 'Depicting the Beckhams as the "New Royal Family" – as they were dubbed by the tabloids – sparked a debate in the UK on the boundaries of artistic freedom when the figures were described as Hindi deities in the media' (RKS). Credit: © the artist

TRI-SUB-CONTINENTAL

KAMILA SHAMSIE

Forget about pets; I can't even consider owning plants. They don't do well on aeroplanes or in the presence of customs officials, and I'm never in one place long enough to see one through the course of its natural life. Since the age of 18, I've spent seven consecutive years at university in the USA, with every summer and winter in Karachi, and in the four years since I stopped being a student, I've been moving constantly between London and Karachi (and to a lesser extent, Clinton, New York). I don't move around so frequently that I never have time to stop and adjust to the routines and rhythms of a city; and I don't stay long enough to really truly get settled in.

But already that's a lie. I feel settled within days of getting to London. I feel settled within hours of getting to Karachi. I am a Karachiite who travels, a Karachiite who feels utterly at home in London, a Karachiite who studied, and now occasionally teaches, in the US. Always a Karachiite. It's really quite that simple.

That is not to say that all the hopping to and fro has made no difference to my life, my opinions, my writing – and yet I sometimes do find myself very nearly saying that. Not so much because I believe it as because I'm reacting against the racism that underlies many people's use of tags such as 'displaced', 'diasporic', 'clash of East and West'. So often the subtext to those tags is: 'She could not have thought of any of these things, could not have held these attitudes of which we approve, if not for the influence of the West.' The 'clash of East and West' bit gets used particularly often in reference to my novels and it's almost invariably used in a context that implies that tradition and class prejudice and familial ties are an Eastern concept, while modernity and feminism and independence are Western.

And all I can think of then is the women of my family.

There is my maternal great-grandmother who was a Member of the Indian Parliament in the 1920s, and who corresponded with feminists in Egypt and Turkey, and co-sponsored a bill in the constitution of her political party, the Muslim League, calling for the greater inclusion of women in politics. She was also, from what I can gather, in many respects a 'traditional' woman when it came to her ideas of etiquette and noblesse oblige and other matters – which only goes to show how absurd the tags about East/West/feminism/tradition are. And she was a Lucknavi – a woman with a strong sense of the city, Lucknow, that was her home.

Then there is my paternal grandmother, who was a Berliner, a Catholic by birth. She married an Indian in the 1920s, converted to Islam, moved to India and then to Pakistan, never went to Germany after 1939, and by the time I knew her was most comfortable speaking Urdu with a German accent.

And my mother, who went to boarding school in England at the age of nine, didn't return to live in Karachi until she was 19, and so spent a good many years feeling more English than Pakistani, though in England she was never allowed to forget that she was, and would always remain, a foreigner.

With such a background is it any wonder that I never really conceived of a life that exists only within the boundaries of a single nation? And by that I don't mean I always knew I would spend much of my life travelling. I mean that the over-used word 'hybridity' – whether it refers to something genetic or something created through travel – is an attribute that I've taken for granted in my life even while feeling utterly rooted. I can trace my ancestry back to the following countries: India, Uzbekistan, Germany, Russia, Mongolia, Arabia, Persia – and while I can't detect any Mongolian, Russian or Uzbek influences on my life (and can't specifically talk about the influences of any of those countries on my psyche) I know that in some tiny, diffused way all those places have contributed to that which I term my Pakistani identity, even though it may not match up exactly with the identity of any other Pakistani except for my sister.

Having asserted all this, let me repeat: that is not to say that all the hopping to and fro has made no difference to my life, my opinions, my writing. If I had stayed in Karachi I don't doubt I would have been a very different writer. On a purely logistical level, this has to do with the people who were so important in helping to define the way I think about language and stories and politics in those impressionable years at university. It's no small irony that the most influential of my teachers was the wonderful Kashmiri poet, Agha Shahid Ali, whom I would probably never have met had I stayed in Karachi. It was through Shahid that I started to read the Urdu poet Faiz Ahmed Faiz and the Urdu short-story writer Saadat Hasan Manto. It was through the influence of Urdu poetry on Shahid's work that I started to learn some of the lessons of imagery and expansiveness that Urdu can teach so well.

It's not just that in Shahid I finally found someone who was able to talk to me about Urdu poetry – it's also that being away from Karachi made me hungry for home and, therefore, ready to listen to those talks. When I was growing up, Karachi was the place I was when I wasn't away on holiday; it was the place I was when I wasn't immersed in a book. That's part of the oddness of growing up with English as your first language in a place like Pakistan – all the books you read are set somewhere different, and so your home is never the place where imagination is located. When I look back now at all the writing I did before I left Karachi, what strikes me most is the absence of Karachi from my writing. I started writing novels when I was 11 (I use the term 'novel' loosely – but I wouldn't have said so then; a 40-page book seems like a novel when you co-author it at the age of 11); by the time I went to university I was working on the fifth novel. But none of them was set in Karachi. They were in dog heaven or ancient Rome or some Tolkienesque land.

But then I left Karachi. And I haven't wanted to write about any place but Karachi since. It started as an act of nostalgia, of conjuring up the place for which I was homesick. And quite rapidly it settled into the only thing that made sense: how could I write about any other place when it was only in Karachi that I could understand the silence between and behind so many utterances?

In all that fiction writing about Karachi during university (which included writing my first novel) I didn't ever write about people who left Karachi – the only piece I wrote that had anything to do with being in a place other than Pakistan was a non-fiction piece (sort of) called 'Mulberry Absences'. It went like this:

> When you grow up among mangoes it's hard to have any regard for the mulberry.
>
> I speak from experience, of course. For the first 20 years of my life I don't think I ever stopped to consider a mulberry for any longer than the time needed to transport it from plate to palate, and in its absence I certainly never missed it the way I miss mangoes when summer is over. I can't remember what made year 21 of my life so different; I only know that one day in 1994, while home in Karachi for the summer holidays, I looked across the dining table at my sister and said, 'What's happened to the mulberry crops? We haven't seen, let alone eaten, mulberries in years.' She regarded me in silence for a moment, the way she does when I say something particularly stupid, and said, 'Nothing's happened to the mulberry crops. I ate mulberries this year. You're just not around during the mulberry season.'

Oh, treachery of mulberries. That a fruit so seemingly innocuous should be the instrument by which the illusion of four years is shattered! Prior to this moment, I'd had no trouble convincing myself that though I was at college in the US, the fact that I returned home for four months of the year meant I was not really missing out on life back home. After all, I was home for at least parts of the crabbing season, the beach season, the monsoon season, the wedding season; home for pomegranates, pears, oranges, apples, chikoos, lychees, watermelons, melons and, yes, mangoes.

Everything was so simple before the mulberries, but after . . . What could I do but become obsessed? I stayed awake all night trying to remember what else I had forgotten. I raced through cookbooks, family albums, old diaries, in search of the once-familiar made unfamiliar by absence. I spent a whole week interrogating people about October at home – and got nothing more than the shrugged-off description 'it's like September becoming November'.

At some point it occurred to me that reacquainting myself with the mulberry would be the only sane way of reclaiming those eight lost months of the year. I started with food magazines; but while there was plenty of space given to berries of the straw- and black- variety, I couldn't find a single mul- in two years of back issues. I did find an entire issue devoted to avocado, and this incensed me immeasurably. What has the avocado ever done to deserve such attention except flaunt its own blandness?

The dictionary was my next stop and, lo and behold! in the parenthetical etymology for *mulberry* I read: 'Middle English *merberie, mulberie*, fr. Middle French *moure*, from Latin *morum'* – and finally – 'from Greek *moron*.'

Moron indeed, I chided myself. A mulberry was never a mulberry to you when you ate it. It was always its Urdu self; always *shaitoot*.

Shaitoot, I say out loud.

The word drips – ripe and purple – from my tongue.

The first thing I need to say about that piece is that I wrote it when I was young and foolish, and that explains my remark about the avocado. Beyond that, what now interests me about the piece is the function of the 'other country'. America is not important for being America – it's only significant that it isn't Pakistan. In my second and third novels, both America and

England get referred to but only because they are the places from which people return to Karachi or to which people go and become cut off from home or fear becoming cut off from home. It's somewhat disturbingly like all those Empire novels that pretend to be about India or Africa but are only really ever about England. Except, of course, there's a different historical context which rather alters the politics of the situation.

The reason why 'the West' is not a more major player in any of my books is that Pakistanis of particular socio-economic backgrounds don't have to leave home in order to feel the influence of certain places beyond our nation's borders. Colonialism meant that language and ideas from far away entered *and became part of* subcontinental life. And so, if I have a character who throws Urdu words into English sentences, refers to Ghalib in one breath and Shakespeare in another and *Charlie's Angels* in another, it's not because of some East–West clash but just an expression of the kind of Pakistani she is – the kind of Pakistani she could be without ever leaving Pakistan. Later, when that character is deciding whether to love a boy of whose antecedents her snobbish, once-aristocratic family will disapprove she's not choosing between East (family) and West (love) as a number of readers (from places outside Pakistan) have suggested – she's just choosing between different aspects of her character and upbringing.

Once more, let me say: I know I'm a different writer for all my time in America and England. I know my relationship with Karachi would be different if I lived there and knew, this is it. This is where I'll spend the next year, five years, ten years of my life. I know all this. But here's something else that I believe: writers never live in the place about which they write.

What I mean by this is that when you live in a place, you don't see it. This is not to say I agree with that oft-proclaimed line that expatriate or exiled writers are able to write more honestly, analytically, accurately about their former homes because distance gives them the ability to see more clearly. To be honest, I find that line deeply offensive to all the writers who write so brilliantly about places in which they've always lived. We write in one way about the lovers we've left, another way about the lovers we're forced to leave, another way about the lovers we meet for a few whirlwind weeks a year, and yet another way about the lovers with whom we cohabit. It's as true of cities as of people.

I'm full of digressions here. So much about this discussion seems to require qualifiers and explanations. The point I digressed from was this: when you live in a place, you don't see it. I mean, you don't notice it. It is the everyday scenery of your life, some background blur. It is what is usual, what is normal, what is expected. But writers – wherever they live, however long they've lived there – are always converting scenes into words. To do that you notice the details, the grains of wood in the doorway of your house. Every time I'm at the beach in Karachi I find myself wondering, 'What is the sound of the ocean?' I've never yet found an answer. How, in words, do you describe the sound of waves breaking in December when the sea is calm, in March when it's getting rough, in July when the monsoons make it lethal? I can hear the waves, right now, as I think about it – but I don't know the words to describe the sound I'm hearing. Once, driving through Karachi, I asked a friend to slow down because I wanted to see some building more closely. She said, 'What a touristy thing to say.' But I wasn't saying it because I had just got back from London after months away; I was saying it because I knew I would soon be writing a chapter set in that part of town and I wanted to have a strong visual sense of it in my head, even if none of those visual details actually made their way to the page. So I believe that there are ways in which writers mimic travellers – outsiders, even – in our ways of seeing, though not necessarily in our interpretation of the things we see.

How does my tri-continental living affect my writing? I don't know. I do know that it does affect it. I do know that it doesn't affect it in the way many people assume it does. So many words are spent on discussing writers in 'multiple locations' as though there were something that simultaneously binds us together and separates us from writers who've lived in 'single locations'. But really, how can any among us who read and, in reading, lose ourselves (and find ourselves) in countless worlds of fiction, pretend we've lived our lives in a single location? ❑

***Kamila Shamsie** is the author of* Kartography *(Bloomsbury, £9.99, May 2002) 'Mulberry Absences' appeared, in a slightly different version, in* Leaving Home: Towards a New Millennium, *ed Muneeza Shamsie (Oxford University Press, Karachi, 2001)*

ONION

SANCHITA ISLAM

When I walk down Brick Lane I see red-brick council flats, hanging saris blowing in the wind, a chicken bone lying on the street, crisp packets washed up with leaves and bloated jackfruit spilling on to the street. An Asian girl, with a thick black plait, wearing jeans that go up her crack and a top that clings to her flat chest, crosses the road. Another girl, could be a woman, a granny, don't know because she's hidden inside a cave of black. She sees her world through a slit of light and her toes are naked. Three boys with gelled-up hair loiter by a car that is half white and half brown with rust. It has no tyres, no doors, no windows, it's just a shell. 'Hello, nice pussy!' they heckle. 'Give us your number, darling.' Keep my head down, don't dare look up in case I grin. Speed past the Cash and Carry filled with one thousand packets of pink toilet roll and sacks of Basmati rice. Hear a fluttering of a flute, a tink tink, followed by a high-pitched voice and a tabla beat floating from a shop. The windows are plastered with posters of Bollywood stars. Men with moustaches wearing tight white pants. There's a stink of onions and rubbish in the air. Eastenders is filled with locals chewing on kebab rolls drenched in chillies and minty yoghurt. It's a no-nonsense place cluttered with orange plastic chairs and mirrored walls. The owner stands in the doorway, his hair cropped short, his pallor shiny, his clothes worn and his teeth stained red from chewing too much *paan*. He stares at his black Mercedes parked out front and I wonder how many kebabs he had to sell to buy it.

An old man, with a long grey beard, wearing socks and brown sandals, walks with his gaze fixed on his toes. He doesn't notice the Japanese girl with her spiky orange permed hair and fake leopard-print flares. He doesn't notice the guy with dreadlocks spinning some decks outside the Vibe bar or the trendies guzzling down pints. At six o'clock the sound of prayer drifts over Brick Lane. Melodic, profound, guttural and solemn. Pause to listen, even try to join in, but feel self-conscious, like I'm taking the piss, when I'm not. Push my way past the babble and travel to the top of the Truman Brewery. Through the large glass windows see Brick Lane, Canary Wharf, the council blocks, patches of green, distant buildings and a scrap heap of

London, 2002: Brick Lane.
Credit: Sanchita Islam

junk. See a little old lady emerge from a disused hut. She's wearing a pink jacket and slippers. She walks a few steps forward in tiny pin steps and then returns to her hut. Watch until a lump fills my throat and can't watch any more. Instead get out my sketchbook and start to draw. The looming blocks, the sloping rooftops, the wonky windows and the crumble. Draw it all before the scrap heap is cleared away and the old lady kicked out of her hut. Draw it all before the dotcoms and men in suits clean up. There's no room for error, no time to be precious, each mark is indelible, each line leads on to the next. Try to create a style that sums up Brick Lane. An onion style with its layers, its peel, its pinch and stink. A bit of Brick Lane, onion style. ❑

Sanchita Islam *is an artist, writer and film-maker. She heads Pigment Explosion, a company that specialises in live art and international art projects, and has exhibited her work in London, New York, Paris and Bangladesh. She is the editor of and contributor to* From Briarwood to Barishal to Brick Lane *(London Arts publication, July 2002)*

I HAVE NO OTHER HOMES

MIR MAHFUZ ALI

When I cross the blue sea
    a black woman
  waits for me
    under the leaking roof
  where I grew up.

When I cross the black sea
    a white woman
  waits for me
    under an apple tree
  where we first met.

The black woman
    is my old mother,
  the white woman
    is my young lover
  but they never have met.

They are my dust
    harvesting in the wind
  they are my vines
    linking me to the soil
  on which I now grow.

I have no other homes
    beside the hearts
  of these women,
    that's where I want to be
  all my life and in my death.

They are my favourite women,
    do not ask me
  to give them up
    for anything
  because I won't. ❑

Mir Mahfuz Ali *was born in Dhaka, Bangladesh, and studied literature at Essex University. He dances, acts, has worked as a male model and a tandoori chef, and is writing a novel based on his experiences in Britain and Bangladesh*

GOING HOME

ROMESH GUNESEKERA

Tamin paused to examine the brickwork. He was a tall man with a thin plait of grey hair running down his back. He wore a dark suit and a black felt hat. He reached for the bell but before he could ring it the door swung open. 'What the hell are you doing out there? Come in, come in.' Aldo grinned. 'I saw you from the window.'

'You know,' Tamin tapped the wall, 'this mortar is cracking.'

Before Aldo could reply, a woman's head bobbed up above him. It was his wife, Sonali. 'Exactly what I told him, sweetie. But does he ever listen?' She looked down at her husband who was a full five inches shorter than her. 'Rain will get in and ruin the whole house. Then, what will we do?'

Aldo stepped out from under her and opened his palm to the sky. 'What rain? This is the driest summer we have ever had, no?'

'But it will rain, sweetie. I know it will rain. This is England. In this country it can rain any time.'

'Don't be so bloody silly. Now let the man in, will you?'

Tamin bowed thoughtfully and stepped inside. Aldo shut the door behind them. 'How about a beer, huh?' Rising on tiptoe off his sandals, Aldo delivered a friendly slap on Tamin's back.

'Have some tea, sweetie?' Sonali countered.

'Thank you,' Tamin said to Sonali. He checked his watch. 'Afternoon tea would be perfect.' He removed his hat and placed it carefully on top of a stack of London telephone directories on the hall table. The wall behind it was covered in hessian and sported a collection of carved wooden masks, hung like the decapitated trophies of a settled exile. 'Are these our erstwhile Members of Parliament?'

Aldo laughed and waved his hand as if to clear a path, 'Go in, Tamin, go into the sitting-room. Young Dilip is there. The fellow is really excited today about the election back home.'

A muffled roar in the adjacent kitchen, where Sonali had disappeared, subsided as a kettle clicked itself off. Cupboard doors banged high and low. Crockery rattled everywhere.

Sonali had married Aldo when she was young and impressionable. He was older than her. Early in the marriage he had told her that he wanted a house full of children, but despite a ban on contraceptives and a regime of regular, even if monotonous, coupling there had been no issue. 'He thinks it's me,' Sonali complained to Tamin once, 'but I think it's more him than me.' Tamin had suggested ginseng. Sonali's eyes had widened. 'Really?'

Tamin floated into the sitting-room.

'Professor?' Dilip looked up. His face was round, like that of a small bird's. His eyes, magnified behind thick spectacles, looked hurt. He was sitting with his head half-cocked, fiddling with a small, silver short-wave radio. The little beard below his mouth was ruffled. 'Any news? Have you heard? I can't get a thing on this radio.'

Tamin looked at him, but said nothing.

'Pondering, huh, Professor? You already know who will win?' Aldo suggested from behind.

'I also know,' Dilip cut back in. 'I know who will win. Everybody knows.' He tossed the radio on to an empty chair. 'You don't have to be a fortune-teller. This time they made a real cock-up. Why did they call an election so suddenly?'

Aldo snapped his fingers, 'It was a gamble, Dilip, a gamble. Fellows thought no one else would be ready. Nip the opposition in the bud, you know. After so many years in power, defeat was inconceivable to the buggers. What do you say, Professor?'

Sonali shouted from the kitchen, 'Why didn't you buy some tea, mister big spender? You bought everything else in the shop, why not tea? He needs some tea, no, before he can talk. Isn't that so, Professor?' She peeped out from the doorway. 'How are you doing anyway, sweetie?'

Tamin smiled graciously and perched down on a large settee below a print of two kingfishers. When he was with a group he always liked to cultivate an air of expectation around him. He would often let others speak for him until the exchanges reached a point at which everyone became aware that he had not said a word, and that they had all exposed themselves. Then he would say something totally unrelated which, because of the atmosphere created, would be taken as deeply profound. It was a trick he learned in his youth. His companions would be reeling afterwards: 'Why the hell did he say that?' Aldo would ask. Dilip would wag his boxy head, 'A real genius.' But Sonali would admonish them both for misunderstanding the Professor completely and they would argue about his pronouncements for days.

'I was thinking about the shape at the back of your masks in the hall. The negative shape. If we had a real artist, he would be the one to paint these masks from the back. A reverse-mask, you know.'

'Backside painter!' Aldo roared with laughter. 'What do you think, Dilip? Backside painter, like you, no?'

Dilip wiggled his head, settling his round spectacles nearer the end of his beak. 'I don't understand. What do you mean, reverse?'

'The outward appearance, like a politician's party, means nothing. Policies, principles, they all shift. The plumage changes, but the creature inside, the real beast, never does.' Tamin tapped his chest. 'You understand?'

Dilip stared at him in a kind of awe. 'Will they call you back, Professor? This time they really should. General Advisor. Something special. The world's first Minister of Philosophy. They need someone like you, no?'

'Anything is possible. From manic superstition it is but a small step to comic art.' Tamin's face was deadpan. He examined his neatly manicured fingernails, turning his hands over one at a time.

Aldo laughed loudly again. Although he was a short man, he had a lot of belly. 'But what about the leopard and its spots, Professor?' He pulled at the flab cradled by his belt. 'I thought the point was that it can't change its *spots*.'

Tamin gently rocked his head from side to side as if he was comparing cuticles and smiled.

Sonali came in with a teapot. 'We could also have a Minister of Poetry, and a Minister of Disarmament in charge of defence.' She grinned at Dilip and added, 'Luckily I found that tea you brought, Dilip, the other day. Thank God.'

Aldo picked up a big, brown, plastic bottle of beer, warily watching his wife through a corner of his eye. Lately, her presence seemed to diminish him. His face grew grim, as though the thoughts in his head were shrivelling even with her breath. Suddenly he kicked off his sandals. 'Minister of Disarmament? Don't be so bloody silly. What a stupid thing to say.'

'Why, sweetie? Too much is spent on weapons. Poor countries like ours are crazy to do this.'

'What do you know?' Aldo snapped. He leaned forward and almost lost his balance. 'What do you know about defence? About government? What are you talking about? They have to protect property. Against terrorists, insurrectionists, scroungers. There are wars to fight, you know. The real world is a tough place. Not some hogwash utopia.'

'I'm talking about insanity, sweetie,' Sonali sniffed. 'I think the world is going crazy, and you know why? Do you know why? It's because of people like you. Just because some little runt has given you a cut on his gun sale, or whatever, you think it is all fine and dandy. You'd do anything to make a buck, no?'

Dilip looked uneasy, stuck between the couple. He steadied himself against the long, velour arm of his chair, preparing to intervene. 'Actually, Aldo, you know I seem to remember there *was* a Minister of Disarmament. A real one. In Czechoslovakia or somewhere. Before the partition. Didn't Havel have some disarmament business?'

'Bloody right,' Aldo nodded vigorously. 'Absolutely. I'm sure he did. This would not be the first time. It would be nothing special anyway.' He glared at his wife. 'Just bloody imitation.' He opened the bottle of beer and filled a glass. He put it in on the table and gloated.

But Sonali felt vindicated, too. 'See. Then it is not so stupid. Is it, dear Professor? If they had one in Prague . . . Anyway, why not make your enemy an ally? Make them ministers, generals, why not?' She poured a cup of tea for Tamin and placed it next to the beer, slightly closer to him. 'Here's your tea, sweetie.' Tamin looked at her in his rather distant way. Sonali was always seeking allies. Like an ambassador on a goodwill mission, she would hoard surreptitious signals, nods of approval, any hint of potential support, to fortify her resources and free a little bit more space from her husband's burgeoning girth.

Aldo ignored Sonali and turned to Tamin. He rapped on the table with his knuckles. 'Have the beer. It has a *pukka* head. Look at it. Excellent value.' The white froth had risen over the brim of the tumbler. 'Have you seen anything like it?'

Dilip retreated, relieved, and pulled out a crimson handkerchief from his pocket. Perspiration had collected on the lower rims of his spectacles. He started to clean them, glad to have escaped more bickering. 'Isn't it time for the news. There should be something on TV by now, no?'

'Television will ignore us unless there is a disaster,' Tamin announced. 'And by tomorrow it will all seem to have been inevitable.' He stared out of the window as if he was watching his words sink into the parched earth.

'But if the government loses, won't there be a flight of capital, Professor? How will they stop it?' The idea of money flying fascinated Dilip. He had spent eleven years working in the registry of a small investment firm in Holborn, nurturing dreams of sudden wealth. Every Friday night, on his way home, he would buy a lottery ticket in the blind hope that as a result he could stop work the following Monday, and sit in his back garden eating Jaffa cakes and drinking champagne for ever.

Tamin sipped his tea. 'Only the weak will fly. Capital these days has its own wings.'

Aldo leaned back and put his small, now bare, feet on the table next to the beer. 'You know, the real business to be in today is international travel. An ocean liner moored just off-limits would be the best. You could sell the berths fivefold to the chaps who want an escape route. They want to be able to get away, on a coconut shell if they have to, if things don't go their way.' He chuckled. 'So, you know what I did? I bought a load of airline tickets.'

'What? What tickets?' Dilip flapped about in the depths of the armchair, a look of panic in his eyes. 'What kind of tickets are you talking about?'

'As soon as I knew the date of the election I bought them. I got a *pukka* rate on the batch. This week's cheapest flights out of the country. You try to get a cheap ticket out now, there is no chance except through my agent. He has the lot and is negotiating premium rates. A lot of people want insurance. An option to fly at short notice. I remember the last time there was a change of government. Oh boy, how the buggers flew. They flew with their gems all stuffed in their butts.'

Dilip struggled to get out of the chair. 'Why didn't you tell me? Why? You never said anything about tickets. You know how much I need a break, no?'

'But you have no dough, my friend. You can't do these things with nothing. You have to have money to make money, you know.' Aldo stood up and patted Dilip on the head.

Dilip was breathing furiously. His lips were trembling. He grabbed the cord beading on the upholstery and hauled himself to the edge of the seat.

Sonali stood up. 'You boys are mad. What are you talking about? Enough of this lining the pocket and kicking everyone else in the teeth. He's joking, can't you see? Nobody's going anywhere. You think those fat cats want to leave? They make money in their sleep, you know, there.'

'But why can't we all make some money, Sonali?' Dilip was nearly in tears.

'But you won't, Dilip buddy, and I will.' Aldo gave Dilip a hard slap on the knee and laughed even louder than before. 'I am not joking, my friend. She knows nothing.'

Dilip clasped his hands around his knees and stared at the carpet.

Tamin finished his cup of tea. 'You should have sold everything you had and gone back three weeks ago, Dilip. House, goods, chattel, shares. You should have sold everything you had and gone with plenty of cash.'

'Why?' Dilip looked bewildered.

'Because you could be buying now, when everyone else is selling. Today you could have bought the whole city for peanuts, everyone is so jittery. In a few days everything will be back to normal. Then everybody will want to buy back everything they sold today, at whatever price you want.'

Dilip let himself slip back into his chair. 'Seems very dangerous, to buy when they sell, and sell when they want to buy. Would you?'

Tamin shook his head modestly, 'I don't dabble in bubbles.'

Aldo scratched the side of his belly a little nervously. 'You think the buggers might really sit tight this time, huh?'

Tamin took a long, deep breath. 'Possibly. The world, I think, is changing. Anyway, I must go now. I am expecting a phone call tonight.'

The other three looked at him, startled. Sonali held his arm. 'Stay, will you, and eat some dinner.'

'We have wine. Some very fine wine. Stay, Tamin, I bought it to celebrate. Special offer. Two for ten quid. Whoever is winning, we can celebrate. They are all the same these days, you know. My agent is absolutely certain, somebody will want to fly out with their secret stash. We can have a fine night.' Aldo winked and rubbed his fingers together rustling a sheaf of imaginary notes. 'Heads I win, tails you lose,' he grinned at Dilip. He reached across and slapped him again on the knee even harder than before. 'What do you say, huh?'

Dilip also appealed to Tamin. 'Stay, please?' He took his spectacles off and blinked.

Tamin shook his head gravely and went into the hall to pick up his hat. 'Thank you, Sonali, for the tea. I only dropped in to say hello.' He pulled at his plait of grey hair. 'It is a very important call I am expecting. Right from the top, you know? Anyway, you people have plenty to talk about. Now is the time to speculate.' He secured his black felt hat firmly in place with a hard tug and stepped out. While the others huddled in the hall behind him, bound together in uncertain dreams, he allowed another small smile to open into the moist air freshening before him. He was going home. ❏

Romesh Gunesekera *was born in Sri Lanka. Before coming to the UK he lived in the Philippines. He now lives in London. His first novel* Reef *was published to much acclaim in 1994. His most recent book is* Heaven's Edge *(Bloomsbury 2002)*

FLYING HOME

SUDEEP SEN

('I love the luxury of secrets', anon.)

I meticulously stitch time through the embroidered sky,
  through its unpredictable lumps and hollows. I

am going home once again from another
  home, escaping the weave of reality into another

one, one that gently reminds and stalls
  to confirm: my body is the step-son of my soul.

But what talk of soul and skin
  in this day and age, such ephemeral things,

that cross-weave blood and breath
  into clotted zones of true escape.

What talk of flight time and flying
  when real flights of fancy are crying

to stay buoyant unpredictably in mid-air
  amid pain, peace, and belief: just like thin air

sketches, where another home is built
  in free space vacuum, as another patchwork quilt

is quietly wrapped around, gently, in memoriam. ❏

From Postmarked India: New & Selected Poems *(1997)*

***Sudeep Sen** was born in New Delhi in 1964 and came to London in 1991.* Postmarked India *was awarded the Hawthornden Fellowship (UK) and nominated for a Pushcart Prize (USA). He lives and works between London and New Delhi*

BEING HERE

AMARJIT CHANDAN

Being is an existential problem; and being with a small 'b' in a so-called alien country with its colonialist past is perhaps not so difficult to divulge with the help of clichéd phrases. The word 'exile' has been a favourite word of writers, artists and political activists. I am here because I had no choice. I think man is an exile everywhere. That's his fate. The real home of a man is where he has dignity, a possible hope or a desperate optimism. A place where one can afford to say No. Being a poet I have that choice. Words like racism and alienation as descriptions of my and other black people's social situation here don't carry the same meaning to me as they did some years ago. I would have felt alienated and marginalised in my 'home', if I were in the Punjab today. I never feel nostalgic about my past. It was hard, too hard. Personal and social reasons made it so. In the Indian collective unconscious, one always returns home. As a good, obedient son, Ram spent 14 years in the forest and when he returned everyone rejoiced. Divali – the festival of lights, the carnival of homecoming – is celebrated every year. Nanak left home four times in search of knowledge and returned. I am not here to uphold my family's honour or to seek knowledge. I have no desire to go back. But the strange leader in the memory game takes me back and on the lane smashes me, as a character in the computer game is done to pieces. Again, I collect my bits and pieces and re-emerge and am again smashed. The cycle never ends and it goes on for ever. I wonder whose hands are the game gear.

I think, feel and dream in Punjabi. My language is my real home, my last retreat. Freud says it's not possible to return to the womb. In another context, John Berger talks about the myth of return. I still have associations with some Punjabi words and the words *ma boli*, mother language, are very close to me. My poems bear witness that the return is possible; and in *ma boli* I feel most secure and at one with my own self. By contrast, just one English word, 'telephone', is very close to me. I was mortified to realise one day that the language in which my beloved children converse with me and the language that gives me my bread and butter is so strange to me. This came as a shock. The loss of my language has been the most severe blow. Again, I don't blame anyone but myself. This is the price I'm paying for being here. It was *my* choice.

There is a catch when I talk of the language. Memories have been the recurrent theme in my recent poems. But what are memories? The slow-motion images that are retrieved or come back in sonic codes. In other words, language – sonic codes – is memory, personal as well as collective. If I find my memories tormenting, how can I feel secure with my mother language?

In my most recent poem, I express the desire to go beyond language and feel free and be silent for ever. Again, I know it's not that easy and there is no escape from memories. Despite my being here, I have no choice.

TROLLOPE & COLLS

Leaning on a derelict pier of the Thames
In the celestial blue neon light
 of capital letters TROLLOPE & COLLS

Unholding her hand abruptly from me
She whispered: 'I make no kiss' &
Lost for words, flicking through
 the English phrase book, continued –

'I feel sad what happen to me tomorrow.
Don't ask me difficult questions
 of why &, but & and . . .'

A boat blew its foghorn.
The tide's waves thumped the bank
& a pair of camouflaged ducks stayed still ❑

***Amarjit Chandan** is from the Punjab in India. He came to the UK in 1996. The above is excerpted from* Being Here *(The Many Press, London 1993)*

FUSSY, MILITANT, REBEL

USHA KISHORE

You want me to be invisible,
I want to be seen; you preach
equality, but I want difference –
You call me fussy . . .

You want me to grin and bear
your affectionate connections
with the Paki corner shop;
I demand an apology –
You dub me militant . . .

You want me to nod assent
when you are rewarded for
my efforts; I call for equality
of acknowledgement –
You title me rebel . . .

I play by your rules and you call
me names – for I am your other,
Your reflection in a dark mirror,
Your consciousness in colour –
I am Caliban, you want to tame me;
I am the exotic, you want to taste me;
When I say I am human, like you,
You get lost in the dual labyrinths
of nature and culture –
But I have come a long way
through space and time –
I want to be seen!
I want to be heard!
I want to be thought of!

I demand non-stop and I get my
difference, my apology and my
acknowledgement!
Somewhere in you lurks the
Sahib, you very soon give in
to the stubborn native in me –
Your atavistic guilt would kill you
otherwise . . . ❑

***Usha Kishore** lives on the Isle of Man*

STRANGERS ON A TRAIN

ROHAN JAYASEKERA

I saw him twice, moving through the carriage. Both times he looked me over, first flicking a look into my eyes as if to provoke a reaction; the second time giving my suit the once-over, as if it puzzled him. He was no one I'd ever seen before, but I recognised him anyway.

The pristine steel high-speed TGV between Paris and Amsterdam is no sane man's Orient Express, but train travel appeals to both my English and Sri Lankan halves. Throughout the early 1980s, I took the train as often as possible when travelling from my news agency HQ in Holland to the bureaus in Paris, Bonn and Brussels.

The man was familiar, not from Paris, but from my reporter's visits to Romania. He had that pressed and shining but worn-out polyester navy blue suit, kept clean and functional way beyond its natural life, that tie, slightly too broad for the day, slightly too red to match the suit. And he wore black tasselled loafers.

Of course, I could have placed him as a Roma from his face, but we had separately chosen to compare sartorial notes as guides to racial origin. On the third sweep he sat down in front of me and asked sharply: '*D'où sont vous?*'

He had been looking at my suit, too. It was Swiss, charcoal grey, relatively expensive (I bought it to get married in), but also unpressed and unnecessarily uncared for.

'England,' I replied, in English.

From his look it was clear he didn't believe me. Being born off north London's Holloway Road does not automatically confer Englishness. 'I'm Sri Lankan,' I said cravenly, '*but* I was born in London.' I nearly said 'British', but his triumphant snort cut off further qualification.

He leaned forward conspiratorially. 'Have you seen any passport inspectors on this train?' he asked.

There, I had it. Sri Lankans were roaming Europe in their tens of thousands, on their way to jobs as doctors and hotel maids, travel agents and grocers, in corners of cities where locals dare not or care not to tread. It was obvious what I was doing. The question was whether I was doing it legally or illegally. And the clue was to be found in the quality of the suit.

He had wives, plural, neither of whom appeared to be aware of each other, two passports and two questions for every one of mine. 'Have you ever seen a passport check on this train? Are you married? How much do you earn? Where do you work?'

But he was soon bored by my answers, as none of them was really much use to him. He was also vaguely annoyed that I wasn't flying from Paris to Amsterdam since I clearly could have got the agency to pay for it. By carelessly dismissing an opportunity denied him, I was somehow being insulting.

And then we were not alone: we were being watched by another furtive traveller, standing at the end of the carriage. And since we were still not far from the subject of daywear, his was styled in the Roma fashion, but in brown and topped by a thick yellow sweater. The Roma waved at him to join us. He sat down. And turned out to be a Kurd from south-east Turkey.

So we chatted together, representatives of the three great travelling peoples of late twentieth-century Western Europe (the Bosnians stayed in Germany; the Maghrebis in France), discussing passports and wives and jobs and my war stories from Timişoara and Trincomalee, Sarajevo and Diyarbakir.

We continued in English for a while, but the Roma eventually began to struggle.

'*Parlez-vous le français*?' offered the Kurd helpfully.

'*Oui. Vous?*' To me.

'*Oui*. Ish.'

'Ish?'

'Never mind. *Ne vous en inquiétez pas. Continuez, s'il vous plait . . .*'

'*Pourquoi vous n'avez pas volé?*' The Kurd, to me, accusingly.

The Roma looked at me, then the Kurd. He rolled his eyes.

'. . . *ainsi*,' he said, changing the subject. '*C'est ma femme . . .*'

'. . . *son oncle a eu l'habitude d'être un policier et j'ai été inquiété . . .*'

'. . . *allez au marché de poisson. Mardi. C'est toujours intéressant . . .*'

The Kurd could manage but he wasn't happy. He cursed softly while trying to remember a word in French, connected to heavy lorries. '*Sprechen sie Deutsch?*' he asked. The Roma nodded and off they went again.

'. . . *Anhänger?*' wondered the Kurd. '*Tja, ich traf sie dort, und sie war fein . . .*'

'. . . *der Inhaber war schmutzig, aber die Garage war vollkommen . . .*'

'*. . . ich kann für drei Reisen pro Jahr vom Geld zahlen, das ich dort verdiene . . .*'

But neither was happy spitting out their flat unloved German, and the Kurd did not demur when the Roma, unheralded, switched seamlessly to Dutch.

'*. . . u moeten overnemen te Toyota,*' he said. '*Op heeft meerder ruim achterin . . .*'

'*. . . weliswaar. Tweetal pizza parlour in zijn geheel jaartal . . .*'

'*. . . mij tevens verafschuwen naar de koffie . . .*'

But something still bothered them both. Neither of them cared much for The Netherlands and still less for its horrible language. They fell silent, hunched, regarding each other's shoes. I had long ago fallen silent, quietly marvelling at the way they had adapted to life between Western Europe's cities of hate, like jungle-hardened commandos patrolling undetected through the deep unforgiving forests.

Then the Kurd's face lit up. '*Parliamo Italiano?*' he whooped.

'*Si! Si!*' replied the Roma brightly. The pair of them chattered away merrily like Neapolitan waiters for the next 100km with barely a breath, and I went back to my newspaper. ❑

Summer 1994

Rohan Jayasekera *was born in the UK of Sri Lankan parents. After considerable journalistic experience, he now works as web managing editor for* Index on Censorship (www.indexonline.org). *He says of himself: 'That exchange on that train was a life-changing revelation to me. It was like the way it suddenly clicks for a pure mathematician. In a flash everything I was seeing happening around me in Europe that year, my nationality, my racial identity, my place on this planet and in England, where I could not physically bring myself to say out loud, "I'm English," everything made sudden sense, like logical functions in a single all-encompassing formula. It was like stepping out into a new skin. For the first time in 33 years I had found a place on earth to stand. I was a migrant. My identity was my very lack of one.'*

DIASPORIC DIARY IN MANHATTAN

SALIL TRIPATHI

Manhattan is full of serendipitous discoveries. One evening in April, when I had gone to see my friend Bharati from Bombay, I ran into P Sainath, the journalist who wrote a classic study about drought and development issues in India. That was the first pleasant coincidence. The next afternoon at a café in the East Village, I recounted that story to my friend Suketu Mehta who simply shrugged with the air of someone who had ceased to be surprised by such things.

I mentioned I was planning to go later that evening to the opening of an art exhibition of Jehangir Sabavala, the distinguished septuagenarian painter from Bombay. Suketu couldn't make it, but said: 'You'll enjoy it; everyone will be there.'

I wasn't so sure. After all, Manhattan has hundreds of art galleries; the gallery hosting Sabavala's show was medium-sized in downtown Fifth Avenue; and it was a sunny Friday evening. Still, I headed for the gallery to, well, meet everyone.

And so it was. I met Jeet Thayil, an old friend from Bombay who worked as a reporter under duress to pursue his real interest, poetry; a bearded painter who turned out to have taught art at the school I attended in Bombay, except that he migrated to the US the year I started at the Montessori school; and then there was this woman that Jeet and I thought we had met before, but she said: 'Well, I have a very Bombay face, you know, and everyone thinks he has met me.' In the end, she turned out to be Maitri, whom I had not met before but who was at business school with my wife.

In no time, this twilight hour at an art gallery in Manhattan, flanked by the sunlit Flatiron Building on its right and with a sylvan park in front, with its leaves shining brilliantly in the unusual heat, turned into an evening that could so easily have belonged to Nariman Point, Bombay, 1986.

It was easy to feel that I was at home again. Even if this home was not a place but time; and the city was Manhattan, the world's melting pot, not Bombay, India's melting pot.

I grew up in Bombay, and since then have lived and worked in five other cities for periods ranging from a few months to years. In each of these cities,

Amrit Kaur Singh, 'Manhattan Mall', 1997. 'A satirical look at the destruction of the Native American way of life by the American Dream' (AKS). Credit: © the artist

I have encountered the Indian diaspora, seeking to reclaim me with its grocery stores in its Little Indias; its video shops and Bollywood posters; its newspapers from home and Alphonso mangoes in season; its *Lijjat papads* and the smell of turmeric. The stores sell nostalgia, a connection with the past, trying to help the immigrant – or expatriate – adjust to the new land. Yes, the landscape around you has changed; the streets are suddenly cleaner and supermarkets are well stocked and there's snow on the street and no servants and it is expensive to call home all the time, but the fridge is full and there's a car in the garage. The world is suddenly, bafflingly, different outside, but you can remain the way you were, in your own mind and in your kitchen. And Little India helps you achieve that: Grey Street in Durban,

Serangoon Road in Singapore, 26th Street in Manhattan, Jackson Heights – or what Indians call Jaykishan Heights – in Queens, Ealing or Southall in London, Mody Street in Hong Kong.

Little India is where the diaspora meets to indulge in nostalgia. There are posters advertising Bharat Natyam classes and faded copies of *Stardust* magazine, announcements of visiting gurus and swamis, and the familiar face of the store's owner, the hard-working Gujarati, who's a one-stop Google search engine, and sometimes works faster than Google itself. He connects myriad strands of people within the overseas Indian network; like the collectors and information mavens Malcolm Gladwell writes about in *The Tipping Point*, he feels he has performed his karmic duty by introducing a homesick student to the lady who'd like to earn extra income by letting a room in her house to someone reliable; by linking the man with an eligible-age daughter with the family looking for a bride for a cousin back home in India, all from a good family, of course, no scandals, same caste even.

In a sense, that Little India is fossilised, its world view set in a period during which most of the Indians left home for this new land. Which is why, in Mauritius, you hear traces of Bhojpuri accents that have refused to submerge in the more Sanskritised Hindi that now dominates the Gangetic plain of India. And in Singapore and Kuala Lumpur, Hindus ritually pierce their bodies and carry impossibly large idols, called *kavadis*, during Thaipusam, a festival rarely seen in southern India these days. And in parts of Britain, parents want to compel their young daughters, bred in Britain, unquestioningly and obediently to marry the groom they've chosen for them, because parents know what's best for their children. There are horrendous repercussions, too, when feudal-minded, caste-obsessed parents force these daughters to marry men untutored in modernity.

But there are good things that emerge out of such fossilisation, too. In the 1990s, Hindus in Durban threw out Hindu preachers from the subcontinent (and Muslims did likewise with Muslim preachers), when they tried to spread their poison of rebuilding the Ram Temple in Ayodhya to people of Indian origin who had moved to South Africa a century before. Saira Essa, an actress I came to know in Durban, told me: 'We told them to get lost. We had a far bigger issue to worry about in the new South Africa – the position of minorities, the fight for justice for all people of colour. Just who did these preachers think they were fooling when they tried to divide us into Hindus and Muslims? Don't they know Gandhi started his struggle here, that he was invited by Muslim businessmen? We told them: You take your hatred back to India; break your mosques and temples there. Leave us alone.'

Saira's India, which is now in the distant past, is the kind of India I had belonged to and which I miss. That's how Bombay was in 1982 when I left it first, to study in the US. But it had changed when I returned in 1986; and by the time I left it again, in 1990, it had begun to move inexorably in the other direction. The virus of the mainland was contaminating the island.

Which is why that evening in Manhattan was so important. It had brought together my diaspora; the kind of people who once belonged to my Bombay, but who were now in Manhattan. We, from the diaspora of Bombay – which is big enough, anyway, and India is far too complicated for any generalisation, including this one – had been clinging not to a place, but a sense of time, an era. Indeed, we could all return to Bombay, and perhaps meet again at the Jehangir Nicholson Gallery at Nariman Point. But it wouldn't be the same. That time which was important to us has gone. The Hindu nationalists and Marathi chauvinists who dominate Bombay's political space have already renamed my city: parochial-sounding, insipid Mumbai. And Salman Rushdie, the Badshah of Breach Candy, has also moved to Manhattan. As Rushdie wrote in his essay on the film *The Wizard of Oz*: 'The truth is once we have left our childhood places and started out to make up our lives, armed only with what we have and are, we understand that the real secret of the ruby slippers is not that "there's no place like home", but rather that there is no longer any such place as *home*: except, of course, for the home we make, or the homes that are made for us, in *Oz*: which is anywhere, and everywhere, except the place from which we began.' ❑

***Salil Tripathi** was born in Bombay and studied in the US. He then lived in Geneva and New York before returning to Bombay. He moved again, to Singapore and Hong Kong, and now lives in London. He is a regular contributor to* Index *and other publications, including the* Wall Street Journal *and the* New Statesman. *He is working on his first novel*

THE LANGUAGE OF EXILE
GAO XINGJIAN & YANG LIAN

WHEN PAIN TURNS TO GAIN

'Exile forces a writer to mature, to be more exacting with language. Being separated from your readership means your work loses all practical significance: there is no connection between writing and making a living. If you still want to write, it has to be purely for yourself and you must make greater demands on your language.'

Gao Xingjian's work focuses on the painful transition of ancient, traditional China into the modern world. The effect of this on Chinese history and culture has never been explored in any depth since the establishment of the People's Republic in 1949. The award of the Nobel Prize for Literature in 2000 recognised Gao's role in demonstrating that Chinese literary culture is still alive and capable of renewal, despite the depredations of the Cultural Revolution and the extremes of social realism demanded by the Party in the interests of revolutionary propaganda.

Gao was able to publish a considerable body of work in China in the 1980s – novellas, short stories, plays, critical essays and four books – though not without problems. In 1982, his play Absolute Signal *played to packed audiences at the Beijing People's Arts Theatre; but in the following year the performance of* Bus Stop *was banned and described by a senior Party member as 'the most pernicious work since the establishment of the People's Republic'.*

In 1987, when Gao left to take up a fellowship in Germany, he took with him the manuscript of Lingshan. *Known in the West under the title* Soul Mountain, *it was completed in 1989 in exile in Paris, where he now lives. Essentially, it is the story of one man's search for inner peace and tranquillity; for the recovery and expression of the self of the individual, all but annihilated in the chaos of the Cultural Revolution. Writers and artists for whom their work was a matter of self-expression were ruthlessly and brutally silenced at that time. When, at the height of the Cultural Revolution, it became too dangerous even to hide them, Gao burned all the several hundred works he had written during the 1960s and 1970s.*

From exile in Paris, Gao continues to write, constantly experimenting with language, bringing together an awareness of the importance of the image and the renewal of language in today's visually oriented world. He is well known throughout Europe and the USA for his large-scale black-and-white Chinese ink paintings with which he largely supports himself.

In the course of his own exile – first in Australia and now in the UK – the poet Yang Lian has met Gao several times. Here we print excerpts from their ongoing conversations on language, literature, the pursuit of the self and the joys, as well as the pains, of the writer in exile.

JVH

Gao Xingjian,
Land of Dreams.
Credit: Schimmel Center for the Arts, New York

YANG LIAN The term 'mother tongue' is loaded with significance: 'mother's language', 'mother's land' both suggest an inheritance. In the past, language was determined by the great group concepts of 'mother' – the motherland, society and the family. Even to say 'intellectual', for instance, in Chinese – literally, 'knowledgeable social element' – emphasises the 'social element' in knowledge. So today, doesn't everyone – especially Chinese writers in the diaspora – have an inescapable duty to take language and turn it upon the self, the individual; to use it to interrogate the self? To put it another way, we do not 'exist' within language, language 'exists' within us.

GAO XINGJIAN What I tried to do in *Soul Mountain* was to express in Chinese the many coexistent levels of experience in modern life, and to present it as a 'stream of language'. Can Chinese do that? After reading Proust, Joyce and Virginia Woolf, I felt that western languages were equipped to write about psychology with such subtlety, but Chinese provides only a structure; the complex psychology exists between the lines, in what we call 'the winsome smile' of the language: in what isn't said. It doesn't trace or describe the inner layers and processes. If I were to try something new with the Chinese language, I'd expend a lot of effort reconsidering its grammatical structure. If the Chinese language expressed the behaviour of consciousness, it would be freer than western languages, more flexible, fuller. But it's much stronger than western languages at expressing strict logical analyses, so, on an analogy with the western 'stream of consciousness', I'd suggest the concept of a 'stream of language' for Chinese writing.

Because a person's consciousness is illogical and so dynamic, so volatile, it can't tolerate the strict tenses and subject-predicates of western languages. But Chinese possesses exactly the characteristics of the behaviour of consciousness. The reason I suggest 'stream of language' is because I think a 'stream of consciousness' is actually unattainable. All that can really be attained is a 'stream of language' and nothing more.

YANG LIAN When I read *Soul Mountain,* I felt it was the only Chinese novel I'd ever read that from beginning to end maintained a distinct awareness of the act of writing itself. Sometimes the writer becomes so involved in the things he's writing about that he forgets these things only exist because of writing. As a result, thinking about 'how to write' and 'what to write' become the same thing, and writing itself becomes the content, intimately linked with the characters' psychology. Compared to this, 'things' become secondary. My long poem *Yi* [the character for *Yi* is an invented composite made up of the characters for *person* and *sun*, corresponding to the philosophical concept that heaven and man are one – *tian ren he yi*], which I wrote in China, I set out using the form and structure of Chinese characters, extending the concept of 'space'. Poetry is a space constructed with language and, as with *In Symmetry with Death*, Chinese myths, legends, history and even the 'I' are all merely words which when thrown into confusion gather and merge together. Because tenses don't change in Chinese, words are rewritten as 'another renewed history' – my own, individual fabricated history. The Chinese language can enable history to exist in the present tense.

GAO XINGJIAN *Yi* is a good, thorough experiment with the Chinese language. It not only seeks a literary form, it also creates a complex language structure. Such experiments themselves embody the efforts to create a modern Chinese language, transforming it into something entirely new, something your own.

YANG LIAN Some writers lay down their pens, others continue to write and others again merely 'borrow' the consciousness, sentence structures, vocabulary and 'flavours' from traditional vignettes, novels and the ancient plays of the Yuan and Song dynasties, just adding a little modern 'spice' and going through the motions of writing. Isn't this because after the individual replaced the group [after the Cultural Revolution], the responsibility on the individual writer to develop language – the pressure of language on the individual – was too great? As a result, while the writer lives, the work collapses.

GAO XINGJIAN Being overseas isn't only non-restricting, it's actually stimulating. Maybe stimulation comes from restrictions. It's possible. When I look back now on the pieces I wrote in China, I find so much that could be changed, such as an impure use of language, or an awareness of language that just isn't strong enough. Conversely, my language now is much cleaner. And, apart from that, my sense of responsibility towards language is much clearer now; it's a creative approach. If we are going to play with language we must play extremely well. There's no urgency now for any current works to be published and no urgency to let other people read them. To put it another way, writing is for the self and for one's own pleasure. I regard writing as the winning of a kind of freedom, a kind of luxury, and so I'm even more aware of the approach to language.

YANG LIAN In China, social and ideological pressures blur or obscure a writer's attention to language. Originally, a writer's most fundamental contradiction was that between the desire to create and the limitations of language. But inside China this is often 'externalised' and becomes a different contradiction: such things as politics, the struggle for rights and social problems are externalised and create a sense of terror of external dangers. And in a collectivised social environment, this then hinders and even destroys the internal connections between the 'self', that sense of terror, and any 'introspection'. As a result, there's no politics and there's no writing. The environment after leaving China resolved both the original suppression and a writer's basic nature, and made the conflict between people and language far more evident.

GAO XINGJIAN When other factors no longer exist, you're left facing only your language. I'd say a writer has a responsibility only to his language; he is not responsible for the 'motherland', or the 'people'. A writer not only becomes removed from the social environment of his original language, he is also removed from his readers and essentially ends up in a state of 'absolute separation'. When you're only responsible for language, your demands on language are far more rigorous. When creating, you have to consider whether or not you're conforming to the characteristics and norms of the Chinese language – and this is manifested in the way you deal with the manuscript. In the past, I used to write all night and hand in a manuscript in the morning. Now, I can leave it to one side as I please and take it out and rework it as I please until I myself feel it's extremely clean; then it's OK. As to the levels of purity in language and experiments with language, I always hope to achieve perfection. If I'm asked what benefit to my writing there is from exile, it is that there is greater peace for a writer, and if my work is read three or five years later, I don't feel there's a problem.

For example, when I received the first year's royalties for a book I'd published in Taiwan, only 90 or so copies had been sold, and only 60 in the second year. In the third year, I went to Taiwan and it rose to some 200 copies, but the publishers had printed 2,000 copies. They were going to take ages to sell. So I wrote an essay called 'Cold Literature'. But exile compels the writer to become 'hot'. Leaving a society and readers makes writing lose all its practical significance. If you still want to write, it has to be purely for yourself. It's extremely valuable to maintain that pleasure and luxury for yourself, and that, naturally, places great importance on it. So your approach towards language becomes an ever more onerous burden. That's the positive side of 'exile'; I'd even say it doesn't have much of a negative side.

All the years I was writing in China, I never planned to publish. That includes *Soul Mountain*. When I started writing it in 1982 I had only one idea and that was to write a book. Perhaps it was a book that couldn't be published in my lifetime – I wasn't counting on that at the time. It was only after I came to the West that it became completely clear.

Going back to the nature of literature, what I call 'cold literature': whatever's said about Cao Xueqin [*Dream of the Red Bed Chamber*] and Shi Naiyan [*Journey to the West*], they never thought about being published when they were writing. One, they didn't depend upon it to eat, and two, they weren't looking for readers, it was only for a few close friends and associates, even just for themselves – purely for pleasure. I think this is fundamental to the nature of literature. So many other things are appended on to the body of literature that it becomes pressurised to such a degree it can't breathe.

China 1966: Red Guards destroy a Confucian shrine. Credit: Xinhua News Agency Beijing / Endeavour Group UK

YANG LIAN Whether in or out of China, I often feel people have a kind of misconception that sees literature as a 'necessary' thing, something 'needed' by society or by reality. I see those writers as needing society as a kind of 'intravenous drip', where the conflicts and aims in their work are all placed outside and they collude with society in an 'external circulation'. As soon as the 'drip' is removed, the writer's death is proclaimed. As far as we're concerned, perhaps the earlier the drip is removed the better. The earlier it's taken away, the better the opportunity to adjust the relationship between creative impressions of existence and language, thereby forming an 'internal circulation'. When I was writing poetry in China, I'd always consciously create a distance between language and the superficialities of life in society. I always wrote as though every piece was the last I'd write and, since these were to be my last words, I had no alternative but to 'vomit' everything out from its deepest place, and to present it all in language. You don't take into account whether people will understand or accept it, you care only about whether poetry can allow you to 'exist'. After leaving China, even though there was a language barrier to face, experiences were never interrupted and the process of feeling every kind of emotion was never disturbed. The connections between people and language became ever more balanced, subjective and clear, and that's what I base my writing on.

GAO XINGJIAN Because of that, we don't have to worry about the critics, it doesn't matter if there is or isn't criticism, if there is or isn't a readership. There are just a few good friends reading my books, but luckily a few other people show an interest. It's a conversation with no response. Something is dropped into the ocean and it creates no ripples, so why do you want to write? It can be understood only in terms of the satisfaction you yourself gain. I sometimes sit in front of my desk and just write what I want to write, and that's enough. As a result, the purpose of writing is very pure. Writing that has no readers and has no audience is not necessarily a bad thing. But when I write plays, I still consider the audience. Why? Because it's fundamental to the dramatic form itself. It requires an awareness of the audience, otherwise it cannot be drama. A good play demands a relationship between the audience, performers and roles. If I want to use this form, I need an abstract audience, though it doesn't matter whether it's a Chinese audience, a French audience or an audience from wherever.

YANG LIAN I already had an awareness of language when I was in China, but thoroughly cutting myself off from the group as an exercise in thinking, and to posit my own writing as an antithesis to myself – as an exercise in thinking – is something to be done outside China. This 'individualisation', this 'subjectification' is an enormous gain from a life of exile. I'm even prepared to tell friends that it's an essential process that takes away the necessities of social superficialities and replaces them with the individual's own internal necessities.

GAO XINGJIAN The ultimate reason for the existence of serious literature, non-commercial literature, is within the literature itself and not in its market value or the reactions of readers and society. I feel this gives rise to a certain human pride – that people live in the world but only want to express themselves. So-called writing is nothing but the individual's small posturing challenge to the world in which he exists. Whether people pay attention or not should be of no consequence whatsoever. To put it another way: to write is to complete the self. With writings outside China, it's not only the language that changes but objectives also change, even the way material is handled. After *Soul Mountain* was finished in September 1989, I felt as though I'd got over a 'China complex'. The background to *Soul Mountain* was all in China, and completing it was like coming to a full stop: it ended my nostalgia for China. It was actually just for myself – a way that prevented me from turning into a loner far from home. Everything was inside me. This 'self-completion' was extremely fulfilling. After I had experienced it, I can honestly say that I hardly ever dreamed about China again, whereas previously, in my dreams, there was so much 'China' in the background and in my subconscious. Now, it's of immense benefit to my psychology, an exiled writer not belonging to any 'country' and roaming the world. What's so bad about that?

YANG LIAN What I find interesting is that I left China without a word of English and went through almost exactly the same psychological processes in my writing as you. In China, I started five years' continuous work on *Yi*. The first draft was finished in May 1988 and the second from last poem was called 'Returning Home', with the last line, 'All non-persons when unable to return, have arrived home.' In August, I went to Australia, and then in 1989 in New Zealand I revised *Yi*. I've been in exile ever since, and reality has confirmed the curse of poetry. That poem was just like a long-distance journey through language, and it's only when you come back that you realise what you've gained from it. Not only is the complex of 'motherland' not necessary, even 'mother tongue' is simply accidental. And chiming with this approach to language is an encompassing rootless psychology, where life is like a journey in a faraway land, where everywhere is the same, including China. In reality, live anywhere for a year or more and you're anxiously thinking about leaving or moving, afraid of once again putting down roots, once again becoming subservient to a piece of land. I can say it with two lines of poetry I wrote – one in China, 'Stretching into the earth to touch death' ('In Symmetry with Death'); the other abroad, 'The sea so sharp it snuffs you out makes you the you of this instant' ('Where the Sea Stands Still').

GAO XINGJIAN You're right. It's just a human instinct. And what kind of instinct? One where people always want to challenge. That includes the way I'm not willing to be associated with French culture or even the French language [Gao Xingjian spoke fluent French before he left China]. Even though I write in French, I still make French 'exceed what is proper', and write French with a certain 'strangeness'. If, in future, people say there was a foreigner who invented a new word that was accepted by the French audience, it'd only be the same as me toying with the Chinese language. This is a common approach to language. I think both of us share this point of view: we're not only against 'motherland', but also against any other kind of nationalism. When the French right wing takes to the stage, there's a strong flavour of nationalism. I find it repellent and really don't want to be associated with that kind of French culture. Most of the great writers of the twentieth century had experience of exile, but not one of them was solely a patriot.

YANG LIAN Almost all foundations of philosophy and literature of the twentieth century – such as Marx, Freud, Joyce and Mann – were built on a sense of exile, and this has profoundly affected knowledge of the self and existence.

GAO XINGJIAN This has never happened to the Chinese people and is only now beginning to appear.

YANG LIAN Couldn't it be said that today, at least for some Chinese writers, an opportunity has appeared genuinely to connect with the twentieth century's spiritual history? Through individual consciousness and the spiritual significance of exile, as opposed to its physical or political significance, we could break out of those group structures – those anti-individual Confucian cycles – and treat the exploration of forms of literature as a part of the exploration of humanity.

GAO XINGJIAN Someone who is totally aware of themselves is always in exile. Once you peel away those layers that other people attach to you and reinforce, you gradually but firmly establish your own worth – and this includes self-doubt.

YANG LIAN You could call it 'individualism' or 'selfishness'. It's a paradox: your own return makes your writing ultimately of benefit to other people. Today, when this endless superstitious fight for a new form of literature has become meaningless, what kind of literature are we searching for?

GAO XINGJIAN It could be the old phrase: 'Shakespeare will never fade away.' He perfectly described the spiritual activities of people, he analysed humanity and had everything you could wish for – form, content, modernity and eternity. All discussion loses its significance when faced with his works. What we need is a kind of literature that doesn't have any attributes: such genres as 'pure literature', 'serious literature', 'experimental literature', 'modernism' and 'post modernism' have no meaning. We are still going through our own existence, concentrating on doing what the first person does. ❑

***Gao Xingjian** and **Yang Lian** met and talked on 18 September 1993 in Australia. This is an edited version of their conversation. Gao Xingjian's latest book is* Yige ren de shengjing *(Taiwan 1999), to be published in English as* One Man's Bible *(Harperperennial Library, September 2002). Yang Lian's latest collections are* Yi *(Green Integer, Los Angeles 2002) and* Notes of a Blissful Ghost *(Renditions, Hong Kong 2002)*

Translated by Ben Carrdus

ADVICE FOR SOMEONE GOING INTO TRANSLATION

RICHARD McKANE

After 'Advice for Someone Going into Prison' by Nazim Hikmet

First, select your writer then read him thoroughly, find a friend as consultant, make a list of vocabulary. Campaign for your poet if they're in prison, persecuted, in the War Zone or Small Zone, for this too is the art of translation. March their poems out like peace demonstrators, as David McDuff and others with Ratushinskaya or Sarah Maguire with Zakaria Mohammed, holed up, beleaguered at home in Ramallah. Take liberties in translation only when the risks are justified, for ultimately 'the language will judge', as Peter Levi said. Retranslate the classics, but only look at your precursors at the end of the process, then declare if you steal a word or 'happy phrase'. Write notes at the back or foot: this is an original part of the work. Surf the waves of centenaries. Each new translation should be greener than the last. Work slowly, or work fast – you will establish a rhythm that will become your template. Use the best dictionary in the language: this, though expensive, is your stonemason's trowel. Read your versions aloud – doing that is a test that will save embarrassment later when you read them in public. Don't fixate on a word, consult and glide on, be mobile and come back to it later. When you feel the pain in the words, be grateful, for the writer suffered it for you, for us; and know that a love poem is a singular gift to you the translator: to open, admire and give on to the reader. Yours are the words, yet the words are the poet's. You are creating, not just communicating. If publication is your aim, the labour can be Sisyphean, rejections can abound. You can't climb on the back of even a famous poet. With computer-ready texts the word 'vanity' should vanish: seek out self-publishing, for instance in India. Translate the poets you feel friendship for, so they should feel less alone, less locked in their language. Favour the bilingual book if possible, though a minority will look at the left-hand page. Remember an anthology from one language could close down the field for other anthologies – even your own – for as much as ten years: so make it comprehensive if you can. Revise the classics every 20 years – they don't change but your language does. The original is virtually immutable. Different translations come and go, but remember, no one is able to write your own poetry. In the same way as it is a compliment to the people of a foreign language to speak it abroad or at home, and it is appreciated, so the English culture is enriched by translation into it. We dream and think in cultures as much as languages. Say the word Akhmatova, the word Hikmet and you bring to life a poet: you cannot translate proper names. What did Dante and Shakespeare mean to Lozinsky and Pasternak in Stalin's times? Is interpreting older than the oldest profession with its body language? The Home Office-interpreted interviews sometimes remind asylum seekers of interrogations at home. The voice at the end of the language-link phone for the DSS may miraculously speak a too familiar language of bureaucracy incomprehensible. Exposure to a completely foreign language is exhausting. I used to think that the more people who are learning a language the easier it makes that language. Minority languages are dying. The quality of language is on the decrease. How vital then to refresh languages with concepts from other languages, rather than flatten them. Rule Englishiana, Englishiana rules the world, yet still we need to translate into English, to make the alien word understandable: the purposes are different: to catch out or approve an asylum seeker at interview, to treat the tortured with therapy and counselling, or to get across a novel or poem. These are powerful roles performed by a singular minority. Unfortunately, minors are too often in the stressful position of being family interpreters, yet you wouldn't entrust your life or living to a 12-year-old doctor or nurse. Perhaps literary translation remains the best example of the global drive into English, for the texts retain their foreign culture – their evocative landscapes, cityscapes, seascapes. Long live the Other, Hybridity, as Reza Baraheni would say, or exoticism as others might say. Our languages are not tired: it is we in our tiredness who are tiring others out with them. Fresh motifs, fresh ways of saying things can come through translation. The Kurdish *saz* poet Ashik Veysel who sang in Turkish told me the old Turkish proverb in 1972: three languages – three persons. ❑

***Richard McKane** has interpreted Turkish and Russian for the past 14 years at the Medical Foundation for the Care of Victims of Torture. His recent poetry and translations are in* Poet for Poet *(Hearing Eye)*, Nazim Hikmet*, co-translated with Ruth Christie (Anvil) and* On Wings Over the Horizon, Poems of Negar *(Russian and English, Anglo-Caspian)*

THE MIDDLE EAST

Dewsbury, northern UK: waiting for the bus.
Credit: Abbas / Magnum

THE KILLING OF THE PUBLISHER

SAMIR EL-YOUSSEF

In the evening, when he had killed the publisher, he went to see the film *The Lost Honour of Katharina Blum* for the second time.

He thought that if he hadn't seen this film the first time, he wouldn't have had the courage to kill. But then he thought that if he hadn't gone to the dentist that morning, all this wouldn't have happened at all. And if he hadn't sat in the waiting-room for such a long time, he wouldn't have resorted, out of boredom, to leafing through the magazines piled on a side table. But then he wouldn't have stumbled on that interview with the publisher and read it out of curiosity.

Great things happen this way, he said to himself, just like in his stories where the course of things changed completely as a result of a transient event, and a word or even a gesture turned things upside down. The situation could roll along in this way for ever, he said. He had come across an interview with the publisher to whom he had been sending manuscripts of his stories and novels for many years, without ever having had the good fortune to get any of them published. Until that morning when he had read the interview, he had had a ready and acceptable explanation for why none of his books had been published, and for not even receiving a letter or note letting him know that the manuscripts had arrived at the publishers.

In the beginning, he had assumed that the publisher must receive dozens of manuscripts every day, and that he was not prepared to write dozens of letters or replies. The fact that they were not published was an adequate reply in itself as to their unsuitability for publication, and the author should try again and keep sending manuscripts non-stop.

He had gone on in this way for years until he realised that this explanation was not convincing, since he was sending manuscripts of varied content and style. He had intended, with a lot of skill and proficiency (so he told himself later), to make them different from one another, so that it would be impossible for the reader to know or even suspect that the author was the same person. In spite of this they were not published. It's impossible that all of them are unfit for publication, he said to himself. At this point another explanation sprang to mind that he found more convincing. He decided that one of the publisher's assistants, who received the manuscripts, must have picked out his works and thrown them aside at the mere sight of his name. This assistant was certainly a writer himself and, out of jealousy and envy, must have lain in wait for his manuscripts. Whenever one arrived he would pounce on it and hurry to slip it under his clothes, then go outside pretending that he was going to buy something and throw it in the rubbish bin in the street.

The publisher must be very stupid to allow that writer to work with him and wreak havoc with the work of others in this way, and to expose himself to exploitation for the sole benefit of that writer and his friends.

Arriving at this conclusion, he had become tired of walking and, although he liked to think on foot, sat down on the pavement bench and thought silently that it was not the publishers alone who were stupid, but also newspaper proprietors and their editors who entrusted writers and poets to run their cultural pages. These people then proceeded to use the pages in their own interests and that of their friends, and thus turned the business into a 'cultural mafia', as was rife these days.

At this point the young writer had smiled, congratulating himself, and decided that from then on he would send his manuscripts addressed expressly to the publisher, and no one else (especially the damned assistant) would be allowed to open the envelope, thereby ensuring that they arrived in the hands of the publisher, who he had been certain would not disappoint him this time. However, more years passed without any sign to show that anyone was taking an interest in his many manuscripts.

Once, he had sent a letter to the publisher asking after the fate of his novels and stories. However, the fate of the letter itself was no different from that of the manuscripts and stories before it. He continued to write letters to the publisher alerting him to what was going on in his establishment and under his very nose or, rather, what chaos and frivolity he imagined was going on there. He began to incite the publisher against his assistants and adjutants and then turned to exposing the conspiracies and corruption in the world of culture.

One morning, he suffered a deadly pain in his wisdom tooth. It was a dismal rainy day. The streets were empty on his way to the dentist and he wished they would stay that way. He didn't have an appointment so he was forced to sit more than two hours until the dentist was finished with his other patients. He felt terribly bored, and his pain had eased a great deal.

He picked up a magazine and began to skim through it quickly. Then he hit upon the interview with the publisher. He read it quickly the first time, then reread it slowly to be sure that what he had read the first time was correct. This time he set about underlining some sentences in which the publisher said, 'We don't overlook any manuscript that comes to us . . . We read it carefully and attentively and lose no time in notifying the author whether it is suitable for publication or not . . . We don't reject manuscripts without giving sound reasons for rejecting them and most of the time we even offer constructive criticism of the work.'

Astounded, he left the clinic. He forgot his pain and began to think of revenge. He sat in a street café and ordered a black coffee. He drank it in silence while he began to envisage numerous methods of revenge.

At first, he thought of sending the publisher a booby-trapped package that would explode in his face when he opened it. Then he thought he would send him a large envelope in the shape of a manuscript with a poisonous snake inside. He liked this idea very much; however, the impossibility of finding a poisonous snake in the city made him abandon it. He kept thinking of ways to murder the publisher until he concluded that there was nothing better than to run him over with the car while he was leaving the publishing house.

But he saw the film, *The Lost Honour of Katharina Blum*, which was showing that day, so he procured a pistol and went to kill the publisher.

He sat in the waiting room. The publisher was busy meeting visitors. In front of him, the secretary was typing a letter with astonishing speed. The publisher was inside talking loudly and laughing. When the visitors left, he stood up, ready to face the publisher. The secretary looked at him in amazement, but he ignored her and went inside. He told the publisher his name, took out the pistol and fired.

It was evening when he left the publishing house and went to see *The Lost Honour of Katharina Blum* for the second time. He pondered how if he hadn't seen the film he wouldn't have had the courage to kill. ❏

Samir el-Youssef *is a Palestinian writer born in Lebanon in 1965 and now living in London. He published his first collection of short stories,* Humum A'iliya (Domestic Affairs)*, in 1994 and a novel in 2001. From* Banipal Magazine of Modern Arabic Literature. *Translated by Fiona Collins*

Opposite: Samuel Shimon in 'You are a film, my son.' Samuel Shimon was born in Iraq in 1956 into an Assyrian family. Since 1978, he has lived in Amman, Beirut, Nicosia, Tunis, Paris and, finally, London. These photographs and an accompanying text by Shimon appeared in Banipal*, Autumn 2001. Credit for all: Matthias Munsch*

THAT RAINY DAY

SA'ADI YOUSSEF

Not because a rainy day is knocking strangely at my window like a thief. Not because I am dwelling in this watery steppe. Not because the sun has dwelt in the books of travellers and poets. And not because . . .

I say: I am burdened by waiting angels; the trees are only trees, while I am looking for shade. The falling rain is not deep waters. Through the skein of its pulse surge rivers, ships of timber and boats of papyrus. The rain does not reach me. The rain does not moisten my lips. But the green railings over there are shimmering with watery light. And in the distance flowers and headstones are quenching their thirst. No more squirrels or birds. My very pores open to the music.

She was on the balcony. The sun rose in the corner of her garden, a bower for grassy tones and dry, rustling leaves. The woman was neither looking nor being looked at. The woman was absent. I, alone, was collecting the fragments of her image, her limbs, and the memory of a kiss one day in the corner café. What planted this green in the blue? Music. A sun from volcanic islands. The woman is about moving, about taking a form. Now I glimpse a tress of straight hair, I glimpse the fullness of a lower lip. Music. The balcony becomes the balcony of a house: a small table, two chairs, a bottle of wine, two glasses and some Spanish peaches. And in the corner a cactus. The woman turns. Now we are two. We shall dwell on the balcony. The sun will come to our glasses. We shall see the moment. Music.

Sa'adi Youssef. Credit: Samuel Shimon, Banipal

The falling rain *is* falling.
We are behind the balcony's glass screen. The room is a bit cold. Her room was charged with the smell of paint and the aroma of the Kirghiz carpet.

The wetness of the day is sticky beneath my shirt. The woman gave me the ember of her lips. Did she slip the ember under my shirt? I feel like a wanderer in a land of hot springs and tors.
My breathing is the continuous music of strings. My fingers are the bars. My breathing is the continuous music of strings. The music throbs.
I don't see any rain. A crystal light falls across the glass screen.

But the falling rain *is* falling.
This falling rain *is* falling.

I feel the hot rain.

Minutes.
Minutes only, and I shall make with your love a narrow bed.

Music. ❑

Sa'adi Youssef *was born in Basra, Iraq, in 1934. He has translated a good deal of Engish literature into Arabic and now lives in London. This poem appeared in* Banipal, *Autumn 2001. Translated by the poet*

OLD RADIO

AMJAD NASSER

Looking through the storage room (dwelling
place of things that neither die nor live) for the
books I fled the country for, to see just what had
enthralled me, I found it: the same old radio,
Philips, with the green eye that would shine
through the rare sleepless nights of my father,
the military man from the tank corps.

Silent, tattered, stripped of its esteem as the most
important member of the family.

The fine mesh that poured out emotions, intrigues
and lies is broken. The strong black leather is
cracked. The old stations (London, Washington,
Berlin, Moscow, Tirana) that stirred the peoples
and turmoils of the East with long tongues, are
quiet as gravestones covered in dust.

The needle my father often warned me from
moving too fast – for fear of setting it loose from
the proper orbit of the universe – is stopped at
Radio Damascus, which the family only tuned
into during Ramadan to hear the child-voice of
Sheikh Tawfiq al-Munjid.

I didn't find my secret books. My family no
doubt got rid of them immediately after my
departure. For what need is there in Al-Mafraq
for *The German Ideology* or *What is to be done?* But
I found my stifled adolescence stuck there, living
on rapacious waking dreams. The Babylonian
sounds rise, reclaiming a life lived only in songs. ❑

From Banipal, *Spring 2002. Translated by Camilo Gomez-Rivas*

Amjad Nasser *is arts editor and managing editor of* Al-Quds Al-Arabi *in London. He has published eight books of poetry, a travel book and selections in French and Italian*

A HUNGRY ORANGE & OTHER STORIES

NASRI HAJJAJ

A HUNGRY ORANGE

I am a martyr. I was killed in a small war for the sake of the homeland. Before enemies killed me, I used to love many-coloured butterflies – friends of red, yellow, white and purple flowers. I loved birds that sang in open skies. And I loved oranges. After life left me I started to dream in death. I climbed an orange tree to reach for the sky and gather a star, but a hungry orange saw me and devoured me.

In front of a crowd of people a grim-looking man stood up and said, 'The martyr was a hero.' Then he drank a glass of orange juice.

Credit: Kalil

MY MOTHER, MY FATHER, MY WIFE AND HER FATHER

My mother gave me a blow that made sparks fly from my head. She accused me of being stupid and spat in my face a gob that stuck to my cheek then mingled with the thick, coarse hair of my beard. My wife, gathering the courage to give my mother a hand, took off her right shoe and threw it at me, hurling the worst possible curses. It felt as if my left eye had been wrenched out of its socket and rolled on the ground. She then pulled off her left shoe and threw it at me, and I saw my right eye being wrenched out of its socket also. My vision was blurred and I started to see things from the bottom up. Then my son got off his potty and started cursing me, saying I was good for nothing except to play with the children of the neighbourhood. He then threw a hammer at me, hitting me between the eyes. Blood flowed copiously, covering my face and clothes and my dreams one by one. As for my wife's father, who is an elegant and well-behaved man, he said he would take away my chocolate for a whole week.

The only human being who stood by me during this calamity, and who did not consider that my staying away from the celebrations for the independence of the homeland was a crime worth all this punishment, was my grandmother. She gathered my eyes from the floor and put them back in their sockets. She put ground coffee in the haemorrhaging hole between my eyes. She gave me a lira to buy chocolate and said, 'Go play with the kids in the neighbourhood.'

My father was already dead.

SOUP FOR THE CHILDREN

My father ordered me to go to the cemetery to wash the grave of my martyred brother, remove any harmful weeds that grow around neglected graves and water the geranium plants that give such a distinctive aroma to our homes and graveyards.

A few moments till dawn. I was standing in front of the cemetery gate, but I was not the only one to come at this hour of the night. There were thousands like me carrying weeding scissors and watering pots, and their drowsiness. The gate was locked and it appeared that the watchman had not yet arrived, even though today was the Day of the Martyr that we all celebrate to honour those who died for the sake of the homeland.

The birds were the first to wake up and we heard their song; but did not rejoice. Then dawn sneaked softly through the pines, cypresses, larch and chinaberry trees, and the graveyard trees appeared like giant warriors.

A black-and-yellow butterfly flew up the high wall of the cemetery and, looking up at it, we realised how faded the colour of our graveyard wall was. The butterfly landed on a branch in the cypress, then soared up in the distant sky and disappeared from sight.

The crowd became restless as sunlight began to break through the branches of the trees, catching the dew on the leaves. The shine touched us with nausea. The waiting men and women started to grumble, and the graveyard watchman had not yet arrived.

A man in the crowd cried out, 'This is annoying!'

A woman shouted, 'This is boring!'

Another man said, 'We've lost hope!'

Another followed up with, 'We've given up on everything!'

A child not yet two years old came forward and said, 'I'm in despair.'

Credit: Kahil

The moment the sun's rays ripened, the massive crowds plunged headlong to the cemetery gate and shook it loose from its place. The people spread out among the graves, each to his own, and they set to smashing them up. Then they started digging up the graves, reaching for whatever was left of the bones of the dead, which they removed and placed in plastic bags like the ones used for rubbish. They carried them on their backs, filling the streets of the city as sweat poured from their bodies. I was among them, carrying my brother's bones in a black plastic sack. We heard our collective breathing in and out as though it were the breathing of a monster being chased by armies of flies and mosquitoes.

We crept along Martyr Street first, then came to Liberty Avenue, which led to Independence Square. And there our movement began to slow, as if we had all asked the same question of ourselves at the same time, 'Where to now?' At this moment, there emerged from among the crowd a man we knew to be one of the wisest and craftiest; he addressed us in a stentorian voice that could be heard all over even without a loudspeaker:

'Today, you have carried out one of the most glorious deeds for the sake of the homeland. You have got rid of the graveyard. He who has died is dead, and the homeland is in need of every square inch of land to house the living and plant their food so that we can be in a position to build a free and independent economy. Bless you, and bless your hands!'

We all applauded, shouting long life to him and to the homeland. Then we set out from there, singing the national anthem with all the strength we had, and when we finished singing, the child who was not yet two years old cried out, 'And what are we to do with the bones of our dead?'

The wise man answered calmly and confidently, 'Grind them and make them into soup for your children.'

And that's exactly what we did.

THE MAN WHO DEVOURED HIMSELF

Alone in his room, the man eats what remains of the sauce and congealing fat at the bottom of the pot. Sometimes he scrapes at the food with an old, rusty knife and at other times with his nails. It had been a while since the pot was full of appetising food. Now the remains were scanty and rotting. To bring back the pleasure of the past, the man eats what sticks underneath his nails.

Tomorrow he will devour his fingers, arms and legs; and then he will eat the pelvis, stomach, liver, intestines, kidneys, lungs, windpipe and his chest.

In a few days he will consume his spine, neck and head. But he flings off one of his molars, and it rolls down and crashes into the ground. Its crash will make a deafening roar, shaking the city. Buildings will crack and tumble down; roads and bridges will collapse. The police will come to arrest the man and charge him with destroying the city.

LAILA'S FACE

It was evening. We went to sleep, Laila and I. We were lovers. The evening melted into our bodies, and then it was night. A spider came and started weaving its web over our naked bodies. When the night patrol came by they didn't wake us up, for the spider had finished weaving its house. And when the devil passed he complained about us to God. But the poet looked at us and said, 'Let it be known that nakedness is more beautiful than poetry!' And when my mother saw us she said, 'How silly of me! I forgot to look after my little child.' As for God, He said, 'How can I not love those who see me in the radiance of the naked body?'

At dawn, Laila got up. She rubbed her eyes, slid the bolt back from the lock. She opened the spider's house, took my body and went away.

As for me, I am still sleeping without a body, playing with a little child who has Laila's face.

HEBRON (AL-KHALIL)

Ayn el-Hilwe. Night. A child is crying. The quilt is pushed aside. Light flowing from two small feet. I look out from my window. Men on the land of Al-Khalil. They carry pickaxes, mattocks and hammers. They speak a strange language. They are demolishing the face of the earth. They chatter and laugh. They are happy. The earth is in extreme pain. That's what the graveyards of Al-Khalil told me. ❑

***Nasri Hajjaj** was born in Ayn el-Hilwe Palestinian refugee camp, and was educated at UNRWA schools in the camp and in Sidon, Lebanon. After his degree at Beirut Arab University he took an MA at Middlesex University, London, and worked in the UK as a journalist. He has also worked as a journalist in Beirut, Cyprus and Tunis. These stories first appeared in the cultural pages of the Beirut newspaper* Al-Nahar *in 1994 and 1997*

Translated by Ibrahim Muhawi

ZIBA

ZIBA KARBASSI

this that I make black about my eyes
this that I rouge on to my reddening lips
and this wild ivy of my hair that I plait in two
    strands with their miniature tulips
        of love

this that I'm wearing bright winter clothes
and they suit me
this that I paint my nails each with different colours
this that I love moonlight
    that brings dreams
        this that I love dreams
where they take me out of myself
this that I dance like a roma dancer
    swaying in the wild-why of the wind
and then more crazily still in the hi-hi of the hurricane
        in the humour, in the
            laughter

    in the language

this that I am tall and as tall as all this that I must
            achieve

and again this: that from the everything –
    out of the nothing – that you have, I
            want no part

and this: that the taller I am and the more I have
I have to love

this that I say poem and then that love will feint
        inside the words

this that I know sudden stress is another name for
            crisis

this that I suddenly become like a crazed one
    and I strip in front of your eyes
        and the poem becomes the craziness
of my crisis
            and I become the storm stress of
                the poem

and I make love all the time
            make love with the poem

this that you've become gob-mouthed and round-eyed
                just looking at me

this that your language stutters in the gap and water
            dries in your throat and your
                mouth stays wide o
                    and says:

Ziba

Zi-Ba

Zii-

Baa

Aaa ❑

Ziba Karbassi *was born in Tabriz, Iran, in the late 1970s and came to the UK in the late 1980s. She has published four poetry collections in Farsi and one in bilingual Farsi/English,* Water or the Blue

Translated by Ziba Karbassi & Stephen Watts

SCHOOL

REZA HIWA

'School' is written over a painting described in Arabic as 'painted in Palestine' and sent to the author from there. The poem was written during the siege of Jenin on a train from Waterloo, 11 April 2002

***Reza Hiwa** is a Kurd-Franco-Iranian born to Kurdish parents in Tehran where he learned to lie about his identity. He never learned how to read or write in Kurdish. In 1984, he reached Paris where he married and now has three children. In 1995, he came to London, and has been commuting between the two cities ever since, as his 'train poems' testify. He writes in Farsi, French and English*

FATHER'S ABSENCES

CHOMAN HARDI

The second daughter remembers the day
she always cries retelling the story
the father does not
he remembers many more trivial things
but however much he thinks and tries
he cannot recollect that very moment

even the mother does not
she remembers crying and cooking him soup
how the two men brought him, holding his armpits
and left him convinced that he will die

The four of them were playing in the garden
each a year taller than the next one
from the moment he arrived in the yard
he stared at them with his fully open eyes

He was struggling for a breath, a word
and could only call them by a gesture of his hand

They stood by the wall
each trying to hide behind the others
none of them went to hold his hand
or give him a kiss. ❑

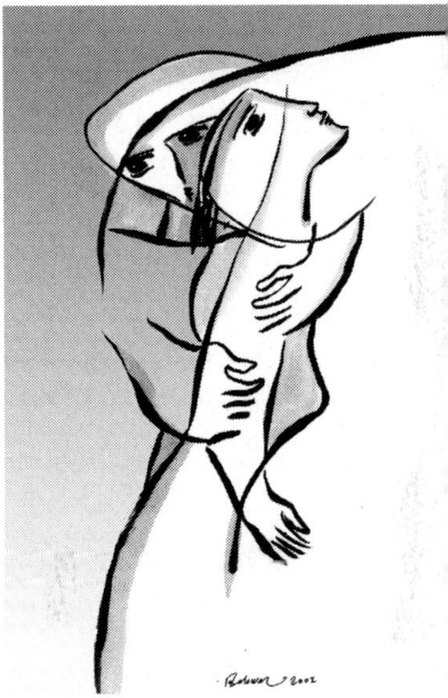

Credit: Rebwar, a Kurdish artist working in London

Choman Hardi *was born in Sulaimanya, southern Kurdistan, in 1974. She lived in Iran and Turkey before coming to the UK in 1993. She has published two poetry collections in Kurdish,* Return with no memory *and* Light of the shadows. *She is the chair of the London-based Exiled Writers Ink!, an organisation that works to represent writers who are unrepresented in UK publishing and media*

MY BLACK FRIEND

KAMAL MIRAWDELI

To Izzaddin Qera, 'Black Izzeddin', from the city of Kirkuk, who was martyred fighting for his homeland

My black friend
Here we are: you, I and the universe
Singing the song of silence again.

Credit: Rebwar

I and night, you and the world
Rehearsing together the melody of alienation.
This song hands me over to the wind
And carries me away to smell all the burnt roses
In search of a nightingale.

It makes me hold the grip of every mountain
In search of a tomb.

It turns all my senses into ears
For hearing the news of an earthquake.

They say your ashes would never come back
To become the henna for the wedding party of your lovers.

This fire is waiting for you
How long will your sleep last?

O my black friend!
This sand has smothered your breath
All the waves are asleep. All the fish have died of thirst.

What a sea, my black friend!
What a sleep, my black friend? ❑

***Kamal Mirawdeli** is a Kurdish poet and writer who left Kurdistan for the UK in 1982 after threats to his life by the Iraqi regime. His native village and town were obliterated in Saddam's chemical assault on Halabja in 1988. He returned to his country in 1993–4 but is once again living in the UK. He has published three collections of poetry in Kurdish. His first collection in English,* Passage to Dawn, *was published in May 2002*

TIME TRAPPED IN THE STONE

BEJAN MATUR

I In the courtyard where sick horses
circle to recover,
a puny youth
his neck thinner than the neck of a sick horse,
stands in the middle of a stone bridge
in long black clothes.
The censer swinging at his neck
shows how far he must travel,
but his horse is sick,
unable to go
and the moon must not enter his sleep.

History must move on
and find its place.
The word must find its subject.
His hair must grow long
and be damp and fragrant.

II Time trapped in the stone
told him,
when it's dark
you'll be driven from here.
But we will remain.
The eagle's beak
snow water
in the well.
Remember your ancestry,
they say history will end
frozen in a photograph.

Man creates his own face
and so there is wind.
A place weeping enters our sleep
and never leaves. ❑

Credit: Rebwar

Zeytun/Mara 1987–8

***Bejan Matur** is a Kurdish woman from Turkish Kurdistan writing in Turkish. She now lives in London*

WAR AND PEACE

NEZAM GHALEBI

My name is Nezam Ghalebi and I am 17 years old. I am living in London. I am from Afghanistan. I lived in Afghanistan for about ten years and then I went to Russia.

In the past, my family was rich and my father was a member of the government. When I was born, there were schools in Afghanistan, but I didn't go to school because of the war. Before the war Afghanistan was a beautiful country. Before the war my four brothers and three sisters and my father and mother were living together with all of my family. The war broke out in 1991; there was terrible fighting with guns and aeroplanes and other weapons. That war lasted one year.

The second broke out in 1992, the year I was nine. My father was killed when I was six months old and I have never seen him. We were in the middle of the fighting in Kabul in 1992. I saw dead and injured people with my own eyes. I never forget that moment. Our house was destroyed by a rocket. It was disastrous, devastating. We were all screaming and running down the stairs in shock and panic. I was very afraid of dying. That was a traumatic time for me.

I was looking at our house, and suddenly a rocket fell close to me and injured my leg. I fainted and woke up in hospital with the doctors, and my mother and my brother looking at me. My mother was crying. One month later I was feeling better. My brother died in battle. He was a soldier. When I was ten years old we decided to leave Afghanistan. After two weeks we left and travelled to Pakistan. We lived there about one year. In Pakistan we lived in a small house. We paid rent and felt very poor and homesick; we knew we had lost everything we had. It was too hot and the people were not friendly. 'Why are you here? Go to your country,' they said over and over again. We had no choice but to stay: the war in Afghanistan was so bad we couldn't go back there. The situation for my family was unbearable.

Then my brother decided to leave Pakistan and travelled to England. After one year we too decided to leave Pakistan and go to Russia. My brother was in Russia studying. We lived in Russia about five years with my brother. After five years we decided to leave Russia and come England. We

Afghanistan 1996: a coach leaves Kabul after Taliban occupy the city.
Credit: Chris Steele-Perkins / Magnum

had no choice but to leave because in Russia the government didn't pay us any money and they didn't give us a home to live in.

My brother really loved England so we came to England. Now we are living here in London. I am happy here but I miss my country and I miss my father, too. I ask myself, why did he die? I go to school every day and I live with my mother and my brother. But I am happy because I am living in peace in a country where I can't see war any more. ❑

***Nezam Ghalebi** came to the UK in 1997 and is at Whitefield School in north-west London*

LEAVING; ARRIVING

ZUHRA BAHMAN

The first time the Taliban came to my city was in 1997. I was at school. My chemistry teacher walked into my class, looking paler than usual. She went straight to her sister who was in my class and whispered something in her ear. Then they both left. All 40 of us sniffed the tension in the air and knew something was happening. Minutes afterwards, we could hear heavy artillery fire from somewhere nearby. It was frightening. We could not decide whether to leave the safety of school and risk being kidnapped, raped or killed on our way home, or stay in school hoping for the fighting to finish. Finally, the vice-principal came into the class. She told us to leave the school immediately and head straight home. Not even she knew what was going on.

We all ran like mad on the street. Walking as fast as I could, I wished I was invisible, the thought that anything could happen to me and my parents would never know, was killing me. It was like a nightmare. The sound of heavy weapons was getting nearer every second, and the distance to the safety of home looked further. I was almost running but the land was slipping away, my feet felt tons heavier. Around me were all sorts of people almost running, shopkeepers closing their shops, old women in burkas searching for their sons. There was the same look of confusion on everyone's face; nobody really knew what exactly was going on. Sadness, helplessness and insecurity could even be felt in the air; it was thick with the sound of gunfire and full of the smell of death, fire and gunpowder. Twenty minutes' walk to my house seemed a lifetime but I finally arrived home. My mother was waiting for me at the door. My brother was still at school, which was right in the middle of the city, the place likely to be hit first if the fighting came closer. My uncle had gone to pick up my brother and had not returned. We waited for another hour or so, tuning the radio to check if there was any news about what was going on. But no use: the local city radio was playing patriotic songs one after the other and the international channels were not even mentioning my country. I turned on the TV; the local channel did not start until about four in the afternoon so it was off air. Nor did the international channels we received through satellite say anything about the war in my city.

My brother, uncle and father came an hour after my arrival. My father's office had been closed until further notice. Their bosses had already fled the city on the only flight allowed out; they were given priority as non-Afghans. The office was left with the security guard. My mother brought food but we could hardly eat. The sound of the arms was now so near that I could distinguish between a shot being fired and the sound when it actually hit the ground. My father was tuning the radio to get *Voice of Iran* when something exploded so near it shook our windows. The explosion was followed by a few brief seconds of pure silence, and then the firing carried on as usual. My uncle thought the explosion was a bomb dropped by a plane that had hit a neighbourhood next to ours called Sayedabad. Most of my friends lived there, and the primary school that I went to was there as well. I hoped with all my heart that whatever it was, it had not killed anyone I knew.

I cleaned up the room and piled the dishes in the kitchen, trying to ignore the constant sound of weapons that was now coming from all directions. In a few hours, when the sun was setting, my mother told me to clean the kerosene lamp. When I was cleaning the delicate glass around the lamp, I saw my parents gathering all the little gold jewellery my mother had and the little money we had, and tying it in a little bunch and hiding it under the stones near the well in the yard. I felt grown-up as my parents did this in front of me, but I felt a little funny as well looking at two grown-ups trying to find a place to hide their money in darkness in their own backyard. At about eight at night, the local radio announced that the Taliban were in our city but the opposition was defeating them. It was far from the truth; the fighting was getting heavier. By the time we sat down to eat that night, the fighting got so near we decided to get our plates and go to the basement. Our house was literally in the middle of the battlefield. Behind our house was the city prison, a huge, castle-like building of raw brick and mud. There was a tower on each corner of the building that was used to keep an eye on the prisoners and the surroundings of the prison building. The prison was occupied and used by the military men of the warlord that controlled my city. They used it both as a military base and as a prison for criminals and prisoners of war.

It seemed that one of the factions had taken over the prison and was using it to attack the area right in front of our house, which was a Hazara group's stronghold. The Taliban particularly oppressed Hazaras so they were fighting as hard as they could. It was a war between those who had weapons. Ordinary people of all ethnic groups were living in my area and they were the ones suffering most. The bullets that hit people were not necessarily shot by the enemy; many ordinary Pashtuns died by Taliban weaponry and many Hazaras by those who were claiming to save them.

We spent a few hours in the basement trying not to look in each other's eyes just in case we saw hopelessness. Everyone was quiet. My father looked decades older then he was, standing in one corner of the basement looking from the little window at the little red lines in the sky that each bullet left. I felt like crying but tears did not come. My brother was playing with marbles and looked at me with nervous smiles. We stayed up the whole night, waiting for the fighting to ease up. But it got worse and worse. We could now even hear the voices of military men shouting orders at each other. We decided to sleep in the basement, so my father, uncle and brother went upstairs to bring the blankets, pillows and mattresses. I went along. The room that my brother and I slept in had a window right at the top of the wall that overlooked the street. We heard some sounds coming from the window so we climbed a table and looked from the window. In the moonlight we saw that a teenage boy was desperately pushing a handcart on which a wounded woman was lying, bleeding and moaning. My brother and I felt paralysed. For the first time I felt that home was not safe after all, I could die any minute and even my father could not save me. We did not tell my parents. We went back to the basement and lay in our bed. I fell asleep quite late. All night there were blood, wounds and death in my dreams.

Next morning my mother woke me up. She had already packed. My father had contacted one of my relatives from the village and he was coming to pick us up in a taxi and take us to the village, which was much safer. We were to stay there until things calmed down. We packed in a hurry. I wore an old brown burka that we had at home just in case it was needed and set off to our village.

We returned from the village after a few weeks. The Taliban were defeated in the city. My city reminded me of when I was a child and I used to put water on the little ants' nest and they desperately tried to save their house and food. The same was happening with my people in my city: someone had destroyed our houses, shacked our souls and left us behind to rebuild all we had lost and mourn for what we would never get back – until they returned to destroy everything again.

The city had not recovered fully from the first attack but it was trying its best to put the conflict behind it. The huge holes on the walls of my school had just been repaired and painted white and gave out a strong smell of *gach*, a white powder mixed with water used to paint walls. The number of students in the school had suddenly decreased. There was enough space for the students to sit, we did not even have to squeeze in six people to one bench. But the number of teachers was also less than it had been. After a few days, the number of students grew back to normal. Those who had fled the city were returning and, as the 40 days' mourning period for those who died in the conflict was over, people who had lost loved ones were returning as well. Soon things got back to normal, but still I felt as if there was something to come. I could not sleep and even if I did I felt as if I would never wake up. I could not start a long book fearing that I might die leaving the book unfinished. It was happening to everyone; a bang on the door, dogs barking, breaking of glass, any unusual sound was enough to make us jump.

It was not long before the Taliban returned. They hit harder this time, taking revenge for last time's defeat. This time it was harder: we could hear their progress as they approached our city. The radio stations were reporting contradictory news of the Taliban's movement towards our city: some said they massacred entire villages; others reported people celebrating Taliban successes.

They were soon in my city. But we were prepared this time. We had enough food at home; we had hidden our TV antenna in the water well. My mother had bought two old burkas for us. We had accepted our defeat and had prepared ourselves to be ruled by the Taliban.

What went on in the streets after the Taliban captured them was unknown to us. But there were dead bodies all over, both Taliban and the opposition. The city had started to give out the smell of death and dead bodies. People could not dispose of the dead since they feared the Taliban might disapprove. After conquering the city, they set up rules. They smashed video and music shops, they hanged petty thieves in the main square of the city, they lashed women on their ankles, they slapped young men on their faces, they took away kites, footballs and school from children. Under the Taliban, our city existed but did not live.

Everyone was trying to get out, so did we. One afternoon, while I was sleeping – there was nothing else I could do – my mother woke me up. She told me to pack: we were going to Pakistan. My father's friend who knew someone at the airport had arranged for us to take a plane to Pakistan. We had to get ready in less then an hour. I could not decide what to pack, there was just a small bag to fill. I had 16 years' worth of belongings. We left in tears. We left the house with my uncle.

At the airport, accompanied by my father's friend, we boarded an old military plane. The only passengers apart from us were some Arabs who sat well away from us. Flying over my country, I saw its full beauty. When I flew over the mountains with the snow still on its peaks, I fell a pleasant cold chill all over my body. I flew over bright blue lakes, identical villages and cities until the scenery changed to a large city full of traffic. It was Peshawar, in Pakistan. We landed in a deserted area of the airport. Nobody asked us for our passport, or anything. We found a gate and got out to the main road, got a taxi and went to my grandparents' home.

At school in Mazar i Sherif 2002. Credit: Carlos Reyes-Manzo / Andes Press Agency

Pakistan was strange, hot and noisy. To keep cool we had to wash ourselves several times a day and lie under the ceiling fan. We soon moved to Islamabad which was cooler but still strange to us. My father remained in Afghanistan. He worked and sent us money; we studied. Although life was better, there were still problems for Afghans in Pakistan. The fact that we did not belong, the constant and painful process of adapting to the Pakistani culture while protecting our own was hard. Pakistani police were also anti-immigrants. They arrested young Afghan boys for no apparent reason and unless they were paid huge bribes they were not let off. The police arrested my brother, who was only 15, several times; each time we had to pay money to release him. The Taliban were equally powerful in Pakistan. As the border between Pakistan and Afghanistan is virtually non-existent, the Taliban came back and forth as they chose.

I left Pakistan for the UK. I arrived at Heathrow at the end of March. It was cold and foggy. I had a three-month visa and I wanted to use it before I actually applied for asylum. I wanted to be sure to look into all the possibilities that existed for me if I lived in any of the three countries I could. Making a decision was hard: by living outside Afghanistan I felt I was running from what everyone else I knew was going through.

My parents, aunts and uncles persuaded me to stay in the UK and not return. So, finally, I decided to apply for asylum. I packed my bags and took the train to the Home Office in East Croydon. I arrived mid-morning at the Home Office; I was the last person in a queue that stretched round and round the metal barriers. Suddenly I felt at home: people around me looked like those from my country. There were young men with grey hair, there were women wearing clothes that did not match the surroundings; children shyly playing around, speaking a language they'll forget in no time. I knew I was in my new home. ❑

Zuhra Bahman *is now at school in the UK*

CYPRUS: CAUGHT OUT

AYDIN MEHMET ALI

'They caught him with his lover. His mother and his wife's brother set a trap for him and caught him. He had this extra flat. His wife and he bought it from the money from their wedding. You know what it's like . . . They collected all that money pinned on to their clothes . . . and they bought a flat with it. His wife had a flat already, her grandmother used to live in it and she died or something, I don't quite know.'

'How did they catch them?' she asks.

'Someone must have twigged that something was going on and they set a trap for them. They caught them in bed together. Screams, shouts, the whole family became involved, a big scandal! The family reported it to the police, the lover was deported. You should have seen it! It was so messy . . . Turkish films have nothing on this!'

'What happened to the lover?' she asks.

'What can the lover do? In Cyprus, waiting for him to sort things out from this end. The lover obviously wants to come here, but not much chance with these immigration laws.'

'Oh! Vay vay vay! What a surprise! Hosgeldiniz! Hosgeldiniz!'

The expansive mother wearing the latest fashion garment from the front covers of magazines opens the door and smiles. She welcomes her guests. She is happy and although she says it is a surprise, it isn't at all. She knew they were coming and was well prepared for them. She leans over and kisses her brother who has just arrived from Cyprus. She has dressed to make a good impression on him and his family. This time he's only here with his son.

She doesn't want to give the impression that all they do is work long hours. She wants him to think they know how to enjoy themselves. It isn't all about killing themselves working in the shop or the factory, just to be able to show off their car, their expensively decorated house, the excessive amount of food and drink. Her pink painted cheeks are flushed, her hair is straw-tinted to hide the grey appearing among the brown; gold bracelets and chains and rings ceremoniously put on to complete the picture.

She embraces her brother's son, who is barely 20. He has smooth skin, dark hair and dark soft eyes. His aftershave reminds her he is a man. She is conscious that her breasts have rubbed against his body. He smiles at his aunt and tells her she's looking younger than the last time he saw her.

'What is it? Is it the water, the soil, the air of this London that makes women look young and beautiful?' She laughs him off and leads him in.

Her daughter kisses the cheeks of her cousin formally. Lest there is talk about even the most innocent of contacts. People talk. People make things up.

Wake up get the children ready send them off take them to school go to work enter that sweatshop early in the morning listen to crap from the boss who keeps telling you to work harder or else you know there are many people out there ready to jump in go to the shop work your guts out trying to make a living go shopping pick up the kids go home cook for the evening eat sit in front of the TV and fall into bed get up in the morning . . .

. . . and at the weekend go to a wedding and engagement reception a circumcision party sit at rows of tables sometimes not sure whether you are in a wedding engagement circumcision party the same food is served the same music played the same dance danced the same money is hung on the breast of the bride groom fiancé circumcised boy you show off your daughters make sure their goods are exhibited to the world ready for the payment from the highest bidder sometimes trouble strikes these young women nowadays go off the rails fall for some penniless nobody because they are good looking what sort of choice is that what sort of life would good looks bring how long do good looks last . . .

Cemaliye kisses her distant cousin's cheeks with the appropriate degree of propriety. Distant because they haven't met often and they don't know each other well. Cemaliye was born in London, in Islington, when it was home to Turkish Cypriots in the late 1960s. Her father was an auxiliary policeman in Limassol. Soon after the declaration of independence in 1960 he took the handout package for services delivered to the Great British Empire and came to London. The package consisted of a British passport for him and his wife who was two months pregnant, two tickets and £1,000 pocket money to start a new life. Compared to what he would have faced – possible reprisals from all those Greek Cypriots he had beaten the shit out of and imprisoned under instructions from British officers – it was a good package. England promised a new life where no one would know who he was and no one would care.

She was the third daughter and her childhood passed in her parents' working men's café in Islington. She remembers forever smelling of greasy chips sausages bacon and fried eggs. And bacon was not supposed to be allowed in the house, let alone cooked and served by Muslims. Her father moved from one job to another, until he settled in a grocer's shop in Haringey.

Her cousin was handsome. Slim. He had beautiful eyes and long eyelashes, a dazzling smile . . . and full lips. He brushed his curly black hair back. He didn't seem to be aware of the effect he had on the women around him.

Cemaliye's husband shook hands heartily and welcomed the father and son. He too was a second-generation Cypriot but came when he was one, and grew up in Haringey with African-Caribbean boys: they were more daring and got up to more tricks than anyone else. He didn't like the English boys because they didn't like him. They called him 'bubble-n-squeak, Greek', even though they knew he wasn't a Greek Cypriot, but it was all the same to them. He picked up Jamaican language, swear words, and one of the best collections of reggae records. His mother shouted at him for going around with those 'Arabs'. Why couldn't he stick with his own kind or, even better, with the white boys? But she was polite to the boys when they came to call for Ahmet, and offered them things to eat. In her heart of hearts she knew they were nice boys. But what would the neighbours say if they saw Ahmet hanging around with them? It would be all over the community, that she wasn't able to control her own son. Her reputation would be damaged. What reputation, Ahmet would ask her? It's just that she didn't want gossip, and it would affect the reputation of his little sister. She was only six but if he continued to hang around the 'Arab' boys and they were to come around when she was older . . . no! That wouldn't do! She wasn't going to have the 'kismet' of her daughter cut off because of his nonsense.

Then he was married off to Cemaliye. He gave in to pressures from his mother to marry. He tried to resist but in the end he ran out of excuses. He held out until he was 25, and then his father joined in.

They wanted him to stop running around with his friends, disco here nightclub there wasting his money wasting his life he needed to settle down a wife would do him good and a couple of kids would settle his madness he was getting old no woman would have him soon he was wasting his life he would be too old to have children and be a proper father did he want to be a father for at 40 he wouldn't even be able to kick a football around in the park with his sons if he left it any later he would be an old man his hair was going to fall out soon and women don't like bald men he had to make up his mind was he going to get involved in the business.

All he did was to say yes when they pointed her out at a cousin's wedding. She seemed OK, lively, was dancing with her friends, she looked at him teasingly across the tables. The boy she secretly loved had married a richer girl eight months earlier. She was devastated, thought about committing suicide, went to Cyprus for five months. And she came back knowing she had to find someone to be married to, maybe the feeling of being married and having children would make the heartache go away. She loved children. She wanted to have one as soon as she was married. And in time she might love her husband. That's what the elders kept saying. In time she would love her husband and forget about her love.

Do you think we loved them, they would say, we just married them and here we are. What's so different about you lot? Just because you are younger and you have a bit more freedom to say yes or no. But nothing much has changed for women. It's the same story. In the end you'll marry someone, you'll serve him, you'll cook for him, clean his house, have his kids, put up with his funny ways and just get on. No use moaning or groaning about your lot and thinking you can do something about it. He is your husband, he has to look after you. That's it! Don't talk about love. What's love got to do with anything?

They were married six months later. That was a year ago. She couldn't complain. He didn't have bad habits. He went to see his mum a lot. He went out with his friends a lot. They played football together for one of the teams in the Turkish League. Most were married like him. Her own marriage wasn't exciting. He didn't take her out as much as she wanted. And she was getting bored on her own in the house. She was working half a day at the dry-cleaners but that was just to get her out of the house and contribute to the bills. She wasn't enjoying it, she wasn't enjoying married life. She felt lonely. At least at home she had had her sisters. She went to her mum's a lot.

And a baby? Well, it wasn't happening. Every time she wanted it he moved away. At first he tried and she didn't know what she was supposed to do. She thought she was doing something wrong, putting him off. She would hug him and caress him and he would get excited and come inside her, then all of a sudden she would realise that she couldn't feel him. She would try her best, open her legs wider, try to hold him. They would both struggle and after the struggle he would roll off and leave her bewildered lying on her back in the dark, because it was always in the dark, not knowing if anything had happened, if he had come, if this was all there was to it. She would lie there afraid to do anything, feeling hunger rising from her cunt, unsatisfied, unfulfilled, screaming with hunger. He would say nothing, turn his back on her. Sometimes he would turn around and hug her, wrap her in his arms and kiss her hair. She felt maybe he loved her then. In time they would learn how to do it and in time they would have children and then everything would be OK. Her mother told her to be patient.

She had nothing to worry about he wasn't beating her up was he wasn't spending his money on whores and other women especially English women was he he went out with his mates every weekend and that was normal men like going out with their friends for a drink he was looking after her providing for her wasn't he not all of them are good at it you know they might brag about it a lot show off and put themselves about and walk around to show what a big bundle they had but when they have to do it when it counts they shrivel up don't worry about it she would laugh wiping her tears from her eyes doubling over and slapping her hands at her own explicitness secretly worrying that her daughter had not been sexually satisfied was living with frustration who knows what might happen if she continued to be sexually frustrated if only she'd get pregnant that would take her mind off things she would be occupied God forbid she might want to divorce him or worse go with another man she would die of the shame of it wasn't it crazy all these years she was like a mad woman making sure that nothing happened to her daughter that nothing happened to her thin membrane her virginity symbol stretched across her vagina's entrance and here she was now that damn membrane didn't matter she wasn't doing anything and wasn't enjoying anything wasn't life a fuck-up!

Everyone piled into the meticulously kept guest room, *misafir odasi*. The best china is in the glass cupboard, so are the crystal glasses for whisky, wine, water, perfectly lined up small china ornaments, glass tall vases figurines dancing playing the violin an inevitable map of Cyprus made into a clock, coffee cups plastic flowers in vases dotted about the room brand-new reproductions of heavy palace furniture . . . all tasteless. The big glass chandelier may even be crystal. And the obligatory untouchable drinks cabinet containing collections of whiskies, wines, miniatures, all lined up leering at the guests with the knowledge that they will never be drunk. Everything else in the room belonged to her, she had chosen it she had arranged it, but that belonged to him. She wasn't even allowed to clean it.

Her uncle tells Cemaliye that marriage seems to have done her good, she's looking good. He makes the usual sexual innuendo and jokes with Ahmet, who laughs heartily. Yes, indeed once you give these women a bit of . . . they blossom thanks to us. Cemaliye shifts her shoulders and smiles as befits a modest married woman. Her eye catches her cousin's smiling eyes, which move from Ahmet's laughing face to her uneasy smile.

During dinner, Ahmet and her cousin sit next to each other. She watches them loosening up as the evening progresses and is pleased. Her husband isn't usually so friendly towards her side of the family. It's also the influence of the drink. By two o'clock in the morning all the men are drunk, the women tipsy and laughing a lot, humouring the men.

Men are telling stories of their youth and telling the younger ones they don't know what life is about. Did they live through EOKA, did they live through TAKSIM and VOLKAN? Lining up 14-year-old schoolboys in the schoolyard and telling them they had to be soldiers and protect the *Yavru Vatan*, baby country, and that *Ana Vatan*, the motherland, had ordered it.

'I shit on you! You pimps! If you thought fighting was easy, why didn't you come and do it?' demands Cemaliye's father of long-suppressed ghosts. He swings his hand across his chest, pointing to the space between his feet. 'Oh yeah! Easy innit? You sent your sons to safety in Turkey, pretending they were at college or university, and you told everyone else to send their sons to fight. They are sacrificial lambs – but not your sons. If your arse is tight, come and fight and let your sons fight, too!'

The uncle tells of the officer from Turkey who came to the village and forced everyone to turn up for duty the following night. 'The village shepherd didn't because no one had told him. He was such a gentle person I suppose no one thought of telling him. They found him dead after a few days, near his animals in the valley. The Turkish officer blamed the Greeks for the bloody murder but everyone in the village knew it was the officers from Turkey.'

He sniffs, trying to suppress tears. Let's drink, he shouts as he staggers across to the whisky bottle – a dash of Coke takes the bitterness away. The music goes on, Turkish, Greek and a bit of English. The young dance, the older ones collapse on the sofa. Ahmet is trying to dance with Cemaliye's cousin. Their arms and legs move exaggeratedly slowly. They look like rams horn-locked in a fight with one arm against each other's neck the other hand holding on to a whisky glass. Once the dance finishes they hug and slap each other on the back, holding each other up laughing with eyes closed, almost passing out in each other's arms. Congratulating each other for still being on their feet. 'How beautifully you dance, kid. Is this what they teach you in Cyprus?' Ahmet holds the cousin's face in his hands.

'How beautifully you danced that night. I couldn't keep my hands off you. I couldn't keep my eyes off you. I trembled each time I thought of my lips touching yours. I don't know how I kept my lips off you. I don't know how I managed to control myself in front of all of them.'

'You do though . . . don't you? You learn to do it as soon as you realise you desire someone. You mustn't let anyone suspect a thing . . .' The cousin reaches out and touches the hands holding his face.

They're on the mattress on the floor in the middle of the room. The white sheet acting as a curtain filters the sunshine coming into the room. They are kneeling facing each other. They are naked. Ahmet holds Cem's face in his palms as he did that night they met, his heart beating wildly. He breathes in Cem's smell. He touches his cheeks, eyes, nose, temples, hair, mouth, lightly, with slightly parted lips. Kissing him gently, afraid of the violence of his own passion. His lips move down to kiss his neck, his shoulders, his chest. He takes his nipples between his lips and plays with them with his tongue until he feels them harden. He moves his hands down Cem's shoulders, then to his waist, to the small of his back, exploring with his fingers the crevice between his buttocks. He lays Cem on his back, trembling, touching him gently, afraid he may break him, his fingers moving to caress the smooth warm skin across his abdomen, navel, down the inside of his legs. Ahmet takes Cem between his legs and on his knees, leans over and kisses this body he adores. He sinks his face into his curly sweet smelling mound of hairs and sucks Cem's offering of himself. He fills his mouth with love juices. He turns Cem gently over on his side and nearly cries out as he enters him.

'Well they had a key, didn't they. The mother had a key because it was her mother's flat. So the mother and his wife's brother found them in bed together. Well you can imagine the scene! Especially from the mother . . .

the mother informed on the boy so he was deported. Ahmet is desperate. And frankly, no one wants to help him, because he cheated everyone. And he's gone crazy! You see him in the cafés, gambling what little money he has. He thinks he will make it big one day and he will bring his lover over. He lives in cloud-cuckoo-land. As long as he stays away from me I don't mind. I tried to help him but it's no use . . . he's a liability, he's lost it . . . he should have told his mother right at the beginning. She would have shouted and screamed but she would have accepted it eventually.' ❑

***Aydin Mehmet Ali** was born in Cyprus and now lives in London where she works as an international education consultant specialising in multiculturalism and bilingualism, and is the chair of Hackney Action for Racial Equality. She has published a book on the educational under-achievement of Turkish-speaking young people and her short stories have been included in a number of anthologies, notably* Weeping Island, *a collection by Cypriot writers living in Cyprus and in the diaspora. The complete version of this story will appear in a collection to be published by Arcadia in January 2003*

MAYA JAGGI

LITERATURE REBORN

INFLUENCE IS MORE THAN A ONE-WAY STREET

History, says a character in Romesh Gunesekera's novel *Reef* (1994), is 'always the story of somebody's diaspora'. The impact of diasporic writers on British literature has been widely remarked since the early 1980s, with the garnering of literary prizes by writers from former colonies, from Salman Rushdie and VS Naipaul to Timothy Mo, Caryl Phillips and Ben Okri. Yet these authors form part of a far longer tradition at the heart of British writing, stemming from patterns of migration and cultural exchange that are an integral – if often forgotten – part of the country's history.

'English literature has, for at least 200 years, been shaped and influenced by outsiders,' writes Caryl Phillips in *Extravagant Strangers: A Literature of Belonging* (1997). His anthology of writers born outside Britain who have nourished the canon ranges from Conrad and Thackeray, Kipling and Orwell, to Doris Lessing and Rushdie. It demolishes the myth of a hermetic national tradition only recently 'reinvigorated' by post-war writers from the receding empire. Descendants of colonisers (Britain's own 'diaspora' forged a global empire) and colonised appear alongside writers from the Irish and Jewish diasporas, and those outside the empire, such as TS Eliot and Kazuo Ishiguro.

A selective amnesia has occluded both the centuries-old black presence in Britain and its cultural creativity. The first wave of the African diaspora on these shores, brought by the slave trade, had its writers. Ukawsaw Gronniosaw, a West African sold into slavery, published his *Narrative* in 1770, while Phillis Wheatley's poems appeared in 1773. Ignatius Sancho, born in 1729 on a slave ship in mid-Atlantic, is thought to be the first 'Afro-British' prose writer; *Letters of the Late Ignatius Sancho, An African* (1782), his posthumously published epistles to London society friends such as David Garrick, Laurence Sterne and Samuel Johnson (he sat for Gainsborough), was a best-seller in its day. Olaudah Equiano's *Interesting Narrative* (1789), also a best-seller, was among autobiographies of literate former slaves that lent weight to the abolitionist movement.

Left: Portrait of a Negro Man, Olaudah Equiano, *1780s, by an unknown artist. Credit: Bridgeman Art Library*

Opposite: 1820: plan of a slave ship to enable masters to 'maximise' their cargo. Credit: AKG London

Indians voyaged to Britain even before the empire claimed its 'jewel in the crown', at least since the East India Company was formed in 1599. Sake Dean Mahomet's *The Travels of Dean Mahomet* (1794) was an early instance of travel writing on Britain. The logic of empire made the metropolis a magnet for would-be professionals and intellectuals, such as the Trinidadian CLR James, who came to Britain in 1932. Given the dearth of publishing in the colonies, the goal for aspirant writers had to be London, which was simultaneously the engine for educating colonial elites and a subversive hub of national independence movements. Nor was the culture altogether foreign; many would-be writers arrived bearing British passports, schooled in Wordsworth and Shakespeare, as is illuminated by the anthology of writers' memoirs, *Voices of the Crossing* (2000), edited by Ferdinand Dennis and Naseem Khan.

Though writers from the colonies remain invisible in orthodox histories of literary modernism, some were championed by their contemporaries in London. EM Forster's preface for the Indian writer Mulk Raj Anand's *Untouchable* (1935) enabled the novel's publication after it was rejected by 19 publishers. TS Eliot and the Bloomsbury group admired the Indian GV Desani's ground-breaking novel, *All About H Hatterr* (1948); his 'rigmarole' English is a precursor of Rushdie's 'mongrel' tongue. Attia Hosain, author of tales of pre-partition India in *Phoenix Fled* (1953) and *Sunlight on a Broken Column* (1961), was a familiar BBC broadcaster in London.

The founding father of the African novel in English, the Nigerian Chinua Achebe, wrote *Things Fall Apart* (1958) while training at the BBC staff school in London. Pronounced the 'best first novel since the war' by a reader at William Heinemann, it became the launch title in 1962 of Heinemann's African Writers Series – a budget paperback imprint that emulated the Penguin revolution down to its orange covers. The series was like a starting pistol to African writers, according to Achebe, who chose its first 100 titles as series editor (shockingly, a job he performed for ten years without pay). Many titles were by Africans studying or working in Britain, including the Nigerians Wole Soyinka and Buchi Emecheta, and the Kenyan Ngugi wa Thiong'o. Flight from economic collapse and repression in independent Africa brought a more recent wave of African writers, including Abdulrazak Gurnah of Zanzibar and Ben Okri of Nigeria.

Fledgling writers often came to study, as did VS Naipaul at Oxford. But mass migration, inaugurated by the docking of the SS *Empire Windrush* in 1948, spawned a West Indian literary movement headquartered in London. In the 1950s and early 1960s alone, West

Indians published more than 130 novels in Britain. Sam Selvon, Trinidadian author of *The Lonely Londoners* (1956), and George Lamming from Barbados, author of *The Emigrants* (1954), stepped off the same boat, having fought over a single typewriter on the transatlantic passage.

Naipaul and Selvon were among 'East Indian West Indian' writers – belonging to both South Asian and Caribbean diasporas. The dislocations of slavery and indenture ensured today's 'double diasporas', as Africans were transported to the Caribbean, South America and the United States, Indians to East and South Africa, the Caribbean or the Pacific islands – before their descendants made the 'final passage' to Britain or North America. GV Desani was born in Nairobi and moved to Sindh [today in Pakistan], before arriving in England, contributing to a fertile triple perspective. Expatriate writers from the Caribbean, a 500-year-old melting pot, in a sense write from a double displacement, with ancestral links to Africa, India, China or Europe – often combined in one individual. The St Lucian poet and Nobel laureate Derek Walcott has likened Antillean art to a restored vase, lovingly made anew from 'our shattered histories, our shards of vocabulary . . . pieces broken off from the original continent'.

The border-crossing migrant is now widely held up as a metaphor for modern man – the Everyman of the late twentieth century. Edward Said in *Culture and Imperialism* (1993) described a shift in creative energy from 'the settled, established and domesticated dynamics of culture to its unhoused, decentred and exilic energies', whose 'incarnation today is the migrant, and whose consciousness is that of the intellectual and artist in exile, the political figure between domains, between forms, between homes and between languages'.

Yet while diasporic writers in Britain have been startling artistic innovators, their critical reception has not always kept pace. They may be read solely in terms of loss and nostalgia, the wistful backward glance, or the quest for 'home' and 'roots' – readings that constrict and sanitise, assuming fixed binaries of here and there, home and abroad, rootedness and exile. Rushdie has scoffed at the pressure to pander to a taste for exotica and 'otherness'; at the 'bogy of Authenticity', a 'folkloristic straitjacket'. He helped popularise ideas of hybridity and 'mongrelism' as an alternative to the 'absolutism of the Pure' ('mélange, hotchpotch, a bit of this and a bit of that is how newness enters the world'.)

Far from the cliché of being caught in a no man's land between cultures, diasporic writers may claim a 'doubling rather than a split', as the Pakistan-born short-story writer Aamer Hussein expresses it. Many writers such as Hussein, or the Bengali Sunetra Gupta and Amit Chaudhuri, enjoy what Kwame Anthony Appiah has called a 'rooted cosmopolitanism', being confidently bilingual or multilingual, and 'at home' in more than one culture. As successive 'second-generation' writers – beginning with the poetry of Linton Kwesi Johnson and Ravinder Randhawa's novel *A Wicked Old Woman* (1987) – have shown, the problem may not be one of cultural identity but the cold welcome offered by Britain.

An anthropological curiosity about diasporic literature can obscure the artistic innovation that the 'culturally ambidextrous' – those with 'stereoscopic vision' or a 'double consciousness' – can bring. The aesthetic innovations of migrant writers have shaped the literature of the metropolitan centre, just as Rushdie's *Midnight's Children* (1981) helped internationalise the British novel. While post-colonial writers have been driven to rewrite history from another perspective – the 'empire writing back' – white authors have begun to participate in this recovery of British history, as seen in Barry Unsworth's and Marina Warner's fiction on slavery. Others, such as Maggie Gee in her novel *The White Family* (2002), shortlisted for the Orange Prize, have opened their eyes to the multiracial inner city.

Diasporic literatures in other languages have sometimes thrived in Britain. Abdullah Hussein of Pakistan, who wrote many of his books while working in a Clapham off-licence, is widely held to be the greatest Urdu novelist. Hanan al-Shaykh of Lebanon, the translation of whose novel *Only in London* (2001) was shortlisted for the *Independent* foreign fiction prize, writes only in Arabic. Others have enriched the English language. Achebe, Rushdie and Anita Desai were among pioneers in rendering the language of another culture in English. Achebe's solution was to use different registers of English to express Igbo, while Rushdie invented a literary version of urban India's spoken hybrid. By a creative sleight of hand, Selvon's characters all speak Trinidadian English, no matter where in the Caribbean they come from.

Diasporic histories may lend themselves to polyphonic, fractured rather than linear narratives, moving back and forth in time and place, as in Phillips's formally innovative novels of the black – and Jewish – diasporas: *Higher Ground* (1989), *Cambridge* (1991) and *Crossing the River* (1993). Like Phillips, the Sri Lankan-born Romesh Gunesekera reconstructs diasporic histories through individual stories in his novels *Reef*, *The Sandglass* (1998) and *Heaven's Edge* (2002), as does Abdulrazak Gurnah, in *Dottie* (1990) and in his asylum seeker's tale, *By the Sea* (2001). The diasporic writer may have a privileged insight into the fragmented nature of memory or the fiction of 'home' that has universal resonance. While Rushdie spoke of the migrant's 'imaginary homelands', others point out that nations are themselves only 'imagined communities'.

Since the Greek derivation of diaspora means 'to scatter and sow', it concerns both dispersal and settlement. Yet a literature of settlement is not new, as the freed slave narrators who married Englishwomen in the eighteenth century attest. The mixed-race characters of Hanif Kureishi, Zadie Smith and Hari Kunzru have forerunners in Desani's H Hatterr, Jean Rhys's Creole heroines and the writings of Aubrey Menem, born in Britain in 1912 of an Indian father and an Irish mother.

There are pitfalls to the notion of diasporic literature. A glib celebration of hybridity can obscure individual trajectories and complex lives, as well as the differing perspectives of class and gender, or of ethnicities that resist the catch-all of 'South Asian' or 'black'. There is growing resentment that diasporic writers are sometimes held to stand for national literatures – notably the Indian writers in English who virtually monopolise fiction on India – simply because they have been anointed by western publishers.

But a key problem for writers may be how they are read. *The Nature of Blood* (1997), Phillips's framed narratives on figures resembling Shylock, Othello and Anne Frank, was lazily seen by some as simply making common cause between victims of persecution, when it insistently questions the very nature of the Europe that persecutes; the fortress that has for centuries built a mythic identity on bogus notions of racial and cultural 'purity', by stigmatising or destroying those it defines, in the teeth of history, as outsiders. Such misreading is a cautionary reminder that diasporic writers are of value not simply for what they tell 'us' about 'them', and their painful if 'colourful' journeys, but for what their often penetrating gaze reveals about Britain, and about ourselves. ❑

Maya Jaggi *is an award-winning feature writer and reviewer for the* Guardian *and editor of a forthcoming anthology of fiction by women who span continents (Random House USA). Some of her literary profiles appear in* Lives and Works *(Atlantic Books, 2002). Twice named national newspaper writer of the year in the Race in the Media awards, and feature writer of the year in the EMMA awards, she was formerly literary editor of* Third World Quarterly

LATIN AMERICA

London 1997: salsa club.
Credit: Alex Majoli / Magnum

POINT OF ARRIVAL

ANDREW GRAHAM-YOOLL

To London, and to all of England, I owe many lives – my own, my wife's, our children's. The new life that we were given at Victoria Station Customs Office on arrival cancelled the past in all but the remoteness of memory.

Flight into exile produces an impression of victory by creating a sense of relief; but the successful escape postpones realisation that exile is defeat. England does not understand exile. Hence she demands coming to terms with her rules immediately. All former rights are lost in the attempt to enter another's land. There is no one to turn to. Solidarity is non-existent among the tired tourists who carry their bags under their eyes and pant their bad breath with the hostility of insult.

I wanted to shout at the visitors that we were alive.

'Please, look, we survived; we escaped being killed; we are not travelling for fun but out of necessity.' But there was no response. Yes, we all have problems, a man seemed to say.

That was at the end of 1976. Another life started after passing through Immigration.

I think I have been here before, but know I have not. Writers, like expatriates, know that a person can return to a point of departure he or she has never been to or never started from. Even if this point is a place that has never been occupied physically, writers and expatriates retain in their mind scenes from a past that is not theirs, and report on its dynamic humanity and inspiring energy as if it were their own. But not always can they convey this rich imagination. A city has poets to paint it and artists to describe it, but how do they discover and uncover and reveal what has been gazed at often by many? In 'The Philosophy of Sight-Seeing' in the book *The New Jerusalem* (1920), GK Chesterton found – ahead of my exploration – that everything to be discovered had been seen before. 'It may be called a contradiction in terms to expect the unexpected,' he wrote. 'It may be counted mere madness to anticipate astonishment, or go in search of a surprise.' Yet in London it did not seem unreasonable to seek the unforeseen, for that was also what Chesterton sought. 'I wanted to be entertained at the firesides of total strangers, in the medieval manner, and to tell them interminable tales of my travels.'

Andrew Graham-Yooll, 2002.
Credit: John Fernandez

If brought up on selected passages of George Orwell, such as extracts from *The Lion and the Unicorn* (1940), the stranger is offered the revelation that the England arrived in has always been and will not go away. 'The gentleness, the hypocrisy, the thoughtlessness, the reverence for law and the hated uniforms will remain, along with the suet puddings and the misty skies.' Orwell went on: 'It needs some very great disaster, such as prolonged subjugation by a foreign enemy to destroy a national culture . . . But England will still be England, an everlasting animal stretching into the future and the past, and, like all living things, having the power to change out of recognition and remain the same.'

Writers like Browning, Auden and Orwell offered a strong sense of nation, and plunged the newcomer into intellectual confusion. It remains difficult to understand the English sense of national identit – there is no reverence for a flag, no beliefs outside of the palpable narratives of heroism at war nor a decently composed anthem – yet one is assured vehemently that a sense of nation exists.

This is why the English do not understand exile. They have the only country in the world to which a native-born son or daughter has always been able to return. They are convinced that their country has no past to expiate, no memory that could or should threaten that of others or make the present uncomfortable. There have been no pogroms here, no concentration camps, no holocaust. England has never been closed to the English, as so many other borders were shut to their own nationals. To the English, exile is romantic, at times titillating, at times a source of impatience; for, once the alien has gained a safe haven, why should the lamentations continue? Thus exile is a state of mind with which many find it impossible to connect. With words of sympathy used for any occasion, such as a discussion of the weather, a person can sidestep, skirt and avoid the small matter of foreign difference.

Before my arrival, England had been a place of other people's memories. Their experiences were the past, but the place of my future. England has been an immovable rock to which dying expatriates from colonial careers and foreign postings returned. The dreams of expatriates were of future days remembered, and which may never have existed. Fantasies had been set in green gardens bathed in a summer sun. In some Buenos Aires houses I knew, one clock had been set at Greenwich Mean Time as a reminder of 'home'. Picture calendars – ordered from Harrods in London – fixed the woodland colours and countryside contours that for ever fired the imagination. The expatriates longed for return to a 'home' about which absence had made them almost ignorant. And when that dream future arrived and became the present – in the planned retirement, with a small pension in a southern county – then, in turn, the expatriate past became brighter. The chintz of the distant colonial sitting room, kept as it had been at 'home', in retrospect looked cleaner in the long-vacated remote company house. The past could again be safely smiled at.

In Argentina, the gentleman described by the social historian Mark Girouard in *The Return to Camelot: Chivalry and the English Gentlemen* (1981) was the epitome of Englishness.

> He was always ready to give up his own time to come to the help of . . . those less fortunate . . . He was an honourable opponent and a good loser; he played games for the pleasure of playing, not to win. He never boasted. He was not interested in money.

This was what any Anglo-Argentine, perhaps any neo-colonial, aspired to. And in the camaraderie of the club bar it was compatible with the humorous definition of the English abroad as given by Major CS Jarvist, CMG, OBE, in *The Black Garden of Allah* (1939).

> From the outside world a variety of wayfarers descend; missionaries desirous of having their throats cut in their proselytising zeal, straying politicians . . . and last but not least the ever-present menace of a type of person that can best be described as the Travel-Monger. A Travel-Monger is a male or female, clad in shorts, shirt, revolver and topee, who travels not for pleasure but for profit, and the 'female of the species is more deadly than the male' because besides being very much in the trade she almost invariably suffers from what is known as the 'First White Woman' complex, and this is a most trying mental malady.

John Russell, in his 'Portrait of the British' in the *New York Times Magazine* (9 March 1986) confirms the impression that the British like to have of themselves:

> In airports, in hotels and on beaches, an Englishman stands out by reason of his dress, his bearing, his speech and his immunity to ridicule. As far as he is concerned, what an Englishman does is right, and to hell with everyone else.

The country I wanted to be in was one of good, clean fun – a mixture of *Carry On* films, 1960s ingénue, and innocent sex with Rita Tushingham in Richard Lester's film *The Knack* (1965).

I tried to cease to be an Argentine, to train to be an Englishman – not even a Scot of the land of my father, for I did not speak the language nor understand Scottish football. I was the expatriate son of an expatriated father. London is packed with similar people who have forgotten their points of departure and have to be reminded of their origins. Such is the fate of expatriates, exiles, foreigners and strangers.

How does a person become an Englishman? The novelist VS Naipaul tried. And as a reward for his efforts he was made a knight, Sir Vidiadhar Surajprasad, in 1989. He had travelled a long way from his father's house, with the Indian lions and elephant trunks in the masonry, at 64 Main Road, Chaguanas, in Trinidad. Naipaul once said to me that he was not an exile and the idea that he should be considered one irked him. 'Exile is an involuntary situation. I came to Britain voluntarily,' he said in 1981. He had found England comfortable and had stayed.

The people of my first English years were also exiles, men and women who had two or more lives. To avoid administrative confusion, they will own up to having one only. We have all lived more than once, for many were the times we fugitives thought that we had come to an end and then were born again into exile.

I like life here. A place becomes likeable when it offers the possibility of personal peace, not just personal gain, in whatever social and political upheaval is affecting the lives of the natives. England has, for all arriving exiles, the mixed surprises of new senses and very old customs – an explosion of fresh feelings that scatters and vanishes into routine and predictability.

The novelist Salman Rushdie said in an interview in 1981 that he too liked it here.

> I am very settled. I hold a British passport. I am, actually, more settled here than I thought I was. The accidents of my life make me feel – not displaced, not alien – simultaneously an insider and an outsider in as many as three countries: Britain, India, Pakistan. I was not a child in Britain, so I enter this culture at an unusual angle. All this makes, I think, for a good 'position' to write from. I don't expect that the feeling of exile ever goes away, not from me or from my stories. I like it where I live. I also like it at White Hart Lane, the ground of Tottenham Hotspur Football Club. And at Lord's in summer.

Can you strip a city of its many layers to show the body below? A wine bar in Bowling Green Lane, once the least respectable public house to be found off Farringdon Road is, in memory, my starting point to explore the English. It was and still is called The Surprise, and was probably so named because it was around the corner from the Greater London Record Office and Library – a place of serious study and full of surprises. My search was an exploration in the manner of the English in foreign parts. Those travellers toured the world and scoffed at the shortcomings of the natives or were amused by their lack of logic. In other words, I set out to be narrow-minded. The public house is the kingdom's leading landmark, and inspection of its interior would reveal the human content of the land.

Among the men who entertained me with conversation and guidance was a priest, who announced an introduction, 'I may be a man of the Church but I am a sensual man. You should hear some of the things I have to listen to. Jesus wept, what nonsense. I enjoy the relaxation of the scene here. Quite harmless . . . What am I having? I'm a Guinness man, myself.'

There was also a Pakistani functionary from the World Bank, who went to The Surprise to escape the formality of his job and to exchange vulgarities in Urdu with the postal workers. There were about half a dozen very well-dressed young men, who seemed to be escaping from somewhere – probably from what they pretended to be in the daytime; there were builders and mechanics, journalists, voyeurs and social workers who had been working late at the council offices nearby. All shared an unspoken feeling of guilt at being at The Surprise in merry conversation about the joys of being inside down-to-earth premises which much of their world outside frowned on.

The Surprise came to an end as the result of an article in the *Sun*. The newspaper ran a story in 1979 or 1980 about a police raid on the place, and soon after the pub had to be cleaned up. The last offending scene had been quite funny. There had always been, closest to the stage, a short bald man who shouted a mixture of obscenities and encouragement. One day a woman sat on the man's bald pate. As the sweat of her crotch gleamed on his head, he cried out, 'Now that must make my hair grow!' The women screamed with laughter and her breasts leaped about as she hiccuped and snorted. They met again in court.

How should writers supply brushes of beauty to paint cities in which grandmothers – old women who once had families – live without company; where old people die alone without care; where unwanted immigrants sleep five to a bare floor until they become millionaires and are then called stinking rich? How do authors create a pleasant vision of, and pay tribute to, a city which ancient poets have populated with fantasies of glory and greatness? Are these writers speaking of the same city as the one in which the grandmothers, the aged, the immigrants are privately reviled and publicly ignored?

What are my regrets? At the end of the age of Thatcherism – when the 1990s were born clichéd with the promise of caring in contrast with the ruthlessness of the 1980s – I fear that it may be too late to realise Orwell's aspiration that 'the Stock Exchange will be pulled down . . . and England will still be England'. It might be too late to overcome the impertinence of greed.

I regret the discovery that nowhere can a person escape the unfeeling meanness of the right as well as the contrived sensitivities of the self-indulgent socialists who play at being fair. I resent the mindless stupidity of the carnival left as well as the social savagery of the right which have ensured that the thinking minority is cowed into showing an incapacity for thought because intellectual reflection is seen to be embarrassing. True, the rejection of ideas has been the salvation of the English from defeat by the empty words that characterised the twentieth century's worst dictators. But it would be comforting to detect a little more respect for intellect. And now, with no respect for ideas, without Priestley or Auden or Orwell, how will the Englishness that always was be preserved?

There had been warnings of change. The first clear signal of an end was seen in May 1979, when Margaret Thatcher was elected prime minister. The historian EP Thompson, in *Writing by Candlelight*, compiled in 1979, lifted the curtain on a new age. England was being pushed 'into a managed society, whose managing director is money, and whose production manager is the police'. What 'is new to the historian is the notion that we should be instructed as to what value we are to put on freedom and democracy, and be instructed by the police'. In the second half of 1980, CP Snow (b 1905) died and one of the century's Renaissance men was lost. In a land that disliked ideas, Snow had cleverly played with the system's curiosity and had bridged the gap between science, art and culture in a country that distrusts all three; he was a pundit in a capital whose politicians disliked punditry.

But wait: the beauty of surviving in a place where survival was made simple is that life is too attractive to loiter either in the litanies of the left or in the corrupt repugnance of the right. England's remoteness from the idea of exile – even though it has harboured many and varied exiles – and from political preoccupation makes it a haven from ideological debate, even from controversial thought, and certainly from the weight of each individual's past. So there is still good in what is wrong, even if the rising tide of wrong is disturbing.

The good, however, can easily be found by the outsider. The exile's guilt at surviving, of coming through safely when others have had both minds and bodies scarred, is irrelevant in London. The pleasure of surviving contains a mixture of guilt and of fear of looking back on the desperation left behind, on the past that one escaped thanks to England's indifference. ❑

Andrew Graham-Yooll *returned to Argentina in 1996 and is now editor-in-chief of the* Buenos Aires Herald. *He was formerly the editor of* Index

Excerpt from Point of Arrival: Observations Made on an Extended Visit *(Pluto Press, UK, 1992)*

'MIND THE GAP'

AGUSTINA LATTANZI

One day last year, two young Argentines decided to follow in the footsteps of many of their friends and try their luck abroad. Which should it be: London or the United States? Maybe because of the spell that Europe still casts over so many Argentines, they settled for London. More than a century ago, immigrants from the old continent came to people this vast southern land. Most were Spanish and Italian, seeking a way out of poverty; others fled from the pogroms and persecutions that characterised late nineteenth-century Europe. For all of them, Argentina represented their dreams and aspirations.

Today, the reverse process is under way as young people flee unemployment, institutional and political crisis and lack of opportunity. Young middle-class would-be professionals are seeking refuge in the lands from which their grandparents escaped.

They are not the first exodus from Argentina this century. At the time of the military dictatorships in Argentina, Chile and Uruguay, thousands of writers, intellectuals, journalists and others fled the dangers of political persecution, death and 'disappearance'.

But back to our young couple, a quite unremarkable pair – except that their story typifies that of 62,880 others who left from Ezeiza [Buenos Aires airport] in 2001. Let's say it was economic exile, unemployment or simply the death of their dreams that drove them away; it doesn't matter. With a few clothes and books in suitcases, they leave home to study or find work in the capital of the world, planning to return with their qualifications in a couple of years. Our couple were excited at the prospect of studying in the best schools of Europe; immersing themselves in another culture; making new friends; and travelling the world before returning. Opportunities seemed endless.

A friendly summer welcomed them to London at the end of August. The attractions of the unknown were irresistible. Everything, absolutely everything was different: language, architecture, weather, food, even the people and their unfamiliar codes. The 'culture shock' made them uncertain, ill at ease, remote from those around them. They began to integrate into London life; but something warned them they should never expect to get too close – that they should, as the loudspeaker in the Underground reminded them daily, 'mind the gap'.

Once at university, they met people from all over the world: English, American, Italian, Spanish, French, Russian, Slovak, Japanese, Latin American. In the week, they chatted to all and sundry, trying out a new language: the English of the others. But at weekends, they went out with their own kind – Argentines, Chileans, Colombians and Peruvians – relaxing in the familiarity of it all: the past became present as it was, always, in their memory. But a memory very different from that of an earlier generation of emigrants.

December arrived and with it the return to Buenos Aires. After a couple of hours there, something became all too clear: Argentina was no longer the country they had left. This was most obvious in the mood of the people, the vacant look in their eyes, the sense that they were crushed under a weight they could not bear. For the first time they could remember, there were no Christmas celebrations in Buenos Aires. No lights, no Christmas trees, no people in the streets – they had taken refuge in their homes. Much had happened in the four months they had been away. After staggering along for years, the nation's economic system had finally collapsed. People's savings had disappeared; unemployment continued to mount. Anger and discontent grew; neither politicians nor the people themselves seemed capable of doing anything.

But suddenly, life returned to the desolate streets of the city. Simultaneously, there were eruptions in different parts of the country: the poor began to loot the supermarkets while middle-class protest took the form of the *cacerolazo* [a popular form of protest expressed in the communal beating of pots and pans]. But they were united in their grievance; apathy came to an end the day that thousands from all walks of life met to express their anguish and fatigue in the Plaza de Mayo, scene some 50 years ago of ecstatic crowds hanging on the words of their president Juan Perón, and today the venue for the Mothers – now Grandmothers – of the Plaza de Mayo, still searching for their children, *los desaparacidos* of the years under the generals.

The superman of the economic ministry was forced to resign and a curfew was imposed. For a moment, the fear of a return to the past gripped people's hearts. But the same day, faced with lack of leadership and the loss of his legitimacy, the president, too, had to go. Five provisional presidents succeeded each other in one week. The chaos was a typical scenario reflecting the critical situation.

'. . . the worst thing is not that I can't have a professional career in this country, but that they stole my dreams,' one friend said.

In December, Hopeless Airways announced 'the departure of 23,000 more young Argentines: no return date specified.' Ezeiza watched them depart, as it had watched so many before.

It was winter in London, harsh and no welcome this time. It would never be the same again. Now their feelings were clouded by nostalgia for a country to which they had no immediate prospect of return; exile was no longer entirely a choice. As the prospect of return faded, memory grew stronger and brought their city constantly to mind in the words of the greatest of all Buenos Aires writers, Jorge Luis Borges:

PARTING

Three hundred nights like three hundred walls
must rise between my love and me
and the sea will be a black art between us.

Nothing will be left but memories
O afternoons earned with suffering,
nights . . . for the sight of you,
fields along my way, firmament
that I am seeing and losing . . .
Final as marble
your absence will
sadden other afternoons.

From *Fervor de Buenos Aires*, translated by WS Merwin ❑

Agustina Lattanzi *arrived from Argentina last year and is studying in London – 'as long as the money holds out: my grant was in pesos and it's worth nothing now'. She is also a volunteer assistant at* Index

POEMS

DIEGO DE JESÚS

Credit: Óscar Ruiz

Entristece llegar a Londres
Sin lluvia
Cargar el paraguaras en vano

It's sad to reach London
without rain
Carrying my umbrella
in vain.

Translated by Amanda Hopkinson

Vete a escanciar sobre los huesos
de tus muertos, pídeles perdón
por la calidad del vino. Ay,
que no se hable de le sequía
de nuestros vasos: eso ques oyes
al anochecer es un río
de sed

You must drench the bones
of your dead, ask their pardon
for the poor quality of the wine. And
let's not have more talk of dryness
of our glasses: that sound you hear
when night comes is a river
of thirst

Pideles permiso para sacarles
la lengua, di lo tuyo y calla,
todavía tienes mucho que contar:
eso que ocultas es un río
de risa

You must ask their permission to put out
their tongues, saying what is yours to say
and then no more, even though you have
  a lot to tell:
what you are hiding is a river
of curled laughter

Vete a escanciar la virtud del vino,
si nadie aparece echa abajo le puerta
de la taberna del cementerio

You must drench off the wine's goodness
and if no one appears you must knock
  down the door
of the tavern, the door that leads out to
  the cemetery ❑

Translated by Stephen Watts

***Diego de Jesús** was born in Mexico in 1965 and came to London in 1989. He teaches language and translation at University College London. A bilingual selection of his poetry was published by Libros De La Mancuspia in 1998*

'KARIBU'

NONI, JORGE

OUR JOURNEY

It was a typical day, spring was awakened and the cherry trees were showing their best blooms. The sun was shining and the days were getting longer and warmer. Even though my life was in chaos and the country was like a pressure cooker ready to explode, that day I felt happy and content. As every morning, I got up early to get the children ready. After breakfast, I put the babies in the pram and we walked the two older boys to school. Once back at home, I sat to relax for a few minutes.

At no moment did it cross my mind that my life was going to change with a knock at the door. A person asked to see my spouse. He looked worried and agitated. He was talking fast and mumbling erratically. 'The military police are looking for the entire unionised workforce, and they are being taken to jail. Tell your spouse he must leave the country as soon as possible.'

That day, my partner was out looking for a job. When he came back home we sat down for dinner and talked throughout the night, trying to find a solution to this new problem. He thought he should go away on his own and, when he found a job, send me the tickets to travel with the children.

I wasn't happy. I said to him, 'We are a family and we should be together. Wherever you go, we all go.' And that was what we agreed. In three days we tried to sell all our possessions. On Saturday morning, we left our home with four children, two potties and my grandfather's suitcase full with clothes and ten blankets, with an unknown and uncertain future waiting for us.

When we arrived at the coach depot and I saw this little bus, no bigger than a hopper, my heart sank to my feet. The coach was packed when we left. I did not see the view or the towns we passed on our journey. I was too worried about the unknown.

We went up and down hills and mountains, until we arrived at the top of Cuesta de Caracol (Snail Hill). I was so deep in my thoughts that I didn't realise that we had been riding for hours. The view from the top was majestic, breathtaking. One could see for miles around. The sun reflected in the mountains with their peaks covered with eternal snow, giving them an aura of peace and harmony. Once out of the coach, everyone walked towards the border crossing. There was a big statue of Jesus Christ with his open arms in welcome to all travellers crossing two vast countries.

***Noni** is from Chile. She wrote this in 1999*

LEAVING QUITO

Everything here is new for me: the people, women, children, country are very different from my country, because my country is very poor. I come from Quito, the capital of Ecuador, in the north of the country. My house is big: it has two floors and I live with my father and mother, brother and sister. I am a graphic designer and I work for a company and have my own small business.

In Quito, people sleep on the streets, children beg on the bus, old people are abandoned, there is no work and the police are not good. The president who left in 1996 was corrupt; today, Jamil Mahuad is president. We have very high inflation: the price of gas was US$3.50 but now it is US$25.

I made posters for my political party, Moviemento Popular Domocratico. Last February, the founder, the leader of my party was killed.

In 1996, the president ran a telethon to raise money for the poor at Christmas. But he took all the money and gave it to his brother who wanted to become the mayor of Quito. I was in a taxi with a friend, investigating the telethon, when I noticed three people following me. The taxi driver went fast but they intercepted my car. They told us to get out and come to their car. They had police guns. They blindfolded me and my friend and told us they would kill us. They asked for our MPD documents, but I said I hadn't got my documents with me. So they said they would kill me.

We drove for 20 minutes and stopped on a bridge. We all got out. They tied our legs and threw us over the bridge.

We hung there.

'Give us the documents or we will kill you.'

'The documents are in my house,' cried my friend.

They pulled me up alone. We went to my friend's house and they told me to go and find his documents. 'Or we will kill the people in the house.' I was very frightened.

I looked but I couldn't find the papers. I didn't know what they would do. But they said, 'Go away. We will kill you later.'

My friend hung from the bridge the whole day, until some people came to help him. At the end of the week, I left Quito. ❑

***Jorge** is from Ecuador. He wrote this in 1999*

This work appeared in Karibu *magazine, part of WEA London's Looking Glass Writers project for refugees and asylum seekers*

APPRENTICESHIP IN ASSIMILATION

URSULA OWEN

Ursula Sachs at 18 months, 1938: the 'single journey only' pass to exile

I seem to start my apprenticeship in assimilation in the womb. My parents are German Jews, born in Frankfurt in the first decade of this century. Neither family is Orthodox and both are highly assimilated into German bourgeois life. My family has never denied their Jewishness. On the contrary, my parents often made a point of it, even after they became converts to Christianity. No one in my wider family supports the Zionist movement; many of them see assimilation as a positive good. It is easy to dismiss this as a craven desire to belong, but nothing as simple as that makes sense.

Is it justified to feel an exile in a country to which I came at the age of 18 months? In fact, the odd thing is that I have felt so English for so many years. My parents spoke with strong German accents and small English vocabularies, we ate German food, our social and family life is almost entirely German in its patterns and habits. Looking back, I see how hard I work at being a little English girl. I live a double life without being conscious of it. It isn't until I am in my 20s that I really begin to understand that I am in an important way a foreigner. And it isn't until my late 30s that I begin to see that being an outsider is a sort of gift, bringing a particular sort of energy for which I am grateful. It takes me some time, too, to realise that politics entered my life long before I had the faintest notion of what politics was.

The English are, after all, a decent people, and they will give some people refuge from some situations, sometimes. But, like most host nations, they have problems when immigrants stand out, don't become enough like them, don't fit in. In 1989, I hear the historian Bill Williams give a talk on Jewish immigrations to Britain at the turn of the century. He describes a list that was produced by the indigenous *Jewish* community for the new immigrants, telling them what to avoid: speaking their own language in public places, talking loudly on buses, wearing the wrong clothes – in other words, anything that made them appear un-English. Nothing changes much.

My parents discover this very early. We, their children, will be their English representatives in their new-found land. They will not try to be English themselves – they are shrewd enough to know they'll never succeed. Ours is a bilingual household – they speak German to us, we speak English back. We learn each other's languages and, much later, I realise I don't feel quite at home in English, that I speak in translation more than I thought.

I turn out to be a brilliant assimilator. A conformist child, I take to it like a duck to water. I am duly embarrassed on buses with my relatives, who do talk loudly, sometimes in German. My parents' conversion to Christianity soon after they arrive in England must help, though I am not greatly conscious of it. My parents are confirmed at the same time as we are christened and my mother actually teaches Sunday school in St Mary's, Oxford, when we are evacuated there.

At school, I am extremely shy and very silent. An early report says: 'Ursula seems to be an intelligent girl but she does not speak.' In my teens I gravitate towards the most English of friends. But I also live a sort of split life, becoming close to two girls whose parents have also come from Nazi Germany, and spending time with their families. They make me feel uneasy. The accents, the food, the aspirations – they are deeply familiar, and yet they jar. I am busy with my apprenticeship in assimilation. They are not the root to belonging.

I grow up feeling confusion about what language can do. My parents express nuance and humour in German. But my attempted subtleties are earnestly imitated from friends. I have no real confidence in my ability to express precisely what I am feeling. I use words experimentally, testing them out on what I think of as my critical audience. (I was well into my 30s when an irritated friend told me that I used swear words as if I was a child, with a desire to shock but without any real conviction. I was shaken as much by her irritation as by her insight.)

When Eva Hoffman's book *Lost in Translation* comes out in 1989, I feel an extraordinary lurch of recognition:

> My speech, I sense, sounds monotonous, deliberate, heavy – an aural mask that doesn't become me or express me at all. This willed self-control is the opposite of real mastery, which comes from a trust in your own verbal powers and allows for those bursts of spontaneity, of response, that can rise into pleasure and overflow in humour. Laughter is the lightning rod of play, the eroticism of conversation; for now, I've lost the ability to make the sparks fly . . . I become a very serious young person, missing the registers of wit and irony in my speech, though my mind sees ironies everywhere.

Even so late in my life, when I think I have dealt with much of all this, I am deeply comforted by reading about something so recognisable, and still surprisingly painful.

Surely I exaggerate these feelings? After all, I enjoy my school life, I am popular, I have friends. And I get pleasure from some of the things I am good at. All children have to assimilate to something and I am not unique in this respect. But I am precarious in particular ways. I am not making sense of the two worlds that I am growing up in. I am never sure why people like me or whether they will go on liking me, whether I will go on being clever or in the school teams. One skin too few, someone once said about me. I need too much to be part of things, things I don't feel are available to me. Much later, of course, I want to discard a lot, some of the very things I wanted so much to belong to then.

When I leave home, I decide that I am going to reinvent myself. I will be free of difficult family circumstances and uncertain cultural messages. I will create myself from scratch. Oddly enough, this crazy project helps me to gain confidence. Spontaneity has not been my strong suit so far but I begin to feel freer to discover things. And I no longer feel so responsible to others for my behaviour.

I still want to be part of the mainstream, but here is a stream that is something to do with me as a separate person. Some part of me decides that reinventing myself will involve using language. I begin to talk less tentatively, to try out new words more confidently. I become intoxicated with words, discover what I think by saying it out loud, worry less about getting things wrong. I feel I might have a place in the scheme of things.

Somehow my opinions and feelings begin to belong to me. There is still a sense of danger: if I let go the opinions I think I ought to have, it would be to acknowledge that I can never be an insider, ever. But even that begins to seem an acceptable possibility.

But as I write about this change I wonder whether taking on one's own past can ever ring true. My retrospective understanding of my apprenticeship in assimilation seems to teeter on the edge of a fiction. Perhaps it's because I am putting together this story from fragments. My memories come in fits and starts. It is often the briefest, oddest incidents that stand out, sharp and powerful, and that seem to me to demonstrate larger truths about the past. I am comforted by what Salman Rushdie says: 'Meaning is a shaky edifice we build out of scraps, dogmas, childhood injuries, newspaper articles, chance remarks, old films, small victories, people hated, people loved; perhaps it is because our sense of what is the case is constructed from such inadequate materials that we defend it so fiercely.'

Perhaps the difficult part comes later. What became of this person who tried so hard to belong and who begins, in complicated ways, to like being an outsider? ❑

***Ursula Owen** is editor-in-chief of* Index. *She came to the UK in August 1938. This is an edited version of an article that appeared in* New Writing, *edited by Andrew Motion (Minerva, 1993)*

AFTER NATURE

WG SEBALD

III

We know, there is a long tradition
of persecuting the Jews in the city
of Frankfurt, as in other places.
Around 1240, the records tell us,
173 were either slaughtered
or died of their own free will
in a conflagration. In 1349
the Flagellant Brothers instituted
a great massacre in the Jewish quarter.
Again, the chronicles tell that the Jews
burned themselves, and that
after the fire there was a clear view from
the Cathedral Hill over to Sachsenhausen.
Thereafter the Jews only hesitantly
returned to the city on the Main.
In the mid-fifteenth century
a clothing statute is issued,
yellow rings to be worn on the tunic,
later a grey circle the size of
an apple, for the prevention of all
carnal intercourse between Christians
and Jews, for a long time to come
under the pain of death.
Then, at the expense of Frankfurt's
high city council, in the train
of civic reform, progressive order
and hygienisation, a ghetto of their own
is built for the Jews near the Wollgraben,
fourteen houses and a new synagogue.
By Grünewald's time, we learn,
there are twenty-three houses, and soon

WG Sebald.
Credit: Ute Sebald

the district counts more than three thousand souls,
without the boundaries having been widened.
Each night – on Sundays at four in the
afternoon – they were locked up, and
might not walk into any place
where a green tree grew,
not on the Scheidewall
nor in the Ross, nor on the Römerberg
or in the Avenue. In this ghetto
the Jewess Enchin had been raised
before – not many months preceding
her marriage to Mathys Grune
the painter – she was christened
in the name of St Anne.
In the compendious book about the historical
Grünewald which WK Zülch DPhil produced
in ancient Schwabach type
in the year 1938 for Hitler's birthday
the story of this extraordinary union
could not be admitted. Grünewald
would have noticed this child,
remarkable, it was said, for her beauty,
when she passed through the Bridge Gate
and the Preachers' Lane on her way
to her workplace just outside the ghetto.
But there is no evidence that it was he who induced
this Anna, betrothed to him a year later,
to change her religious faith.
Rather, it seems that she herself
had facilitated this step,
attesting great strength of will,
of desperation, by looking the painter
straight in the eyes, perhaps
at first merely in love with
his green-coloured name,
a conjunction which to the bachelor
master, who meanwhile had given up
the Mainz Court Painter's appointment
in favour of the great Isenheim altar

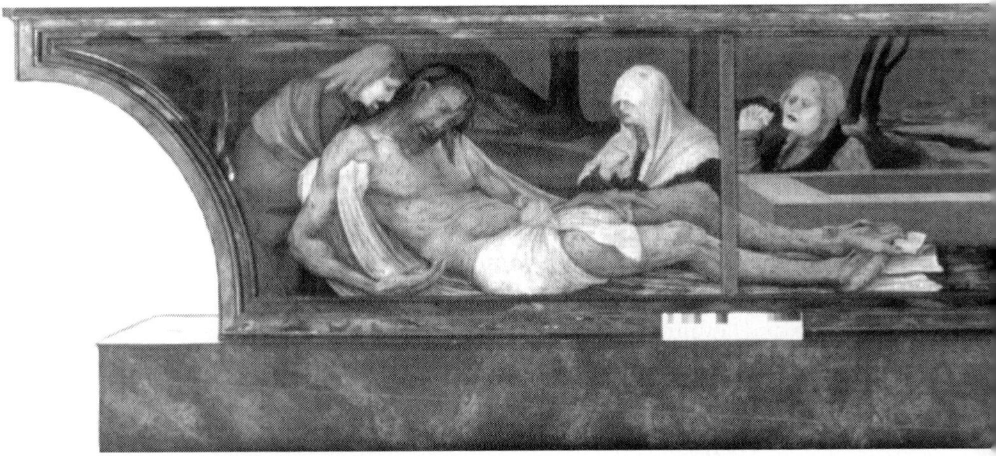

Mathias Gothart Grünewald (1470/75–1528), 'Burial', from the predella of the Isenheim Altar. Credit: Unterlindenmuseum / AKG

commission, would not have come amiss,
for without a household of his own
he could employ no assistant
or apprentice for his work.
When Grünewald buys a house
very close to the cathedral
on December 17 1512
for twenty-three guilders
twelve shillings, already,
the documents record, he has taken
to wife the baptised Anna.
The much admired young proselyte,
who for the Frankfurt Christian
community, which even for her baptism
had overwhelmed her with gifts,
was no mean acquisition,
could have founded Grünewald's fortune.
If it came out otherwise, for one thing,
it was because the painter,
who later lived as a recluse
and almost underground, himself
made impossible his recognition
by his community; and,
for another, as his pictures prove,
he had more of an eye for men,

whose faces and entire physique
he executed with endless devotion,
whereas his women for the most part
are veiled, so relieving him of the fear
of looking at them more closely.
Perhaps that is why Grünewald's
Anna grew shrewish, ill, a victim
to perverse reason, to brain fevers
and to madness.
In the end, awaiting recovery,
she is placed in hospital, where
at the time of the painter's death
still she lives on, infirm
in body and mind.

IV

In his excitement about the truly
boundless growth
of industry, the statesman
Disraeli called Manchester
the most wonderful city of modern times,
a celestial Jerusalem
whose significance only philosophy
could gauge. Half a life ago now
it is that, after leaving my remote home,
I arrived there and took lodgings
among previous century's
ruins. Often at that time
I rambled over the fallow
Elysian Fields, wondering
at the work of destruction, the black
mills and shipping canals,
the disused viaducts and
warehouses, the many millions
of bricks, the traces of smoke,
of tar and sulphuric acid,
long have I stood on the banks
of the Irk and the Irewell, those

mythical rivers now dead,
which in better times
shone azure blue,
carmine red and glaucous green,
in their glow reflecting
the cotton clouds, those white ones
into which without a word the breath
of legions of human beings had been absorbed.
And the water carried them downstream
together with salt and ashes
through the marshland out
to the sea. Those silent mutations
clear the way to the future.
In the course of three generations
the working classes of Manchester
had become a race of pygmies.
Volunteers who in wartime attempted
to escape into military service
were rejected by the selection boards
as unfit, unless they could be accommodated
in one of the so-called bantam battalions
which recruited diminutive soldiers from the city
and throughout the surrounding area.
In either case they were
part of the obscure crowds
who fuelled the progress of history.
From my workplace I thought
I could see the will-o'-the-wisps
of their souls, as with tiny lanterns
they haunted the rubbish dumps
of the City Corporation, a smouldering
alpine range which, it seemed to me,
extended into the beyond.
In the dusk I often saw
the searchlight beams from
bulldozers creeping about there
that pierced the void, and aeroplanes,
our grey primeval brothers,
rose with infinite slowness

from the lagoon and the bogs.
I recall that these images
often plunged me into a quasi
sub-lunary state of deep
melancholia and that then
I heard the incessant monotonous
vibrations of a Jew's harp
and repeatedly had to step out
of doors in my oppression.
Whole days long in the basement
of the university library I read
the works of Paracelsus, in which
it is written that from septentrione
nothing good emanates and
that the body is dyed
by illness like a piece of cloth
by an extraneous colour.
Often on my wanderings
through the streets I resorted
to one of the many infernally
glittering hostelries, for preference
to Liston's Music Hall
where a radiantly blue-eyed,
down-and-out heroic tenor,
who always wore a winter coat
too long for him and a Homburg hat,
sang *Tannhäuser* arias, accompanied
by a Wurlitzer organ. And to
the Gospel Chapels I went
from time to time, witnessing
how row after row of the sick,
amid the congregation's shrieking,
were healed and even the blind
had their sight restored.
Once, while searching
for the star-shaped Strangeways
Prison, an overwhelming
panoptic structure whose walls
are as high as Jericho's, I found

LS Lowry (1887–1976), 'The Canal Bridge', 1949.
Credit: Bridgeman Art Library / Southampton City Art Gallery

myself in a sort of no-man's-land
behind the railway buildings, in a terrace
of low houses apparently due
for demolition, with shops left vacant,
on whose boards the names
Goldblatt, Grünspann and Gottgetreu,
Speigelhalter, Soloman, Waislfish
and Robinsohn could be made out.
In the wind a door moved
as if as a sign. Stuck to it
was an old placard
for the musical *Oklahoma!*.

The entrance to nature's theatre
stood open. I still strained
to hear ethereal waves
when, with martial brass music,
bugle horns and drums,
a procession of olive-green
child soldiers marched
down the street, passed
by me and suddenly vanished
as though swallowed by the earth.
If I told Mr Deutsch
about these things
he shook his head
and said: 'Strange, very
strange.' Mr Deutsch,
born in Kufstein, had come
to England as a child
in nineteen-thirty-eight.
There were many things he could not
remember; some others he could not erase
from his mind. He had never
mastered the English language
although for years, day in
and day out, he followed
on TV with an expression of
the utmost attention the entire
television schedule, as if
at any moment he expected
a message that would
change his whole life.

VII

Lord, I dreamed
that to see Alexander's battle
I flew all the way to
Munich. It was when darkness
crept in and far below me
I saw the roof of my house,

saw the shadows falling
on the East Anglian landscape,
I saw the rim of the island,
the waves lapping at the shore
and in the North Sea the ships
motionless ahead of the foam-white wakes.
As a stingray hovers deep down
in the sea, so soundlessly I glided,
scarcely moving a wing,
high above the earth
over the Rhine's alluvial plain
and followed upstream
the course of the water
grown heavy and bitter.
Cities phosphorescent
on the riverbank, industry's
glowing piles waiting
beneath the smoke trails
like ocean giants for the siren's
blare, the twitching lights
of rail- and motorways, the murmur
of the millionfold proliferating molluscs,
woodlice and leeches, the cold putrefaction,
the groans in the rocky ribs,
the mercury shine, the clouds that
chased through the towers of Frankfurt,
time stretched out and time speeded up,
all this raced through my mind
and was already so near the end
that every breath of air made my
face shudder. A high surf,
the mountain oaks roared on the slopes
of the Odenwald, and then came a desert
and waste through whose valleys
the wind drove the dust
of stones. A twice-honed
sword divided the sky
from the earth, an effulgence flowed

into space, and the destination
of my excursion, the vision
of Altdorfer, opened up.
Far more than one hundred thousand,
so the inscriptions proclaim,
number the dead over whom
the battle surges for salvation
of the Occident in the rays
of a setting sun. This is
the moment when destiny turns.
At the centre of the grandiose thronging
of banners and flags, lances and
pikes and batons, the breast-plated
bodies of human beings and animals,
Alexander, the Western world's
hero, on his white horse,
and before him in flight
towards the sickle moon
Darius, stark terror
visible in his face. As fortunate
did the clever chaplain, who
had hung up an oleograph
of the battle scene beside
the blackboard, describe the outcome
of this affair. It was,
he said, a demonstration
of the necessary destruction of all
the hordes coming up from the East,
and thus a contribution to the history
of salvation. Since then I have
read in other teachers' writings
that we have death in front of us
rather like a picture of Alexander's battle
on our schoolroom wall.
Now I know, as with a crane's eye
one surveys his far-flung realm,
a truly Asiatic spectacle,
and slowly learns, from the tininess
of the figures and the incomprehensible

Opposite: Albrecht Altdorfer (1480–1538), 'The Battle of Issus', 1529, depicting the victory of Alexander in 333 BC over Darius and the Persians. Credit: Alte Pinakothek, Munich / AKG

Roman mosaic, Pompeii, imperial era, depicting the Battle of Alexander at Issus. Credit: AKG / Erich Lessing

beauty of nature that vaults over them,
to see that side of life that
one could not see before. We look
over the battle and, glancing
from north to south, we see
a camp with white Persian
tents lying in the evening glow
and a city on the shore.
Outside, with swollen sails
the ships make headway, and
the shadows already graze
the cypresses, and beyond them
Egypt's mainland extends.
The Nile Delta can be made out,
the Sinai Peninsula, the Red Sea
and, still farther in the distance,
towering up in dwindling light,
the mountain ranges. ❑

***WG Sebald** (May 1944–December 2001) came to Manchester University as a* lektor *in 1966. He settled in East Anglia four years later as a lecturer in German at the University of East Anglia where, in 1989, he became the founding director of the British Centre for Literary Translation. The above excerpts are from* After Nature, *to be published in July 2002 by Hamish Hamilton*

Let Paul Robeson Sing !
Gadewch i Paul Robeson Ganu !
celebrating the life of Paul Robeson and his relationship with Wales
i ddathlu bywyd Paul Robeson a'i berthynas â Chymru
TREDEGAR HOUSE
Newport
1 JUNE – 1 SEPTEMBER 2002
Wednesday – Sunday
10.30 – 5
Tel: 01633 815880
Newport
COUNTY BOROUGH
BWRDEISTREF SIROL
Casnewydd
INDEX
for free expression
Cynulliad Cenedlaethol Cymru
The National Assembly for Wales
AREM MEDIA
UNISON
the public service union
THEATRE MUSEUM
AMGUEDDFEYDD AC ORIELAU CENEDLAETHOL CYMRU
NATIONAL MUSEUMS & GALLERIES OF WALES

DEMOCRACY AND THE MILITARY NECESSITY

When former Afghan king Mohammed Zahir Shah broke his silence in late May, letting it be known he was ready to serve as the country's head of state, he was effectively pre-empting the Loya Jirga, the national gathering of tribal and ethnic leaders held in June. They had been assembled to choose a transitional government ahead of elections in 18 months' time and, despite public expectation, the king's silence had been preserved precisely to avoid any suggestion that he and his supporters were sidelining the process

The king's statement was taken as proof that the Loya Jirga had been stitched up in advance. It was, said almost everyone, the only way to guarantee the peaceful participation of the *jihadi* warlords, holy warriors against the Soviets and later the Taliban.

The ethnic Tajik Afghan warriors from the Panshjir Valley who dominated the anti-Taliban Northern Alliance had been handed control of the country's power ministries – defence, interior, foreign and information – at the December 2001 Bonn conference. They dug in deep, using their new authority to protect their interests and cow the country's ethnic Pashtun community, from which both Zahir Shah and the Taliban spring. Other warlords in the western provinces were making millions by levying tolls on traders trucking over the border from Iran.

In violent confrontations across the country, and through the frequent abuse of the democratic process set up to select candidates for seats at the Loya Jirga, it was made clear that these men would not gently give up their privileges to a new Pashtun-led government set up to replace the old Taliban-led one, ousted by the US military onslaught in the wake of 11 September.

But a week truly is a long time in politics, even for an ex-king who enjoys widespread popular support in Afghanistan and who had been billed by the United States as the man to deliver Pashtun support for a process so visibly manipulated by their ethnic rivals from the north and west. By the time the Loya Jirga opened, the horse-trading had settled on a different scenario. The former king was persuaded to withdraw his candidacy, apparently in return for the parallel withdrawal of the Northern Alliance's preferred alternative, pre-Taliban president Burhanuddin Rabbani.

That cleared the way for the then interim president Hamid Karzai, close ally of the US, to take the top job. Interim foreign minister Abdullah Abdullah had to face down allegations that the deals had been forced on them by Washington special envoy Zalmay Khalilzad, who announced the king's withdrawal three hours before Zahir Shah himself.

The US needs to recompense the Northern Alliance, essential partners in its short-, medium- and long-term military strategy in Afghanistan. The Alliance is also expected to take responsibility for blocking a Taliban or al-Qaida resurgence once the US starts scaling down operations in the region. And they will be the future guarantors of the oil and gas pipelines that Khalilzad's former colleagues from the global oil giant Unocal and others want to run across the country.

An attempt by the CIA to assassinate former Afghan prime minister Gulbuddin Hekmatyar, a man hated by all sides, was cited as evidence of committed US support for the Panshjiris, Hekmatyar's fiercest foes during the savage civil war that followed the collapse of the old Soviet-backed government in the 1990s.

There were uncomfortable echoes of America's past careless alliances: with the feeble Christian Maronite Amin Gemayel in Lebanon in 1983 and with Darod opponents of the Somali Habr Gidr ten years later. Both associations fomented new civil warfare and ultimately dragged US forces to terrible defeats. But the Afghans were not quite prepared to let this partiality go unremarked. As soon as the Loya Jirga opened, delegates began to question the participation of the warlords and their battle 'commanders', forcing the vote for head of state to be pushed back by at least a day. The vote that eventually gave the presidency to Karzai was held by secret ballot at the request of delegates.

'This country is uneducated, but is not ignorant,' said former exile Hashmat Ghani Ahmadzai, a member of the Pashtun Kochi nomad community. 'Even a ten-year-old boy from this country can no longer be deceived. My vote is mine, and mine alone.'

The pre-Jirga preparations have also brought women, academics, intellectuals, journalists and scores of ordinary citizens into political life. They have gained a taste for public service and will make their presence felt at grass-roots level in village and city institutions. The current Loya Jirga process has added new elements of broad-based participatory democracy to this ancient system. But the true test of the strength of this Afghan hybrid may come when its exponents challenge the warlords' writ in their own tribal lands. Washington may then be forced to choose between tradition and embryonic civil society, or keep its commitment to the warlords as agents in the war on terrorism and defenders of US oil interests. ❑

Rohan Jayasekera *in Kabul*

A censorship chronicle incorporating information from Agence France-Presse (AFP), Alliance of Independent Journalists (AJI), Amnesty International (AI), Article 19 (A19), Association of Independent Electronic Media (ANEM), the BBC Monitoring Service Summary of World Broadcasts (SWB), Centre for Human Rights and Democratic Studies (CEHURDES), Centre for Journalism in Extreme Situations (CJES), the Committee to Protect Journalists (CPJ), Canadian Journalists for Free Expression (CJFE), Democratic Journalists' League (JuHI), Glasnost Defence Foundation (GDF), Human Rights Watch (HRW), Information Centre of Human Rights & Democracy Movements in China (ICHR DMC), Instituto de Prensa y Sociedad (IPYS), the United Nations Integrated Regional Information Network (IRIN), International Press Institute (IPI); the Inter-American Press Association (IAPA), the International Federation of Journalists (IFJ/FIP), the Media Institute of Southern Africa (MISA), Network for the Defence of Independent Media in Africa (NDIMA), International PEN (PEN), Pacific Islands News Association (PINA), Radio Free Europe/Radio Liberty (RFE/RL), Reporters Sans Frontières (RSF), Transitions Online (TOL), the World Association of Community Broadcasters (AMARC), World Association of Newspapers (WAN), World Organisation Against Torture (OMCT), Writers in Prison Committee (WiPC) and other sources including members of the International Freedom of Expression eXchange (IFEX)

AFGHANISTAN

It was reported on 6 March that the international peace-keeping force had warned of a threat to kidnap foreign journalists. This followed an attack on Canadian journalist **Kathleen Kenna**, correspondent for the Canadian daily *Toronto Star*, who was injured in an ambush in Paktia province. (CPJ, RSF)

The International Press Institute (IPI) wrote to the Afghan Interim Administration on 15 March expressing concern about its draft media law of February 2002. IPI said the draft created a complicated licensing system that amounted to a licensing of individual journalists. (IPI)

Ebadullah Ebadi, a translator and assistant for the *Boston Globe,* was assaulted on 11 April by Afghan soldiers working with US special forces in Sorobi, 45km from Kabul. (CPJ)

ALGERIA

Human rights activist **Mohamed Smain** was sentenced to one year in prison on 25 February on charges of defamation. Smain, president of the Relizane branch (western Algeria) of the League for the Defence of Human Rights, was accused of falsely linking Mohamed 'El Hadj' Fergane, a former mayor and local chief of a state-armed militia, and eight of his militia companions to the abduction, torture, killing and 'disappearance' of dozens of citizens in the province of Relizane. He was also ordered to pay a fine of approximately US$65 and damages of US$390 to each of the nine plaintiffs. (AI)

On 14 March, police broke up a protest in Algiers against repression in the Berber region of Kabylia, arresting around 140 demonstrators. The march had been prohibited by the Interior Ministry. On 19 March, five demonstrators detained in Bgayet by the police during a protest were condemned to one year in prison and a fine of US$125 each for 'public disorder' and 'destruction of state property'. (*El País,* WAAC)

On 26 March, the Ministry of Defence accused the magazine *Le Matin* of 11 counts of defamation. Editor **Mohamed Benchicou** and columnist **Sid Ahmed Semiane** (*Index* 1/2002) were ordered to appear in court on 9 April to answer the charges. The magazine is already the subject of six complaints by the Ministry of Defence. (WAN)

Fourteen Berbers were sentenced on 16 May to between four and eight months in prison for taking part in anti-government protests. They were among 29 defendants tried by a tribunal in Bouira, in Kabylia, on charges of threatening public order and destroying state property. Tension had increased in Kabylia after a Berber youth died in custody at the end of April. (AFP)

Opposition parties with strong support among the Berbers announced a boycott of parliamentary elections. Foreign media were banned from the region when voting started on 27 May. (BBC)

On 19 May, human rights worker **Abderrahmane Khelil** and his friend **Sid Ahmed Mourad** were arrested while carrying out research for the independent Algerian League for the Defence of Human Rights on the arrest of 19 university students the previous day. They were scheduled to appear in court on 26 May on a charge of 'inciting an unarmed gathering' and faced fines and prison sentences of up to one year. (HRW, AI)

ARGENTINA

The former head of COMFER (Federal Committee of Radio Broadcasting), **Gustavo López**, confirmed on 6 March that he had received instructions to stop television reporting of government violence against people protesting in the Plaza de Mayo on 19 and 20 December 2001. López said former general secretary Nicolás Gallo had been responsible for suppressing the reports but Gallo denied it. (*Página 12*)

ARMENIA

At a meeting in Yerevan on 4 March with editors of the country's media outlets, three visiting Council of Europe media experts expressed concern at parts of a proposed new law on the mass media. They criticised a plan for a government agency charged with 'state oversight' of the media that would also issue and revoke the licences to publish or broadcast. Journalists have argued that the bill poses a threat to media freedom. (RFE/RL)

Main independent television station **A1 Plus** faces closure after a regulatory commission appointed by the president allocated its frequency to an entertainment company, *armenialiberty.org* reported on 5 April. **A1 Plus**'s director, Mesrop Movsisian, said he would appeal against the decision in court. The channel, founded in 1996, has earned popularity with its hard-hitting coverage of the government. Opposition politicians have accused Kocharian of cracking down on independent media to ensure he wins next year's presidential elections. (www.armenialiberty.org)

AZERBAIJAN

A new law on mass media came into effect on 16 March which the Journalists Trade Union of Azerbaijan (JuHi) says is the best media law in any of the CIS countries. Newspapers no longer require state registration or licensing, accreditation cannot be annulled without a court's involvement and authorities cannot restrict media without a court decision. (JuHI)

BAHAMAS

On 29 April the Prime Minister of the Bahamas, Hubert A Ingraham, became the 23rd head of state in the Americas to support the Declaration of Chapultec by signing the document during a ceremony held in Nassau. The Declaration, which contains ten fundamental principles to safeguard a free press, was written during a conference on freedom of expression in 1994 in Mexico. The signing launched a campaign by the Inter American Press Association (IAPA) to obtain the endorsements of other leaders of English-speaking Caribbean countries. (IAPA)

BANGLADESH

On 1 March, the government deployed hundreds of Bangladesh Rifles and police personnel to guard Hindu temples and sensitive areas such as the Indian Embassy in Dhaka and the city of Chittagong. According to the *Hindu*, this followed protests by Islamic groups associated with the Bangladesh Nationalist Party-led coalition against the massacre of hundreds of Muslims by Hindus in the Indian state of Gujarat. The mass killings were in retaliation for the murder of nearly 60 Hindus by Muslims in the Indian town of Godhra on 27 February (*Index* 2/2002). (*Hindu*)

Supporters of the Islamist movement Bangladesh Khelafat Andolan protested outside the Dhaka head office of the newspaper ***Dainik Jugantor*** on 29 March. The demo, the latest in a series of actions against independent media by Islamic groups associated with the new government, was allegedly launched because a short fictional story about the rape of a young village girl published by the paper had 'injured' Muslims. The editors of *Dainik Jugantor* apologised for having 'hurt believers' feelings'. (RSF)

Tehelka.com noted on 15 April that a newly proposed government bill would, if passed, block media access to parliamentary proceedings. The proposed Special Privileges and Powers Act 2002 would make it illegal for the media to publish reports about any public debates, documents or statements made or presented in parliament or as part of the business of parliamentary committees. (Tehelka.com)

BELARUS

On 14 March, the Minsk Regional Court sentenced two former members of the Interior Ministry's special forces to life imprisonment for the murder of five people and the July 2000 disappearance of journalist and cameraman **Dmitri Zavadski**. Reporters sans Frontières has called for an investigation into the the trial, which revealed nothing new about Zavadski's probable murder. (RSF, Reuters)

Fourteen journalists went on trial on 8 April for criticising or protesting against the rule of President Alexander Lukashenka. The Belarusan Journalists Association (BJA) said the journalists had protested against the closure of the independent newspaper *Pagonya* in the town of Grodno in western Belarus. The authorities closed down *Pagonya* after a court ruled it had defamed Lukashenko. Editor **Nikolai Markevich** and senior reporter **Pavel Mozheiko** are to stand trial and face up to five years in prison. (RSF, Reuters)

Belarus's Foreign Ministry warned Russia's NTV correspondent in Minsk, **Pavel Selin**, about 'biased and unsubstantiated information' in his reports, it was reported on 29 April. The ministry demanded an apology from Selin and threatened to cancel his accreditation. The warning may be connected with Selin's reports on a recent wave of emigration from Belarus and an opposition rally on 19 April. (RFE/RL)

The Belarusan human rights organisation Charter 97 reported on 21 May that a new law on religious affairs and church–state relations was likely to be introduced soon. Charter 97 says the new 'politically motivated' legislation will restrict freedom of belief rather than ensure it.

After what amounts to a government takeover of the principal Belarusan literary journals, Eduard Skobelev, the editor-in-chief of the Information newsletter of the Presidential Administration, has instructed the new, government-appointed editors of those journals not to publish the works of the writers **Vasil Bykau**, **Nil Hilevich**, **Ryhor Baradulin** and **Siarjiey Zakonnikau** – the most esteemed figures in Belarusan literature today. (Charter 97, RL)

BELGIUM

José Masschelin, a reporter for the Flemish-language daily *Het Laatste Nieuws,* was jailed on 14 March for possession of a file about paedophilia, a sensitive issue since a paedophile ring involving high-level figures was exposed in 1996. The arrest is in breach of the legal protection for journalists given by the European Court of Human Rights, which defends reporters' rights to protect their sources. (IFJ)

BOLIVIA

María Teresa Guzmán, executive director of *El Diario de La Paz* and wife of Jorge Carrasco Jahnsen, the newspaper's general director, was killed on 10 April when the vehicle in which she was travelling exploded in southern La Paz. Carrasco believes the bomb was meant for him in response to investigations the paper was preparing to publish. The newspaper has suffered 11 violent attacks in the last six months. (IFJ, IFEX, Eldiario.net)

BOTSWANA

The popular talk show '**Live-Line**' was cancelled on 22 April 30 minutes before transmission. The weekly *Mmegi Monitor* said the programme was to have featured a discussion about news reporting by public service media with the National Director of MISA-Botswana, **Modise Aphanyane** as a panelist.

MISA-Botswana has seen several recent cases of pressure on media figures who resist government interference in editorial policies. Two general managers of Botswana Television (BTV) have resigned in recent months.

BRAZIL

A Brazilian judge ordered ***CartaCapital***, a weekly magazine based in São Paulo, not to publish a conversation between presidential candidate Anthony Garotinho and Guilherme Freire, a donor to Garotinho's previous campaigns, it was reported on 26 May. In July 2001, a judge banned the daily *O Globo* from publishing transcripts of taped phone conversations that allegedly showed Garotinho authorising a bribe. The *Jornal do Brasil* has since published the contents of the calls without repercussion. (CPJ)

BURMA

On 25 March, the military government announced that **Dr Salai Tun Than**, a retired university professor, had been sentenced to seven years in prison under Burma's national security legislation. Salai, aged 74, was arrested for conducting a peaceful protest on 29 November 2001. He distributed copies of a petition calling on the government to hold a general election in one year. (HRW)

Nobel Peace Prize-winner and opposition leader **Aung San Suu Kyi** was freed from 20 months of house arrest on 6 May. Aung San Suu Kyi was arbitrarily detained on 22 September 2000, when she and other National League for Democracy (NLD) members tried to board a train to the northern city of Mandalay for a political meeting. The ruling State Peace and Development Council (SPDC) holds more than 1,000 political prisoners, including members of ethnic minority groups and 17 elected members of parliament. (HRW, *The Times*, *Independent*, *Washington Post*)

BURUNDI

The National Communication Council has banned local media from interviewing anti-government dissidents waging war in the country, the official Agence Burundaise de Presse (ABP) reported on 20 May. The ban came after Defence Minister Cyrille Ndayirukiye complained that local **Radio Publique Africaine** had compromised state security by broadcasting details of planned military operations against the dissidents. **Alexis Sinduhije**, director of the station, denied the accusations. (allafrica.com)

IFEX reported on 6 March that two journalists, **Aloys Niyoyita** and **Corneille Nibaruta**, had been attacked while covering a demonstration by activists from the PA Amasekanya group, which opposes the Arusha peace accord. **Niyoyita** was attacked after refusing to hand over his reporting materials and detained for four hours at the first Battalion of Intervention station in Bujumbura along with eight other activists. Nibaruta, an FM journalist, was attacked by police officers but not arrested. (IFEX)

CAMEROON

On 1 March, **Peter William Mandio**, Publication Director of the weekly *Le Front Indépendant*, was arrested in Yaoundé after he reported an alleged extramarital affair between two senior bureaucrats in President Paul Biya's office. Mandio was released after questioning on 4 March. He believes his arrest was linked to his involvement in the Comité National contre l'Impunité (the National Committee against Impunity), which has filed a complaint against the President for 'crimes against human rights' in Belgium. (RSF)

Jacques Blaise Mvié, Publication Director of *La Nouvelle Presse*, is being sought by the security forces for publishing the names of the two bureaucrats. Mvié is in hiding and plainclothes police officers are watching his newsroom. (RSF)

CANADA

An Ontario education authority has threatened to pull advertising from local media if it does not approve of their reporting. The Keewatin-Patricia District School Board made the threat on 18 March after a strike by support workers led to some hostile editorials in the local press. (CJFE)

CHAD

On 30 March, the High Council of Communications (Haut Conseil de la Communication – HCC) banned all political programmes on private radio stations during the campaign for elections on 21 April. An HCC source said it made the decision because it was technically unable to control each political party's airtime on private radio stations and thus avoid any 'imbalance'. (RSF)

CHILE

On 3 May, World Press Freedom Day, government spokesman Heraldo Muñoz announced that the government would present a proposal to the Chamber of Deputies to achieve 'the decriminalisation of crimes of opinion' and 'deal with the crimes of libel and slander to take out any reference to freedom of expression and freedom of the press and opinion'. In 2001, the Chilean legislature passed a press law repealing some of the country's most punitive defamation statutes. But the Penal Code still contains several articles that make it a crime to insult public officials. (CPJ)

CHINA

On 18 March, **Li Yanling**, wife of imprisoned journalist **Jiang Weiping**, was detained. The reason was unclear. Jiang was arrested in December 2000 after writing articles about local corruption for the Hong Kong paper *Qianshao*. (CPJ, *Frontline*)

Bishop Jia Zhiguo, 67, a Roman Catholic cleric from China's underground church in Hebei Province, was detained on or around 20 March on unspecified charges. His current whereabouts are unknown. Beijing refuses to recognise the Pope's authority over China's Catholics. Bishop Jia has spent around 20 years in labour camps for his beliefs and recently came into conflict with the authorities over an orphanage he established. (CKF)

The weekly paper ***Nanfang Zhoumo*** (Southern Weekend) has been censored by the government. On 20 March, the paper stopped printing the 26 March edition, which contained an article about a scandal-hit NGO associated with the government, on the orders of the Propaganda Department. (RSF)

Authorities detained 2,000 followers of the banned Falun Gong spiritual group in Changchun city on 29 April after the group interrupted cable television programmes in the district of Chongqing on 1 January and broadcast Falun Gong documentary films. More than 150 followers were sent to 're-education through labour' camps. (ICHRD)

On 18 May, four Falun Gong followers, **Jin Wei**, **Li Xizngdong**, **Shu Jianqui** and **Li Wei** were sentenced to prison for 16, 15, nine and seven years respectively for organising the interruption. (RSF, AP)

Jasper Becker, a journalist with the *South China Morning Post,* was dismissed from the paper on 29 April, a few weeks after he complained to the editor that the paper was restricting his reporting and failing to cover sensitive issues such as Tibet, labour unrest and Aids. The paper says he was dismissed for insubordination. (*Washington Post*)

A ban on access to news agency websites imposed in November 2000 was lifted on 15 May. It is now possible to access the sites of Reuters, CNN, the *Washington Post*, the *Los Angeles Times*, National Public Radio, the *San Francisco Chronicle*, the *Boston Globe*, and the *Atlanta Journal-Constitution* from Beijing and Shanghai. As of 16 May access was still prevented to Voice of America and BBC websites. (Reuters, *Washington Post*)

COLOMBIA

Seven journalists who have covered high-profile criminal investigations for big Colombian media organisations were threatened with death on 13 March and given three days to leave the country. The journalists are **Jairo Lozano**, reporter for the daily *El Tiempo*; **Juan Carlos Giraldo**, senior correspondent for RCN Televisión; **Julia Navarrete**, correspondent for Caracol Televisión; **Jairo Naranjo**, correspondent for RCN Radio; **Hernando Marroquín**, correspondent for Caracol Radio; **Marilyn López**, correspondent for Noticias Uno, and **José Antonio Jiménez**, a former correspondent for TV Hoy. (CPJ)

Juan Carlos Gómez Díaz, an intern at the radio station La Voz de Aguachica in Cesar department in the north of the country, was found dead on 3 April in the Magdalena River. Gómez had been abducted by two unidentified men on 1 April along with a friend, **Óscar Guerrero**. Gómez's father, Luis Alejandro Gómez, a journalist and presenter at the station for 25 years, received an anonymous call the next day saying that his son had been killed. The intern's death was blamed on right-wing paramilitaries. (IPI)

On 12 April, a cameraman for National Radio Chain of Colombia (RCN), **Héctor Sandoval**, and a driver died after being shot during an army attack on the kidnappers of 12 deputies from the department of Cali. Journalists who survived the attack say a military helicopter attacked their vehicle. (IFJ)

On 23 April, unidentified men threatened to kill TV journalist **Daniel Coronell** and his three-year-old daughter. Coronell, news director of *Noticias Uno*, a current affairs programme on the Bogotá TV station Canal Uno, received threatening phone calls after he aired a report examining possible links between the presidential candidate Álvaro Uribe Vélez and drug traffickers. Uribe has denied links to Colombia's right-wing paramilitary movement. (CPJ)

On 8 May, two men approached journalism professor **Carlos Pulgarínas** of the University of La Sabana in Bogotá as he was walking to work. They warned him of a plot to murder him and the dean of the university's Department of Journalism, **César Mauricio Velásquez**. The threats are the latest in a series following Pulgarínas's exposés of violence by the country's warring factions and have forced the journalist to flee the country on several occasions since 1999. (CPJ)

On 14 May, a former reporter for several Colombian newspapers and radio stations, **Víctor Omar Acosta**, was shot dead near his home in the western city of Yumbo by two men. Acosta's family believe his murder may be linked to his investigations into local corruption. (CPJ)

Nidia Álvarez Mariño and **Ramón Vásquez Ruiz**, reporters from the Santa Marta-based daily *Hoy Diario del Magdalena*, and their driver were kidnapped by the Revolutionary Armed Forces of Colombia (FARC) on 16 May. Álvarez was freed unharmed the following morning but the rebels continue to hold Vásquez and the driver, **Vladimir Revolledo Cuisman**. (CPJ)

DEMOCRATIC REPUBLIC OF CONGO

Journalist **Jose Feruzi Samwegele**, a journalist at Radio-Télévision Nationale Congolaise 2, was arrested on 3 April in Kinshasa. He was accused of circulating a communiqué from the opposition group L'Union pour la Démocratie et le Progrès Social (UDPS). (IRIN, RSF)

Sports journalist **Nawezi** of RTNC's provincial station in Katanga has been detained since 7 May in Lubumbashi after 'making political propaganda for Katoto', a candidate for President of the transitional authority in the DCRC. Nawezi reported in South Africa on a soccer match between the South African Orlando Pirates and the Congolese Tout Puissant Mazembe in which the Congolese team wore shirts with the image of Katoto. (IFEX)

Raphael Paluku Kyana, director of Radio Rurale de Kanyabayonga (RRKA) was arrested in the eastern town of Goma on 9 March. The reason was not clear. On 7 March, the director of Radio Muungano, **Wema Kennedy,** was arrested near the Ugandan border by intelligence service agents, accused of broadcasting a report that the president of the rebel movement was still in Kampala when inter-Congolese working meetings opened in Sun City, South Africa. (RSF)

CROATIA

The bank account of the satirical weekly ***Feral Tribune*** was frozen on 11 March after Zagreb Regional Court imposed a fine of 200,000 kuna (US$26) on the paper for 'moral damage' and publishing 'cosmopolitan opinions and views'. (RSF)

CUBA

On 4 March, independent journalists **Lester Téllez Castro** and **Brizuela Yena** were assaulted and detained by police in Ciego de Avila while protesting in front of a hospital where a colleague was recovering from a police beating. (FCDH)

The health of journalist **Carlos Alberto Dominguez,** from the independent press agency Cuba Verdad, has deteriorated markedly since his arrest on 23 February. Dominguez, who was charged with 'disturbing public order' and 'refusing to obey instructions' was moved to a military hospital on 8 March. (IFEX)

Independent journalist **Jesus Joel Diaz Hernández** left Cuba on 21 March for the USA, where he has been granted political asylum. Hernández was director of the independent news agency Cooperativa Avileña de Periodistas Independientes (CAPI) and had been sentenced for two years in prison for 'dangerousness'. (CPJ)

CZECH REPUBLIC

It was reported on 27 March that the Czech-language publisher of *Mein Kampf* faces imprisonment. **Michal Zitko,** who published the edition in March 2000, was charged under Article 260 of the Czech Penal Code dealing with national, racial, class or religious hatred. In most democratic countries, Hitler's autobiography is available as it is regarded as a valuable historical document. (Article 19)

DOMINICAN REPUBLIC

Dominican lawyer **Tapia Espinal,** recognised for his contributions to the freedom of the press and constitutional law, died of a heart attack on 24 March aged 76. (DR1.com)

EGYPT

Shohdy Surur (*Index* 1/2002), *Al-Ahram* web designer, went on trial on 3 March for posting a political poem written by his late father Naguib Surur on the Internet. The poem, known as the 'Ummeyat', was written over 30 years ago and has a sexually explicit title. It is considered by the authorities to violate laws aimed at protecting 'public morality'. If convicted, Surur faces up to two years in prison or a fine of almost US$2,000. (*Al-Ahram*)

On 5 March, eight people were convicted of 'contempt of religion' for belonging to a sect that tried to 'spread extremist ideas contrary to the principles of Islam'. An emergency state security court sentenced two of the men to three years in prison with labour while the others received suspended sentences. One of their 'unorthodox' ideas was that people should fast during the month of Shaaban rather than Ramadan. (*Cairo Times*)

On 21 March, **Adel Hammuda**, a journalist for *Sawt al-Umma*, and **Essam Fahmy**, the newspaper's managing editor, were convicted of libelling businessman Nagib Sawiris, president of one of Egypt's biggest telecommunications groups. They were sentenced to six months' imprisonment and fined US$100 for an article about Sawiris's business practices. The two journalists are free pending an appeal. (RSF)

On 27 March, two members of the **Church of Scientology**, accused of 'contempt for monotheistic religions by trying to spread a new religious doctrine', were released. A court ruled that the detention of the married couple, an Israeli and a Palestinian, violated their human rights. (*Cairo Times*)

Fifty-four men, including four Britons, were arrested on 1 April and charged with belonging to the outlawed Islamic group **Hizb al-Tahrir** or 'Liberation Party'. The suspects are accused of joining a secret, illegal group that aims to obstruct the legal system and undermine state institutions. The party has branches in many Arab and European countries and possible links with al-Qaida. During February, March and April authorities also arrested 30 Islamists suspected of having links with the **Vanguards of Conquest**, a branch of the radical Jihad movement. (*Al-Ahram, Cairo Times*)

One man was killed and 68 other people were arrested by police on 9 April during demonstrations by Alexandria University students at the visit of US Secretary of State Colin Powell. According to the Interior Ministry, the students threw stones at riot police, who later opened fire. (*Cairo Times*)

On 28 April, the editor-in-chief of the web newspaper *Al-Methaq al-Arabi*, **Ahmed Haredi Muhamed**, was sentenced to six months' imprisonment and ordered to pay a US$200 fine and US$400 in temporary administrative compensation for libelling Ibrahim Nafie, editor-in-chief and chairman of Egypt's largest newspaper, *Al-Ahram*. The charges stem from articles published last year accusing Nafie and other senior managers of financial malpractice. (EOHR)

Dr Saad Eddin Ibrahim (*Index* 2/2002) and six colleagues returned to court on 29 April facing the same charges as last year when they were sentenced to seven years' imprisonment. Ibrahim, Professor of Sociology at the American University in Cairo and head of a now-defunct democracy think-tank, the Ibn Khaldoun Centre, is charged with illegally receiving funds from the EU for monitoring elections in Egypt. (oneworld.net)

It was reported on 23 April that President Mubarak had ordered the retrial of 50 men tried last year in the 'Queen Boat' case (*Index* 1/2002) on charges of sexual immorality – a euphemism for homosexuality. The president said the state security court, where the charges had originally been heard, had no authority in such cases. All but two of the 23 men jailed and 29 men who were acquitted will now stand trial at a lower court. (BBC)

EL SALVADOR

The Assocation of Salvadoran Journalists (APES) complained on 15 February that journalists had been verbally and physically abused by police officers guarding the Legislative Assembly building. The journalists were reporting the arrest of Congressman Orlando Arévalo, who was detained for organising violent demonstrations in support of a bus strike. (Mesoamérica)

EQUATORIAL GUINEA

In early May, authorities barred the Equatorial Guinea Press Association (ASOPGE) from holding a series of activities to mark World Press Freedom Day. A few days later, the Vice-Minister of Information, Alfonso Nsue Mokuy, asked the government to ban ASOPGE, accusing it of operating as a 'parallel government'.

ERITREA

Nine journalists and a photographer began a hunger strike on 31 March to protest against their illegal detention. The journalists are **Yusuf Mohamed Ali**, **Mattewos Habteab**, **Dawit Habtemichael**, **Medhanie Haile**, **Temesgen Gebreyesus**, **Emanuel Asrat**, **Dawit Issac**, **Fessehaye Yohannes** and **Said Abdulkader**. The photographer is **Seyum Tsehaye**. The journalists were arrested in September after all eight of Eritrea's independent newspapers were closed down. (IPI)

ETHIOPIA

EFJA president **Kifle Mulat** has been found guilty in the Federal High Court of violating press laws but was released after paying a fine of Birr 12,000 (US$1,435).The court ruled that Kifle had 'disseminated fabricated information' against the state. (IFEX)

Journalist **Tamrat Zuma** was released from prison on 4 March after ten months. Tamrat, editor-in-chief of *Atkurot*, was charged with violating press laws and detained in Addis Ababa prison for failing to produce bail of US$1,915. The case is still pending. (IFEX)

It was reported on 26 March that nine newspaper editors had been taken to court in recent weeks for various offences. They were **Ato Kebebew Gebyehu Filate** and **Arega Wolde Kirbos Ayele** of *Tobbia*, **Wondwossen Gebre Kidan** of *Ith'op*, former *Ethio-Time* editor **Shimelis Asfaw**, **Abinet Tamrat** of *Madona*, **Gezaw Taye Wordofa** of *Lamrot* and **Tigist Behailu** of *Tinkish*. (IFEX)

EUROPEAN UNION

Leaders of the European Federation of Journalists issued a statement on 23 April accusing Europe's political leaders of 'complacency and cowardice' in face of 'a growing assault on public broadcasting in Europe'. They said 90 per cent of Italy's television market was controlled by its prime minister, Silvio Berlusconi, and in Portugal the government was threatening to privatise the state television channel. (EFJ)

The European Parliament approved legislation on 30 May giving law enforcement agencies greater powers to eavesdrop on telephone calls, read private e-mails and intercept other electronic communications. MEPs bowed to pressure from certain European governments that wanted extra powers for their 'war against terrorism'. (RSF)

FRANCE

Security guards from the National Front party's Département Protection Sécurité (DPS) assaulted a Canal + television crew at a press conference given by the party's presidential candidate, Jean-Marie Le Pen, on 26 April. Journalist **Jean-Paul Lepers** was attacked and technical assistant **Yacine Ben Jannette** was expelled from the room. (RSF)

Ten French journalists initiated legal proceedings on 21 May against their employer, newspaper *Le Voix du Nord* in Lille, for publishing their articles on the Internet without their agreement. The journalists have refused to sign an amendment to their contracts authorising the management to publish their articles on the paper's website. (OJR)

Five employees of **Radio France** went before an Ajaccio judge on 27 February charged with 'racist insults' and 'complicity' in a satirical sketch broadcast on 27 May last year on France Inter. The Union Corsa d'Antibes had accusing the programme of racism against Corsicans. (RSF)

An estimated 500 people demonstrated for press freedom in New Caledonia's capital Nouméa on 2 March. The march was organised to protest against recent assaults on **Etienne Dutailly**, publisher of the satirical weekly *Le Chien Bleu* and **Lucienne Moreo-See**, editor-in-chief at Radio Djiido. (*Les Nouvelles Calédoniennes*)

Members of the French print union CGT Filpac have been trying to disrupt the distribution of the free daily newspapers ***Metro*** and ***20 minutes***, which they see as a threat to

France's media landscape. On 15 March, copies of *20 minutes* were stolen and dumped in the street. On 18 and 19 March, union members halted distribution trucks and seized their contents. (IPI)

Pierre Lescure, the last remaining founder of the popular Channel Canal + still working at the company, was sacked as chairman on 17 April by Jean-Marie Messier, head of its owner Vivendi Universal. (IFJ)

GERMANY

Jews in Germany were advised by police to wear baseball caps instead of the traditional kippa after a wave of anti-Semitic attacks. A girl wearing a Star of David had it ripped from her throat on a train in Berlin, and there have been several incidents of street violence against Jews as well as an arson attack at one of Berlin's oldest synagogues on 28 April. A Berlin Jewish community spokesman condemned the police recommendation as condoning anti-Semitism, saying 'everybody who wants to should openly display Jewish symbols'. Some German Jews have accused their politicians of legitimising anti-Semitism through their criticism of Israel. (*The Times*)

GHANA

Jake Obetsebi-Lamptey, the Minister of Information, stated on 30 March that journalists must clear any stories about interclan violence with the ministry unless they are based on an official press release. This followed a clash on 25 March between two royal clans in the northern chieftancy of Dagbon, in which some 40 people, including the paramount chief, Ya Na Yakubu Andani, were killed. (CPJ, RSF)

GUINEA-BISSAU

The attorney-general ordered all media organisations on 12 April not to publish any information from the Liga Guineense dos Direitos Humanos (LGDH – Guinean League of Human Rights). Two LGDH officials were found guilty of showing 'disrespect' to the attorney-general during an inquiry into reported misappropriation of funds. (IRIN, AI)

HAITI

President Jean-Bertrand Aristide reappointed Judge Claudy Gassant on 1 April as the investigating judge in the Jean Dominique murder case, three months after his original mandate expired. Dominique, the head of Radio Haiti Inter, was killed in April 2000. The leading suspect in the case is a Senator who enjoys parliamentary immunity. Gassant has faced obstruction from the Senate and the police, and has had to flee the country twice because of threats to his life. Reporters sans Frontières urged Aristide to guarantee Gassant's safety. (RSF, AI)

INDIA

The National Human Rights Commission (NHRC) criticised the state government of Gujarat on 1 April for its failure to contain communal violence after the massacre in Godhra on 27 February (*Index* 2/2002). The NHRC did not explicitly hold Chief Minister Narendra Modi's government responsible for the murder of at least 2,000 Muslims by Hindus, but it reminded the government that it 'is responsible not only for the acts of its own agents, but also for the acts of non-state players acting within its jurisdiction'. The NHRC questioned the 'extraordinary lack of appreciation of the potential dangers of the situation' in a state with a long history of communal violence and challenged the Gujarat government's assertion that it had brought the violence under control within 72 hours of the Godhra attack. (*Frontline*)

On 1 April the central government declared Al-Badr and Jamiat-ul-Mujahideen to be 'terrorist organisations' under the controversial Prevention of Terrorism Act (POTA) 2002. The POTA, which was passed by a rare joint session of parliament on 26 March, first took shape in October 2001 as a government ordinance. Opposition parties, which felt the government was trying to exercise emergency powers without declaring an official national emergency, defeated attempts by the government on 13 December last year, and 21 March this year to enact a bill to replace the short-term ordinance. Twenty-seven groups have been banned as terrorist organisations since last October. (*The Hindu*, BBC, *Frontline*)

On 17 April, the BBC quoted **Ragu Dhar**, the business editor at *Zee TV*, as saying that officials from the failed US energy company Enron had tried to bribe him after he had repeatedly criticised its Dabol power plant in the state of

Maharashtra. Enron, which went into bankruptcy protection last December in the United States and is still trying to sell the plant, denied the allegations when they were first made on the US news programme *60 Minutes*. (BBC Online)

Zafar Iqbal, a journalist for the Kashmir-based English-language daily *Kashmir Images*, was shot and seriously injured by three unidentified assailants on 29 May. The assailants fled the scene and have not been caught by police.(CPJ)

Recent publication: *India: The state must ensure redress for the victims. A memorandum to the Government of Gujarat on its duties in the aftermath of the violence* (AI, March, pp12)

INDONESIA

The Indonesian government refused on 10 March to grant Australian journalist **Lindsay Murdoch** a journalist's visa, barring him from reporting for his Fairfax Group papers, the *Sydney Morning Herald* and the *Melbourne Age*. The move is thought to be related to two stories written by Murdoch on Aceh and East Timor. (SEAPA)

IRAQ

It was reported on 2 May that **Safia Taleb Al Souhail**, publisher of *Al Manar Al Arabi* newspaper, published in Iraqi Kurdistan, and Advocacy Director for the Arab and Islamic World at the International Alliance for Justice (AIJ), and members of her family had received death threats after she organised a conference in Jordan that called for the indictment of the Iraqi leadership. She is the daughter of **Sheikh Taleb Al Souhail**, a prominent Iraqi figure who was assassinated in Beirut in 1994 by four Iraqi diplomats. (AIJ, Kurdish Media)

IRELAND

An internal investigation into allegations of brutality by the Garda has begun after the violent break-up of an anti-capitalist demonstration on 6 May. Twelve protestors were injured by Garda batons and 28 arrested, including a photographer from the *Irish Independent* who was covering the event. (*Irish Times*, *Independent*)

The Church of Ireland Dean of Clonmacnoise, **the Very Reverend Andrew Furlong**, resigned from his post on 7 May, the day before his heresy trial was due to resume. The trial, the first for more than a hundred years to be brought before the Church of Ireland General Synod, was initiated after Furlong published an article denying the divinity of Jesus. (*Irish Times*).

ISRAEL

Yaffa Yarkoni, 76, said on Israeli Army Radio on 14 April that she supported soldiers who refuse to serve in the Occupied Territories. The newspaper *Maariv* said she had 'joined the ranks of the new anti-Semites in Europe', the Artists Syndicat cancelled an annual event in her name, and radio stations said they would no longer play her music. (*Le Monde*)

On 3 May, it was reported that the director-general of the Broadcasting Authority reprimanded news director **Rafiq Halabi** for screening an interview with the UN Special Envoy to the Middle East, Terje Larsen. (*MEI*)

On 3 May, it was reported that a directive had been sent to employees of the Arabic-language television channel ordering them not to refer to Palestinian civilians killed in the Israeli military offensive as 'victims' but as 'fatalities'. Statements by Israeli spokesmen were not to be referred to as 'versions' as this suggests a 'casting of doubt'. 'Conquests' of Palestinian lands should not be mentioned, 'unless quoting declarations by Israeli or American personages'. The conflict should not be labelled 'Israeli–Palestinian' or 'Israeli–Arab' but 'Palestinian–Israeli' or 'Arab–Israeli'. (*MEI*)

Dr Ilan Pappe, senior lecturer in political science at Haifa University and the Academic Director of the Research Institute for Peace at Givat Haviva, is being threatened with expulsion from his university. On 12 May, Pappe received a summons to attend a university trial, with the Dean of Humanities as the 'prosecution'. Pappe believes the reason is the position he took on the Katz affair, concerning an MA student who uncovered the Tantura massacre in 1948 and was disqualified for it. (Ilan Pappe) *See pp208–9*

ITALY

On 16 March, 20,000 people demonstrated against the closure of Roman independent radio station **Radio Onda Rossa**. Onda Rossa's closed on 6 February because its FM

IN DEFENCE OF HERESY

ILAN PAPPE

On 5 May, I was summoned to stand trial at the University of Haifa, where I work as a lecturer in the department of International Relations. While the procedures against me were eventually suspended, they were not dropped – and they could be resumed at any time. The issues involved are bracing for those who still believe in Israeli democracy.

The prosecution, represented by the university's Deans of Humanities, had demanded my expulsion from the campus because of a position I took in the case of Teddy Katz. Katz was an MA student who, in 1999, received the highest possible grade for a dissertation that exposed a massacre in the village of Tantura during the 1948 war. It was quite probably one of the worst atrocities committed by the Israeli army in that conflict.

He was sued by veterans from the unit involved, but the trial never took off. First, Katz – under unbearable pressure exerted on him by family and public alike – apologised for fabricating an event. Then, he retracted the apology and asked for the trial to be resumed. He was turned down.

This meant that Katz's thesis had to be examined by a special university inquiry commission; it disqualified him in November 2001. The commission said they had found six misquotations out of several hundred, a quite normal ratio in the works of established historians. No questions were raised about his conclusions, or his findings on the Tantura massacre.

Meanwhile, I challenged the university's conduct, and conducted my own research into events in Tantura. I accused the university of moral cowardice and attributed political motives to its conduct in the affair. Eventually, I published my unequivocal conclusion that a massacre of around 250 innocent Palestinians took place in May 1948 in Tantura, a village that was at the time already part of the Jewish state, hence all the victims were citizens of the new state.

As a result, I became the target of a boycott campaign initiated by the department of Eretz Israel studies, an ideological academic outfit established to provide scholarly scaffolding to the Zionist narrative. The prosecutor in my case came from this department.

Such guardians of official national history could not allow Katz's thesis or my conclusions to be accepted as legitimate academic research. The Tantura affair exposed the brutal nature of the 1948 ethnic cleansing and gave credence to Palestinian demands for restitution and repatriation.

The exposure of such atrocities could affect world opinion and might even plant doubts in the minds of Israelis. The ethnic cleansing that took place in 1948 is directly connected to the peace process today and the shape of any future solution.

While the Katz affair ended half a year ago. I think there are three reasons why the authorities decided that now was the time to settle older accounts with me: my signature on a petition a few weeks before endorsing a boycott by European academics of Israeli institutes; an article about the affair in Hebrew pending publication in a highly reputed academic journal; my proposal to give Israel's first university course on the Nakbah (the 'Catastrophe', as Palestinians call Israel's founding) in the next academic year, a course that would identify with the Palestinian narrative of the Nakbah and discuss openly its implications. In my university, this is heresy.

The timing is also connected to a general atmosphere that can best be described as a conscious desertion of any pretence at the democratic game by government and society alike. This is manifested in two ways. The first is the silencing of any form of criticism – even Israel's national singer, Yaffa Yarkoni, was ostracised when she dared question the Jenin operation; lecturers who support military refuseniks have been prosecuted by the Ministry of Education and, under intense pressure, some critical Israeli scholars have retracted their earlier positions. My colleague Benny Morris was one of those who succumbed. His confessional is now being distributed by Israeli embassies around the world.

The second manifestation is a drive by the political elite to finesse ideologies and discourses of the extreme right into the centre of the political stage. The most notable is the ethnic cleansing of Palestinians, whether they are inside Israel or in the Occupied Territories. Israel's media have willingly served the government, distorted reality and closed down spaces for alternative thought ever since the outbreak of the second intifada.

The erosion of free thought and speech can lead to only one conclusion: there must be economic and cultural pressure on Israel to stop its destructive policies against Palestinians and prevent the region as a whole from deteriorating into a war that would ruin the lives of everyone, Jews and Arabs, in Israel, Palestine and beyond. ❑

Ilan Pappe *is a professor of political science at Haifa University and a notable member of Israel's new historians. A longer version of this article will appear in* Red Pepper *in July* frequency is being returned to its previous licence-holder. Onda Rossa had been an important counter-cultural voice since 1977, broadcasting from demonstrations at the G-8 meeting in Genoa last summer with the organisation RadioGap, and more recently from Palestine. (indymedia.org, *Carta, Il Corriere della Sera*)

Prime Minister Silvio Berlusconi continues his pressure on Italian television. At a press conference in Bulgaria on 19 April, he declared that RAI broadcasters **Enzo Biagi, Daniele Luttazzi** and **Michele Santoro** had made a 'criminal use of television funded by the taxpayer' and should stop or be removed. Santoro has remained defiant, opening one edition of his programme with the left-wing anthem 'Bella Ciao' and inviting Sergio Cofferati, a union leader who led recent protests against Berlusconi's reforms, to appear on 26 April. (*La Repubblica,* RSF)

On 7 May, Italy's governing centre-right coalition asked the RAI inspection commission to suspend four current affairs programmes in the run-up to local elections on 26 May. *Porta a Porta* with **Bruno Vespa**, *Il Fatto* with **Enzo Biagi**, Tg3's *Primo Piano* and **Michele Santoro**'s *Sciuscià* were all accused of unacceptable bias. (*Il Manifesto, Il Corriere della Sera*)

RAI's opinion polling contract has been won by a joint venture by Datamedia and Cirm, part of the HDC group run by trusted Berlusconi adviser Luigi Crespi. The deputy chairman of the winning bid is Gianni Pilo, a former MP for Mr Berlusconi's Forza Italia party. (*Guardian*, RSF, *Il Nuovo*, 'Yahoo! Italy')

JAPAN

The Japanese cabinet approved a draft privacy protection bill on 27 March that media organisations believe may restrict investigative reporting. The draft sets out five basic principles for the collection of personal information, requiring that data-gathering must be conducted fairly and that personal information cannot be used other than for the purposes specified. The Japanese Newspaper Publishers and Editors Association, representing 112 newspapers, 38 television companies and four news agencies, urged the government to exempt news media from the restrictions, arguing that the guidelines could stop the media performing its duties and interfere with the public's right to know. All four opposition parties, as well as several members of the ruling Liberal Democratic Party, also oppose the draft. (*Japan Times*)

JORDAN

Former TV journalist and ex-member of parliament **Toujan Faisal** was sentenced to 18 months in prison on 16 May for slandering state institutions and publishing 'lies that hurt the state's integrity and honour'. In an open letter on 6 March, she had accused Prime Minister Ali Abu Ragheb of having profited financially from a government decision to double vehicle insurance rates. Faisal, who was Jordan's first-ever woman member of parliament, received the maximum sentence on four charges. No appeal can be made against the state security court's decisions but the King can commute or pardon those convicted. (*Al Bawaba*, AI)

KAZAKHSTAN

A number of journalists have been harassed in the city of Almaty. On 1 April, two unknown assailants attacked TAN TV cameraman **Vadim Malakhov** and tried to break his camera. The next day another TAN TV cameraman, **Ruslan Tahirov**, was beaten by three unknown assailants. On the night of 1-2 April, Irbis TV cameraman **Valeriy Pavlov** was asked to stop filming by police. When he refused to hand over his film, he was attacked by militiamen who smashed his camera and confiscated the cassette. (Adil-Soz)

President Nursultan Nazarbaev called for the establishment of a council to monitor the press, protect the rights and interests of both media owners and their employees, and shield individuals from 'prejudiced and subjective' reporting. The Minister for Culture, Information and Public Agreement said the council was needed to check whether the press was observing the rule that at least 50 per cent of its output should be in the Kazakh language. (Adil-Soz)

On 27 May, a court in Almaty, the former capital of Kazakhstan, ordered the closure of the **PR Consulting Company**, publisher of the independent weekly *Respublica*, following an application from the Culture and Information Ministry. Publication of the paper had been suspended in April by a court order on the grounds of 'legal technicalities'. A dead dog, with a threatening note attached, was dumped at *Respublica*'s office and later the paper's offices were destroyed by Molotov cocktails. At about the same time, two employees of another independent paper, *SolDat,* were beaten up by unknown assailants. (RL)

KENYA

Police in Nyeri, north of Nairobi, stoppped the comedy *Ngoma Cia Aka* by the Kenyan playwright **Wahome Mutahi** being performed on 23 and 24 March 'on security grounds' and because they said it contained pornographic scenes. (*East African Standard*)

It was reported on 25 March that the High Court found Kenyan media houses guilty of 'unmitigated and defenceless character assassination' and ordered them to pay cabinet minister Nicholas Biwott KSh 20 million (US$256) as compensation. This is the latest in a series of monetary rewards to Kenyan ministers and officials for injuries incurred by the press.

On 22 April, an order was issued for the arrest of *East African Standard* correspondent **Victore Obure** after he reported the extortion of money from inhabitants of the city of Garissa by police during a crackdown on illegal immigrants. Obure went into hiding. (RSF)

On 8 May, parliament passed a new law aimed at government control of newspapers. The new law imposes exorbitant publishing fees which Human Rights Watch says could muzzle the press in the run-up to elections for a successor to President Daniel arap Moi, who steps down at the end of the year after two decades in power. President Moi said the law would stop 'irresponsible journalism'. The law increases a libel bond required from every publication from US$128 to US$12,800 and penalises vendors and distributors who don't establish whether publishers of all the publications they sell have registered with the government and paid the bond. (HRW)

KUWAIT

Groups in Kuwait opposed to normalisation of relations with Israel demanded the dismissal of **Dr Shafeeq Ghabra** as Director of the Kuwaiti Information Office in Washington DC after he appeared on a panel with Israelis. Ghabra offered to resign in February but the Ministry of Information asked him in April to stay on. (*Index*)

LIBERIA

On 26 April, police shut down ***The Analyst***, an independent newspaper based in Monrovia, and ransacked its offices. Reginald Goodridge, the Minister of Information, said this was to investigate an allegation that the paper had been 'inciting the public to create chaos' during the state of emergency which started in February. Paul Mulbah, the Monrovia Police Chief, said the ban was permanent and refused to give reasons for the closure. The paper published an interview on 25 April with human rights lawyer Tiawan Gongloe and criticised President Charles Taylor. (AP, CPJ, RSF, *Independent*)

On 11 May, **Emmanuel Mondaye**, a reporter for the *Independent Inquirer*, was arrested in the provincial city of Gbarnga by state security forces. He is currently being held at the National Police Headquarters in the Liberian capital, Monrovia. Mondaye had gone to the city to report on fighting between government forces and Liberians United for Reconciliation and Democracy (LURD) who are seeking to overthrow the government. (RSF)

MACEDONIA

Macedonian journalists held a demonstration on 20 May against police harassment of **Daniela Veljanovska**, a reporter from the newspaper *Dnevnik*. Veljanovska and three other people were injured during a Lions Special Police exercise in the village of Leunovo when the Minister of the Interior, Ljube Boskovski, fired an automatic rocket launcher. Boskovski refused to accept responsibility, saying the paper was at fault for sending an inexperienced journalist to cover the exercise. After Dnevnik published an article demanding that Boskovski take responsibility, unidentified people describing themselves as members of the Lions Special Police arrived at the *Dnevnik* offices and Veljanovska's home, trying to intimidate them into accepting the ministry's argument that the paper and the injured parties themselves were to blame. (*Dnevnik*, Skopje AI TV, BBC)

MALAYSIA

In March, journalists from the Internet newspaper ***Malaysiakini*** and web radio **Radiq Radio** were denied access to the press gallery in parliament on the basis that they had not been accredited by the Information Ministry. They called on the government to repeal laws that restrict media operations and expose journalists to sanctions, provide for independent judicial review of administrative decisions relating to the media, and to extend public space for expression of citizens' views, including dissenting opinion. (malaysiakini.com)

MALDIVES

In March, political activist **Mohamed Nasheed** (*Index* 2/2002) lost his appeal against a two-and-a-half-year sentence for theft. Shaheen Hameed, Nasheed's lawyer and a nephew of President Gayyoom, was allegedly pressured by people close to his uncle to drop the case shortly before the appeal. Nasheed had been involved in a peaceful campaign to bring multiparty democracy and ministerial accountability to the country when he was convicted last November. (Maldivesculture.com)

MAURITANIA

A party supporting the rights of ex-slaves and other black Mauritanians, AC-Action for Change, was banned by the government in January, bringing the total of outlawed parties to three in two years. Slavery is officially illegal in Mauritania but the practice is said to continue. (allafrica.com)

Mohamed Fall Ould Oumère (*Index* 5/1998, 6/2000), publication director of the weekly *La Tribune*, was arrested on 12 April. Accused by the government of covering the congress of the underground Mauritanian organisation Conscience and Resistance, the journalist was held for nearly a week in the offices of the State Security Services. He was detained with a businessman and a Franco-Mauritanian professor. The three men were later released without charge. (IFJ)

MEXICO

Assailants fired shots at the offices of the weekly ***Páginas*** on 3 April and threatened the newspaper's employees. The management said that the attack might be linked to *Páginas'* criticisms of the authorities and stressed that acts of intimidation, threats and violence by the Chiapas authorities against journalists have multiplied in recent months. (RSF)

María Esther Martínez of the daily *La Unión de Morelos,* published in the state of Morelos, was arrested on 11 March in the city of Xochitepec. According to the Morelos Independent Human Rights Commission, a non-governmental human rights organisation, she was arrested after criticising the Morelos Attorney-General's Office and the Ministerial Police. She was released the same day. On 14 March, **Jesús Castillo**, of the same daily, received threatening telephone calls after reporting on alleged links between some police officers and drug traffickers and kidnappers. (RSF)

MOROCCO

The 7 March issue of the French weekly *VSD* was withheld from news-stands by the Sochepresse distribution company without explanation. The issue contained a special report entitled 'The man who doesn't want to be king' and made reference to two controversial books, *Notre ami le roi* by **Gilles Perrault** and *Le dernier roi* by **Jean-Pierre Tuquoi** (*Index* 1/2002). (RSF)

Parliament approved a new press law on 12 March. It retains jail terms for insulting the king and royal princes and princesses but reduces the prison terms for those convicted to three to five years, compared with five to 20 years under the old law. Article 29 retains the government's right to ban Moroccan or foreign newspapers if they 'undermine Islam, the monarchy, national territorial integrity or public order'. But it says the government must give reasons for seizing or banning local or foreign newspapers. In 2001, nine newspapers, including seven foreign publications, were censored for reporting on topics such as the Western Sahara, corruption and the king. Parliament also passed a new electoral law reserving 30 seats for women representatives. At present there are just two women out of 325 deputies. (RSF, *El País*)

In March, journalist **Younès Moujahid** was removed from his post at the daily *El Ittihad el Ichtiraki*. Aides of Prime Minister Abderrahmane Youssoufi, who is managing editor of the newspaper, told the journalist, who is also secretary-general of the national press trade union, that he did not appreciate his criticism of the country's counter-espionage service, the DST, and the new press law. (RSF)

Eleven people were arrested and taken to court on 28 March for trying to organise a demonstration in Tamlast against the arbitrary confiscation of land that threatens argan trees. Destruction of the trees means the displacement of the Amazigh people who depend on them for their subsistence. Argan wood, leaves, fruit and oil extract are used commercially, medicinally and in cooking. (WAAC)

On 7 April, a large-scale demonstration in support of the Palestinian cause was allowed to go ahead. The prime minister, Abderramán Yussufi, led a march in Rabat of 300,000 according to the government, or one million according to organisers. A similar demonstration was banned in January (*Index* 2/2002). (*El País*)

On 6 May, all 8,000 copies of the intellectual and political magazine *Wijhat Nadhar* were confiscated by secret service agents without explanation. The issue contained the text of a speech by **Moulay Hichem al-Alaoui** (*Index* 2/2002), cousin of King Muhammad VI and a frequent critic of the monarchy who is second in line to the throne. (CPJ)

NEPAL

On 3 March, **Gopal Budhathoki**, editor of the weekly newspaper *Sanghu*, went missing on his way home from work. After three days of inquiries from legislators and media organisations, the prime minister's office announced that the army had detained Budhathoki for publishing reports that 'encouraged and raised [the] morale of the Maoists'. Budhathoki was released on 26 March. Under the current emergency laws, anyone accused of supporting or aiding the proscribed Communist Party of Nepal-Maoist can be charged with terrorism and sentenced to life imprisonment. (CPJ)

Shyam Shrestha, editor of the left-wing monthly *Mulyankan*, **Mahesh Maskey**, a member of the human rights organisation the Intellectual's Solidarity Group, and human rights activist **Pramod Kafle** were arrested at the international airport in Kathmandu on 16 March. They had been on their way to New Delhi to take part in a conference about the civil war in their country between Maoist rebels and the government. The next day, Prime Minister Deuba confirmed that the three men had been detained but would not disclose their whereabouts or explain why they had been arrested. According to local media reports, the three men are being held at army headquarters in the capital, and their families have not been allowed to see them. (CPJ)

On 23 May, **Tara Neupane**, a columnist for the weekly *Sanghu*, was arrested by police at the Kathmandu office of the Federation of Nepalese Journalists. The arrest continued the crackdown on journalists that started after the declaration of a state of emergency last November. (CPJ)

Recent publications: *Nepal: A spiralling human rights crisis* (AI, April 2002, pp 48); *Nepal: Human Rights Year Book 2002* by the Informal Sector Service Centre (INSEC, April 2002, pp 217)

THE NETHERLANDS

Pim Fortuyn, founder of fast-rising anti-immigration party Lijst Pim Fortuyn, was shot dead in Hilversum on 6 May, nine days before a general election that was expected to bring big gains for the party. Outgoing Prime Minister Wim Kok described the killing as 'a deep tragedy for our democracy'. Fortuyn's rise had been seen as an alarming example of the growth of the extreme right in Europe. He spelled out his central policy quite clearly: 'no more Muslims can come in'. The Lijst Pim Fortuyn party contested the 15 May elections and won 26 of the 150 seats, making it the second-largest party in the Dutch parliament. (*Guardian*)

NIGER

Abdoulaye Tiemogo, publisher of the independent weekly *Le Canard Dechainé*, **Sanoussi Jackou**, an opposition leader and owner of the private weekly *La Roue de l'Histoire*, and **Abarad Mouddour**, publisher of the magazine, went on trial on 28 May charged with defaming the prime minister and trade minister. Tiemogo was acquitted but Jackou and Mouddour were convicted of criminal defamation and sentenced to suspended four-month prison terms and a fine of 100,000 CFA francs (US$136). They were also ordered to pay 2 million CFA francs (US$2,702) in damages. (CPJ)

NIGERIA

On 24 April, Justice Minister Kanu Agabi threatened to prosecute foreign journalists who came to Nigeria and wrote 'malicious falsehoods' about the country. The government's statement followed publication in the European edition of the US weekly *Time* magazine on 15 April of an article reporting that a foreign journalist had been given an envelope containing 50,000 nairas (approximately $400) by the government at a conference on 'good and honest reporting'. President Olusegun Obasanjo said he was outraged at the *Time* magazine article and ordered an investigation. However, several international correspondents have confirmed receiving – and returning – envelopes containing money. (RSF)

PAKISTAN

Reuters reported on 30 April that the trial of four men charged with kidnapping and killing *Wall Street Journal* reporter **Daniel Pearl** (*Index* 2/2002) had been moved because of security concerns. Raja Qureshi, the advocate-general of Sindh Province, said the trial had been moved from Karachi to an anti-terrorism court in Hyderabad because there had been reports of a threatened attack on the Karachi jail where the trial was taking place. (Reuters)

On 1 May, the election commission declared **General Pervez Musharraf** the victor in a referendum on 30 April that he had called to extend his rule. Although the election was highly controversial both locally and internationally and Reuters journalists said they witnessed widespread vote-rigging, the commission also said that 70 per cent of the electorate had turned out to vote and nearly 97 per cent of voters had supported Musharraf. (*Guardian*, Reuters)

On 19 May, the *Washington Post* highlighted Pakistan's repressive blasphemy laws by publishing an article by Professor Akbar S Ahmed on the case of his friend **Mohammad Younus Shaikh** (*Index* 03/2001, 04/2001). Shaikh, who was sentenced to death for blasphemy last August, revived international interest in his case by sending a letter from death row in April to Ahmed and another expatriate Pakistani in the United States. Shaikh was accused of making blasphemous remarks about the Prophet Mohammad during a medical lecture. (*Washington Post,* BBC)

Recent publication: *Pakistan: Insufficient protection of women* (AI, April 2002, pp56)

PALESTINE

The Israeli military assault on West Bank towns in March and April targeted NGOs and media stations as well as the Palestinian Authority, security installations, towns and refugee camps. Scores of offices were destroyed, vandalised and, or looted. Journalists and human rights organisations were repeatedly denied access to West Bank towns, most notoriously Jenin where a massacre was reported.

On 18 March, TV cameraman **Amjad Allami** was shot dead by Israeli soldiers while filming events in his home town of Hebron. (*Jerusalem Times*)

On 31 March, *Boston Globe* reporter **Anthony Shadid** was shot in the shoulder while walking along the street. (*Jerusalem Times*)

On 2 April, Israeli forces occupied and vandalised Al-Quds Educational TV. Equipment was thrown out of fourth-floor windows. Staff were detained for many hours and warned not to return. The TV transmitter was destroyed. Tanks and armoured personnel carriers occupied the compound. (Al-Quds Educational TV)

On 2 April, the Israeli Government Press Office said it had sent letters to CNN and NBC in Jerusalem complaining about their live coverage of Israeli attacks on Ramallah and accusing their reporters of breaking a military order to leave Ramallah.

On 4 April, it was reported that a Palestinian cameraman for al-Jazeera TV had been shot in the head by Israeli soldiers. (*Jerusalem Times*)

On 5 April, it was reported that four Turkish journalists had been arrested in Ramallah by occupying Israeli soldiers and had their passports confiscated. The Israeli troops also expelled a crew working for Abu Dhabi satellite channel, the Link Institution for Media, ABC News and the Yemen satellite channel. **Mahmoud Numan Fatafteh**, Ramallah correspondent of *Al-Quds Daily*, was arrested while working in the paper's offices. (*Jerusalem Times*)

On 6 April, the President and Secretary General of the International Federation of Leagues for Human Rights (Fedération des Ligues des droits de l'homme – FLDH), **Sadiki Kaba** and **Driss el Yazami**, and the Honorary President of the French League for Human Rights, **Henri Leclerc**, were detained by Israeli immigration and security forces at Ben Gurion airport. The Ministry of Interior said it had ordered immigration officials to ask whether visitors were intending to visit or meet Palestinians, and had given them the right to deport such foreigners. (LAW)

On 7 April, it was reported that in the previous ten days, there had been 40 cases of journalists being wounded, injured, arrested, expelled or threatened. RSF said: 'The Israeli army is knowingly targeting journalists in a deliberate policy of intimidation.' (RSF)

On 8 April, among the military destruction of much of Nablus was the vandalisation of the offices of the PLO's **Palestinian Refugee Department** and the **Palestinian National Council**. Hard disks were taken from the PNC offices including all data relating to internal correspondence, personnel and finance. The **Bisan Centre for Research and Development** was occupied and vandalised. Hard disks and a camera were stolen. The **Tariq al-Mahaba** FM station was blasted with tanks despite there being no fighting in the area. (*Palestine Monitor*)

It was reported on 22 April that most of the equipment of the **Health Development Information Policy Institute** (HDIP) in Ramallah had been destroyed by Israeli troops. More than 13 years of research, bibliographic information and databases were looted or destroyed. Computers were broken and computer hard drives, printers and fax machines were stolen. The Ramallah offices of the ***Palestine Monitor***, the **Union of Palestinian Medical Relief Committees**, the **MATTIN** organisation, which specialises in international human rights and humanitarian law enforcement, the **Mandela Institute for Political Prisoners**, the human rights organisation **al-Haq**, the Ramallah **YMCA**, the **Khalil Sakakini Cultural Centre Foundation** and the **National Conservatory of Music** were all pillaged.

The offices and equipment of **Al-Nasr TV**, **Manara** radio station and **Love and Peace** FM radio station were totally destroyed. **Al-Quds** FM radio station was shelled and set ablaze. The offices of **Ajhal** and **Angham** FM radio stations were occupied and equipment destroyed. **Watan** TV and **Amwaj** TV and radio stations were occupied and Israeli soldiers broadcast pornographic material before destroying the studios. The Israeli military denied that it had anything to do with the pornographic programming (also broadcast on **al-Sharq**), and blamed Palestinian leaders. (AFP, *Palestine Monitor*)

PANAMA

On 22 January. President **Mireya Moscoso** announced the approval of a transparency law making all documents related to public processes more available to the general public. (Mesoamérica)

At a meeting convened by the Inter-American Commission on Human Rights (IACHR) in Washington DC, three journalists presented a report highlighting seven main threats to journalists in Panama. Supported by the Committee to Protect Journalists (CPJ), Journalists Against Corruption (PFC) and the Centre for Justice and International Law (CEJIL), the report detailed the absence of public access to information, the so-called 'disrespect laws' and a censorship law inherited from the former dictatorship. PFC said that of 200 active journalists in Panama, 90 face slander charges, 36 of them were made by government officials. (IFEX)

Panama enacted a new law giving citizens free access to public records. The law states that 'every individual or juridical person has the right to request information from the government bodies'. The Inter-American Press Association (IAPA) welcomed the new law but warned that it did not allow access to information on national security and cases under investigation by the Public Prosecutor's Office. (IFEX)

PERU

On 12 May, the new communications manager of América Televisión, Pablo Cateriano, dismissed news programme producers **Alvaro Maguiña** and **Jessica Tapia** and news programme director **Jean**

Pajuelo from the programme *América Noticias*. Cateriano claimed the programme was not profitable but Maguiña accused Cateriano of caving in to pressures to censor the programme. (24Horas.com.pe)

On 21 May, **Pan-American Television** journalists were attacked in Villa Militar de Chorrillos while covering the release from custody of General Augusto Jaime Patiño. Journalist **Yorka Poémape** suffered physical injuries. (24Horas.com.pe)

On 26 March, the editor of *El Búho*, **Mabel Cáceres Calderón**, received a suspicious parcel, which was opened by the bomb disposal squad. It contained a threatening note and a bull's testicles. The incident is the latest threat arising from a series of articles published in 2001 about the finances of the Universidad Nacional de San Agustín. Cáceres has been forced to suspend publication of *El Búho* to enable her to fight a criminal defamation lawsuit brought by the rector of the university. (CPJ, IPYS)

PHILIPPINES

Cable television reporter **Arlyn de la Cruz** was released by her captors on 27 April in Jolo, southern Philippines. De la Cruz, a reporter for Manila's Net 25 and a contributor to the *Philippine Daily Inquirer*, had been missing for almost four months after being abducted on 19 January by former Moro National Liberation Front (MNLF) guerrillas now serving with the Armed Forces of the Philippines. De la Cruz said the former guerrillas thought she had brought ransom money for the release of three hostages held by the Abu Sayyaf Group. Finding no ransom money, she was transferred from one group to another until her release. Officials denied that members of the military had been involved. (SEAPA)

POLAND

Polish authorities prevented three prominent editors and publishers from attending the World Newspaper Congress and World Editors Forum in Belgium in late May. Three executives of the Polish national daily *Rzeczpospolita*, **Grzegorz Gauden**, **Elzbieta Poniklo** and **Piotr Fratczak**, had their passports confiscated by a Polish court in a dispute involving Presspublica, the publishing company of *Rzeczpospolita*, and another company. (WAN)

RUSSIA

Witnesses told of torture, disappearances and killings during an anti-rebel sweep operation by Russian forces in the Chechen town of Staryi Atagi, 25 miles south of Grozny, on 6–11 March. At least ten men 'disappeared' during the operation; the corpses or burned remains of nine people were found, raising fears that they had been murdered. So far, the remains of only one of the 'disappeared,' 26-year-old **Imran Kuntaev**, detained on 6 March, have been identified. His remains were found the next day in a house that had been burned and relatives identified him by his four gold teeth. On 9 March, three more bodies were found in a burned-out vehicle at the edge the village. Under Decree No. 46 of the Procuracy General, officials on sweep operations should compile a list of all detainees, showing why they were detained, who detained them, and where they were taken. They should also inform relatives where detainees are held. A list does exist for the Staryi Atagi operation but the ten 'disappeared' detainees are not on it. (HRW)

Kirill Simonov, the son of Glasnost Defence Fund head Aleksei Simonov, was found dead on 1 April near his house in Moscow. A spokesman for the Moscow Interior Ministry said the 18-year-old student committed suicide by jumping from an 11-storey building. But his father, who is well known for defending independent media from government pressure, said he considers this a 'politically motivated killing'. (RFE/RL)

On 21 March, **Alexander Podrabinek,** editor of the *Express Chronicle* and Prima Human Rights News Service in Moscow, was arrested in Austria along with two Chechens, **Borz Ali Ismailov** and **Abudula Arzanukaiev**. They are accused of being terrorists. The three were in Austria because Arzanukaiev was suing an Austrian newspaper for defamation. The arrest occured in Amstetten, outside Vienna. (*Glasnost Media*)

Marina Popova, correspondent of *Moskovski Komsomolets* in Vladivostok city, was attacked in the street on 28 February. This followed the publication of two articles by Popova on the illegal sex industry and police involvement in prostitution. (*Glasnost Media*)

In Armenia, the leaders of the Airanpetyun and National Democratic parties and the Socialist Armenia union say the government is driving the opposition to break the law by limiting its scope for free political activity. The parties cited in particular the decision of the Ministry for Culture, Youth and Education, prohibiting colleges from leasing halls and auditoriums to the opposition. (*Glasnost Media*)

SENEGAL

The Dakar Tribunal sentenced two journalists on 16 April to four months' imprisonment and a fine of three million CFA francs ($2,740). **Mamadou Oumar Ndiaye** and **Pape Ndiaye**, publication director and reporter with the private weekly *Le Témoin*, were charged with defaming and insulting Victor Cabrita, the director of a Dakar-based Catholic private school in an article published in September 2001. They accused Cobrita of misappropriating funds and of being racist. The same case will be tried a second time on 6 June, because the plaintiff filed two separate complaints. Lawyers are appealing against the first ruling. (IFJ, RSF)

SIERRA LEONE

During the week of 11 March, the Independent Media Commission ordered the suspension of the privately owned daily *Africa Champion Newspaper* for two months. The paper had published a story accusing the president's son of corruption. The managing editor of the publication, **Mohamed D Koroma**, was barred from practising journalism for the same period. The editor defied the order and *African Champion Newspaper* was distributed on 18 March. (RSF)

SOMALIA

On 2 May, authorities withdrew the licence of the **Somali Broadcasting Corporation (SBC)**. SBC manager Ali Abdi Aware said they had been accused by the authorities of breaking the county's press laws. However, IPI believes the broadcaster was targeted for criticising President Colonel Abdullahi Yusuf. (IPI)

SOUTH AFRICA

It was reported on 28 March that the Johannesburg High Court had issued a gagging order against 16 residents of **Steel Valley**, Vanderbijlpark, who have been protesting against alleged environmental spillage by the huge ISCOR corporation. They say residents are suffering numerous health problems because ISCOR is spilling chrome and cadmium into the region's groundwater. The court order prevents journalists from gathering information from local sources about the case. (FXI, IFEX)

According to a report in *City Press* on April 14, journalists **Wonder Hlongwa**, **Mandla Zulu** and **Bongani Hans** from the paper were assaulted by associates of a businessman, Michael Mwangi, in KwaZulu Natal after they published a story accusing Mwangi of criminal activities. (FXI)

Thousands of **Truth and Reconciliation Commission (TRC)** documents were declared confidential in April by the National Intelligence Agency after being unearthed by the **TRC**. The boxes, files and folders contain valuable documentary evidence of South Africa's apartheid history. (FXI)

SRI LANKA

It was reported on 9 March that ten police officers and 31 civilians had been indicted in connection with the massacre of 27 former Tamil Tiger guerrillas on 26 October 2000 at the Bindunuwewa rehabilitation camp (*Index* 1/2001). Army captain **YK Abeyratne Banda**, the officer in charge of the camp, and seven other police officers were acquitted and released because of insufficient evidence. On 26 March, the *Hindu* said that all 41 indictees had been formally charged with 83 offences ranging from unlawful assembly to murder and attempted murder. (*Gulf News Online, Hindu*)

On 13 March, a bomb exploded at the home of **Dr AT Ariyaratne**, the leader of the Gandhi influenced Sarvo daya movement. The attack was believed to be a warning by Sinhalese chauvinists against Sarvodaya's support for the current peace process between the government and the Liberation Tigers of Tamil Eelam (LTTE) and, specifically, the movement's peace meditation event planned for 16 March in Anuradhapura. Several thousand people took part in the event as planned. (*Lanka Academic*)

Anuruddha Ratwatte, former deputy defence minister and uncle of President Chandrika Kumaratunga, was further remanded in custody until 15 April in connection with the massacre of ten supporters of the Sri Lankan Muslim Congress after parliamentary polls closed last 5 December. Two of Ratwatte's sons, Lohan and Chanuka, were also remanded in custody. The 5 December incident sparked several days of riots in the Kandy area between the country's minority Muslim and majority Sinhalese communities. (*Gulf News Online*)

Three masked gunmen claiming to be from the Presidential Security Division broke into the house of **Sarath Chinthaka**, correspondent for the English-language *Daily Mirror* and the Sinhala daily *Lankadeepa*, on 30 March. They demanded that his wife hand over an audiotape which they said Chinthaka had made of a controversial public speech by President Chandrika Kumaratunga in January, in which she said she could end the current ceasefire between the government and the LTTE simply by saying so. RSF said Chinthaka also received several threats by phone. He says he does not have a tape of the speech. (*Sunday Times, Lanka Academic, Times of India,* RSF)

The *Lanka Academic* reported on 22 April that journalists covering a protest march by the National Bhikkhu Front to Prime Minister Ranil Wickremesinghe's official residence had been threatened and prevented from taking photographs of the event by members the Special Task Force, a paramilitary arm of the police. (*Lanka Academic*)

On 30 April, a magistrate in the eastern town of Trincomalee ordered four Tamil men to be held in remand until 3 May in connection with an alleged brawl between them and police officers. The four men had been taking part in a demonstration against the Indian state of Tamil Nadu's decision not to allow Anton Balasingham, the LTTE's chief peace negotiator, to use the state as a base during forthcoming talks with the Sri Lankan government. (IANS)

SYRIA

Members of parliament **Riyad Sayf** (*Index* 1/2002) and **Muhammad Ma'mun el-Humsi** were sentenced to five years in prison in separate hearings by the Criminal Court of Damascus, it was reported on 4 April. The court found Sayf guilty of 'trying to change the constitution by illegal means', forming a secret assembly and illegally convening meetings. Sayf had called for an end to Syria's long-standing state of emergency. El-Humsi had faced similar charges. (SHRC, *MEI*)

It was reported on 30 April that the accreditation of **Maher Chmaytelli**, AFP's bureau chief in Damascus, would not be renewed when it expired at the end of March. Chmaytelli was summoned early this year to the Communications Ministry's information chief, who accused him of putting out negative reports about the internal political situation. (RSF, SHRC)

The state-appointed Damascus City Branch of Lawyers froze the membership of lawyers **Haytham el-Maleh** and **Anwar el-Bunni** for three months with effect from 3 May because of critical statements they made about the trials of Muhammad Ma'mun el-Humsi and Riyad Sayf. (SHRC)

The trial of **Riyad Turk**, 73, leader of the banned Communist League, opened on 12 April. Turk was arrested in September and charged with 'trying to change the constitution by illegal means', 'incitement to armed sedition' and 'undermining patriotic sentiment and national morale'. Economics professor **Arif Dalila** and salon organiser **Habib Saleh** also face charges including 'inciting sectarian and regional strife' and 'spreading lies aimed at harming the state and its economy'. (*CSM, MEI*)

It was reported on 20 May that the satirical magazine ***Addomari*** had had its reporters threatened, its electricity cut at printing time, advertising withdrawn and paper prices drastically increased. (*CSM*)

TAIWAN

The National Security Bureau raided the Taipei offices of ***Next*** magazine on 20 March and seized 160,000 copies of the next day's edition on the grounds that it violated national security. The edition contained an article about secret bank accounts used by former President Lee Teng Hui's government to finance spying on China and to buy diplomatic favours from certain countries. The

21 March edition was still available at news-stands despite the seizure. The author, journalist **Hsueh Chung-Liang**, had his home searched. On 22 March, the editor of the *China Times*, **Huang Ching-Lung**, was charged with endangering national security for republishing the article. (CPJ)

THAILAND

Prime Minister Thaksin Shinawatra could be expelled from office if he is found guilty of abuses against press freedom, the *Bangkok Post* reported on 15 March. A group of 384 academics signed an open letter demanding that the prime minister explain alleged intimidation of the press and the infringement of civil liberties. They also wanted Thaksin to promise he would protect and promote freedom of speech, guaranteed under articles 39–42 of the constitution. A group of 1,195 journalists and reporters had earlier demanded parliamentary inquiries into other actions seen as government attempts to gag the press, including investigations of 35 journalists by the Anti-Money Laundering Office and a ban on Nation Group's radio news programmes. (SEAPA)

SEAPA reported on 5 April that shortly after the Defence Energy Department suspended the Nation Group's news programme, the Thaksin government ordered the Anti-Money Laundering Office (AMLO) to investigate several prominent journalists and publishers and members of their families. Nation Group editor **Suthichai Yoon** and his son, **Prabda**, group editor **Thepchai Yong** and senior editor **Sopon Onkgara** were among those facing investigation. A panel set up by the government concluded that the AMLO order had been wrongfully issued and that the officials involved would face disciplinary action but it failed to establish who ordered the investigation. (SEAPA)

TOGO

Le Combat du Peuple said on 2 April that its news editor, **Lucien Djossou Messan**, had been receiving 'real and specific death threats' for some time. Messan was sentenced on 5 June 2001 to 12 months in prison for 'falsehoods and use of falsehoods', but was released five months later in a presidential pardon. (RSF)

On 4 April, General Sizing Walla, the Minister of the Interior, ordered the seizure of copies of *La Tribune du Peuple*, an independent newspaper, after it reported that two Togolese Armed Forces agents had assaulted a blacksmith suspected of theft. **Kodjo Afatsao Siliadin**, the newspaper's editor and author of the article, faces serious threats and has gone into hiding. Police confiscated more copies of the paper the following week. (RSF)

On 8 April, police seized several hundred copies of the weekly ***Motion d'Information*** from news-stands after it alleged that a dozen student activists with close ties to the opposition had evaded arrest.

On 9 April, several thousand copies of ***Le Regard*** were confiscated after an article about human rights abuses. Abass Derman Mikaila, the editor of this paper, has gone into hiding. (RSF)

Koffi Augustin Amégah, publisher of *Reporter des Temps Nouveaux*, has been hiding from police since 18 April. Amégah's newspaper published comments by a soldier condemning the seizure of *La Tribune du Peuple*. (CPJ, IPI, RSF)

TUNISIA

The Appeals Court on 30 March upheld the conviction of four men found guilty of belonging to the banned Tunisian Communist Workers Party, distributing leaflets and spreading 'false information' capable of 'disturbing the public order', and inciting people to violate the laws of the country (*Index* 2/2002). However, it reduced three of the original prison sentences, giving **Hamma Hammami** three years and two months, **Samir Taamallah** 21 months, and **Abdeljabbar Madouri** 21 months plus an additional two years on a contempt-of-court charge. (HRW)

Jean-Pierre Tuquoi (*Index* 1/2002), a reporter from the French daily newspaper *Le Monde*, was refused entry to the country on 17 May. He had intended to cover the 26 May constitutional referendum. (RSF)

The interior ministry said that more than 99 per cent had voted 'yes' in the referendum to abolish the three-term limit for incumbent presidents and raise the maximum age limit of the president from 70 to 75. Souheir Belhassen, vice-president of the Tunisian

Human Rights League dismissed the result as a 'masquerade'. (BBC)

TURKEY

The Turkish Ministry of Culture banned an Oscar-nominated film featuring a relationship between a retired judge and a young Kurdish girl in April. The film, ***Big Man, Small Love***, was partly funded by the ministry itself and had already been seen by 100,000 cinema-goers in Turkey. **Handan Ipekci**, the film's director, said that the film 'underlines the fact that people can live together on this land despite all ethnic differences'. The movie includes dialogue in Kurdish with Turkish subtitles and depicts a violent police raid on Kurdish activists. (BBC, *Index*)

Three people died in Mersin on 21 March in clashes between riot police and thousands of Kurdish youths after the government banned Kurds celebrating their new year, claiming the event would be 'exploited by outlawed groups to cause provocations'. Two police officers were killed and one demonstrator was crushed to death. More than 100 people were detained. In Diyarbakir, nearly half a million Kurds sang and danced and lit a giant torch – a symbolic burning of the past's impurities – despite thousands of police and soldiers on the roads leading to the city. (CNN)

A last-minute reprieve saved the **GUN-TV** chain, which the High Council for Radio and Television had ordered to close for a year from 22 March for broadcasting two Kurdish-language love songs. A court annulled the decision, saying the songs did not promote separatism. (*Cildekt*)

The trial of the 15 people who published *Freedom of Expression 2000*(FoX), a book containing 60 articles in breach of four laws that penalise free speech, continued on 26 March at the State Security Court in Istanbul. Those on trial include **Yavuz Önen** (*Index*, 4/2001, 1/2002), president of the Human Rights Foundation of Turkey, **Cengiz Bektas** (*Index*, 4/2001), president of the Writers' Union of Turkey, **Mehmet Atilla Maras** (*Index*, 4/2001, 1/2002), former president of the Islamic Writers' Union, **Erdal Öz** (*Index*, 4/2001), writer and publisher, **Etyen Mahçupyan**, writer and journalist, and **Sanar Yurdatapan** (*Index*, 3/1997, 5/1998, 4/2001, 1/2002), composer and leader of the FoX campaign. (International PEN)

The trial of **Abdullah Keskin**, a Turkish publisher charged with 'separatist propaganda' for printing a Turkish edition of a US journalist's book on the Kurds, began in Istanbul's state security court on 3 April. If convicted, Keskin faces one to three years in prison.(CPJ)

Fourteen writers, poets, artists and playwrights known as the Initiative of Intellectuals and Artists (IIA) appeared before Ankara's state security court on 8 April charged with 'supporting an illegal organisation.' The 14, **Ahmet Telli** (poet), **Sükrü Erbas** (poet), **Aydin Çubukcu** (writer), **Zerrin Taspinar** (poet), **Selma Agabeyoglu** (poet), **Ilhan Akalin** (writer), **Abdullah Aydin** (writer), **Ali Balkiz** (writer), **Oktay Etiman** (translator), **Fetta Köleli** (poet), **Hüseyin Sahin** (poet), **Yilmaz Demiral** (actor), **Necmettin Salaz** (poet, writer), and **Kuvvat Yurdakul** (poet, playwright), formed the IIA in protest at the prosecution of photographer **Mehmet Özer** for his condemnation of new 'F-type' prisons. They believe the new prisons will contain more isolation cells, leading to a rise in ill-treatment by prison guards. (*Kurdistan Observer*)

On 9 April, Turkey was fined £25,500 by the European Human Rights Court for banning the pro-Kurdish **HEP** (Working People's Party) in 1993. The Court ruled that Turkey had violated the rights to freedom of assembly and freedom of association, guaranteed by Clause 11 of the European Convention on Human Rights. (*Cildekt*)

On 9 April, a Kurdish driver was given a suspended sentence of three years and nine months in jail for playing a cassette of Kurdish songs in his minibus. The Diyarbekir state security court considered that **Selahaddin Onen** was guilty of 'helping an armed organisation'. (*Cildekt*)

The Kurdish author **Mehmet Uzun** (*Index*, 3/2000) went on trial at the national security court in Diyarbakir on 19 April for 'propagating separatism', based on a speech he had made in December 2000, but was acquitted for lack of evidence. (*Kurdish Media*)

The Kurdistan Workers' Party (PKK) announced on 16 April that it was changing its name to KADEK (Congress for Freedom and Democracy in Kurdistan) and abandoning violence in favour of a peaceful struggle for Kurdish rights. The Kurdish rebel chief **Abdullah Ocalan** (*Index*, 1/1998, 3/1999, 4/1999) was named President of KADEK. 'Whether the PKK changes its name or its form, it still remains a terrorist organisation for us,' said Turkish Industry Minister Ahmet Kenan Tanrikulu. In May, the EU added the PKK to a new list of 'terrorist' organisations, despite the name change. (*Cildekt*)

The Turkish parliament passed a new media law on 15 May, putting army officers on the national radio and TV monitoring council RTÜK, increasing fines for media offences, and authorising RTUK to supervise Internet sites. **Nuri Kayis**, head of the Turkish Broadcast Council, warned that the law would threaten fundamental freedoms and allow already powerful media magnates to run 'out of control'. (*RSF, FT*)

May Day demonstrations were banned in several Kurdish provinces but took place under heavy police supervision in Ankara and Istanbul. In Diyarbakir, police smothered attempts to assemble and ten people were arrested, according to police sources. In Tunceli, there were clashes between police and 1,500 demonstrators and about 20 people were arrested, including the local leader of the pro-Kurdish HADEP party, **Alican Unlu**, after he tried to make a public statement. (*Cildekt*)

Turkey is reportedly submitting a report to the United States and the European Union on 17 organisations in Europe which it accuses of supporting the PKK. They include **Médecins sans Frontières** and **Reporters sans Frontières** which featured the Turkish Armed Forces Chief of Staff, Huseyin Kivrikoglu, in an exhibition in Paris of 38 'predators of press freedom'. (*Cildekt*)

A high court judge in Diyarbakir Province dismissed a case on 21 May in which the state prosecutor had demanded that 21 Kurdish children should be renamed with Turkish first names. However, in Izmir the following day, another trial opened against nine families charged with promoting terrorism for giving their children Kurdish names. (*Cildekt*)

Recent publication: *State violence against women in Turkey*, Kurdish Human Rights Project.

UGANDA

Parliament passed a new press law on 20 March, providing for prison terms of up to ten years for journalists convicted of encouraging 'terrorism' and giving the government the power to deem any organisation a 'terrorist group'. RSF urged President Yoweri Museveni not to ratify the new law. (RSF)

UKRAINE

Oleg Liachko, editor-in-chief of the privately owned weekly *Svoboda*, was arrested on 15 April when he went to the local State Prosecutor's Office to answer allegations of libel against an unnamed senior official from the office. He was charged with 'abuse of authority' and 'resisting the police'. He was released on 23 April after a protest from the Council of Europe.

UNITED KINGDOM

In early May it emerged that media baron Richard Desmond's Northern and Shell company, Britain's largest publisher of pornography, had donated £100,000 pounds to the Labour Party days after the government gave the go-ahead for Desmond's controversial acquisition of the *Express* newspapers. The donation was taken by then Labour Party General Secretary Margaret McDonagh, who later joined Northern and Shell. The controversy went largely unreported not only in Desmond's own titles but also in the *Daily Mail* and *Mail on Sunday*, owned by Associated Newspapers (AN). AN has a legal agreement with Northern and Shell which bars it from referring to Desmond's pornography empire, in return for the *Express*'s silence on allegations about the Rothermere family owners of AN. (*Guardian, Observer*)

Channel 4 News journalists **Alex Thompson** and **Lena Ferguson** could face jail for contempt of court after refusing to disclose to the Saville Inquiry the identities of four British soldiers whom they interviewed in 1997 about the events of Bloody Sunday. (*Guardian*)

A man in Northern Ireland was awarded £12,500 on 20 March by the European Court of Human Rights because he had been denied access to a tribunal to pursue a claim that he had been sacked because he was a Catholic. **Liam Devenney** lost his job as a waiter in August 1992 and complained to a Fair Employment Tribunal. The Crown Solicitors' Office issued a certificate saying that the tribunal had no jurisdiction because he was a police suspect. The ECHR ruled unanimously that his rights had been violated.(*Irish Times*)

On 14 March, the Court of Appeal ruled that the **BBC** acted illegally by refusing last year to screen a party political broadcast by the Pro-Life Alliance which included images of aborted foetuses. Lord Justice Laws insisted, 'This case is about the censorship of political speech.' The BBC said it would take the case to the Law Lords. (*Guardian*)

The Department of Trade and Industry and the Department of Media, Culture and Sport published a draft communications bill on 7 May which, if implemented in its current form, will significantly deregulate media ownership and probably lead to greater consolidation and foreign ownership of media companies. Among the proposed changes is an end to the ban on newspaper proprietors controlling more than 20 per cent of a terrestrial television company. This would allow Rupert Murdoch, who controls several newspapers and Britain's biggest satellite broadcaster, to buy the terrestrial Channel 5. The draft lifts restrictions on joint ownership of TV and radio stations, ownership of more than one national commercial radio licence, and foreign broadcasters buying UK radio and television stations. (*Guardian*)

USA

The Supreme Court on 16 April struck out a section of the 1996 Child Pornography Prevention Act that prohibits any image that 'is, or appears to be, of a minor engaging in sexually explicit conduct', whose broad phrasing could easily be applied to patently non-pornographic works of art. From now on only images that exploit real children are banned. (*Daily Telegraph*)

VENEZUELA

The Inter American Press Association declared on 5 March that Venezuela fails to fulfil the ten principles of the 1994 Chapultepec Declaration, which sets out principles of press freedom for the Americas. The former president of IAPA and director of the Uruguayan weekly *Búsqueda*, Danilo Arbilla, said that President Hugo Chávez regulates the media on a weekly basis, a more dangerous act against free expression than closing down media outlets entirely. Measures against the media include a campaign against **Grupo de Periódicos Capriles** and the prosecution of **Pablo López Ulacio**, the exiled owner of the weekly *La Razón*. (IAPA)

On 11 April, a reporter for the daily *2001*, **Jorge Tortosa,** was shot dead while covering violent clashes between supporters of President Chávez and opposition demonstrators in Caracas. Witnesses said Tortosa was shot in the head by a military sniper firing from the roof of the City Hall. (IPI)

YUGOSLAVIA

On 7 March, a hand grenade was thrown into the house of the acting director of Radio Paracin, **Mihajlo Peric**, but did not explode. Peric heard a loud noise and found the grenade on the floor of his nine-year-old daughter's bedroom. (ANEM)

ZIMBABWE

Zimbabwe's last non-black senior judge, **Justice Ahmed Ebrahim**, resigned on 4 March. A week earlier, **Ebrahim**, who is of Indian origin, led a sitting of the Supreme Court and attacked a law that left elections open to rigging. Elections were held on 9 and 10 March. (*The Times*)

President Robert Mugabe ratified an Access to Information and Protection of Privacy Act on 15 March, that established a Media Commission to register media companies and journalists. The Minister of Information, Jonathan Moyo, said on 21 March that the Act needed to be revised to ban all foreign ownership of the media in Zimbabwe. (MISA)

It was reported on 26 March that **Sikumuzo Dube** faced a year's imprisonment sentence and Z$20,000(US$365) fine for writing and reciting a poem that ridiculed President Mugabe. (MISA)

After the introduction of the Access to Information Act,

Peta Thorncroft of the *Daily Telegraph* was arrested on 27 March. She was accused of operating without credentials, being in possession of an unregistered vehicle, and providing 'false information' about President Mugabe. She was released on 31 March. (MISA)

Geoff Nyarota (*Index* 1/2002, 4/2001, 3/2001), editor-in-chief of the *Daily News*, was arrested on 15 April after being accused of fabricating evidence suggesting that the Registrar General, Tobaiwa Mudede, had announced contradictory results during the election. Nyarota was charged under the Access to Information Act but released the same day. (MISA)

On 15 April, chief reporter **Dumisani Muleya** and editor **Iden Wetherell** (*Index* 4/2001) of the *Zimbabwe Independent* were arrested by the Criminal Investigations Department (CID) for 'tarnishing the image of the first lady' with a headline implying her brother had been involved in a bid to take over a local firm. They were later released. (MISA)

Foreign experts trying to uncover any rigging of the election have been repeatedly denied the election roll, weeks after the end of the election, *The Times* reported on 18 April. **Roland Whitehead**, a human rights activist, found 'huge indiscrepancies in voting patterns' with thousands of citizens using fake identity numbers, according to the opposition Movement for Democratic Change (MDC). (*The Times*)

Lloyd Mudiwa and **Collin Chiwanza** of Zimbabwe's only independent newspaper, the *Daily News,* were arrested on 30 April because of a story on the alleged murder of an opposition supporter by Mugabe militants. (MISA)

On 7 May, **Pius Wakatama** was arrested in connection with a 23 April article alleging that the mother of two young girls had been beheaded by Mugabe militants. (MISA)

It was reported on 10 May that **Joy Television** had stopped transmission of a daily news bulletin from the BBC on instructions from the government. (MISA)

Brian Mangwende from the *Daily News* was arrested on 10 May after writing a 'false' story about the working conditions of schoolteachers in rural areas. Mangwende was released after a few hours with no charges. (MISA)

On 7 May, youth supporters of ZANU-PF reportedly banned any press coverage of a rally headed by Morgan Tzvangirai, leader of MDC. Crews from the **Zimbabwe Broadcasting Corporation** (ZBC) and the **Chronicle** crew, both state-owned, were asked to leave by youths manning the gates of the White City Stadium in Bulwayo. (MISA)

Compiled by: James Badcock (North Africa); Ben Carrdus (East Asia) Gully Cragg (Western Europe, North America, Pacific and Australasia); Fiann Coombs (Central Asia and the Caucases); Avery Davis-Roberts (East Asia); Yasmine Gaspard (West Africa); Hanna Gezelius (South-East Asia); Andrew Kendle (India and subcontinent); Sara Laszlo (Eastern Europe); Agustina Lattanzi (South America); Ramsey Nasser (Southern Africa); Gill Newsham (Turkey and Kurdish areas); Ruairi Patterson (UK and Ireland); Shifa Rahman (East Africa); Neil Sammonds (Gulf States and Middle East); Katy Sheppard (Russia, Poland, Ukraine and Baltic States); Mike Yeoman (Central America and Caribbean), with contributions from Vera Rich. Edited by Paul Eedle and co-ordinated by Natasha Schmidt

WWW.INDEXONCENSORSHIP.ORG
CONTACT@INDEXONCENSORSHIP.ORG
TEL: 020 7278 2313 • FAX: 020 7278 1878

SUBSCRIPTIONS (4 ISSUES PER ANNUM)
INDIVIDUALS: BRITAIN £32, US $48, REST OF WORLD £42
INSTITUTIONS: BRITAIN £48, US $80, REST OF WORLD £52
SPEAK TO TONY CALLAGHAN ON 020 7278 2313
OR EMAIL TONY@INDEXONCENSORSHIP.ORG

Index on Censorship (ISSN 0306-4220) is published four times a year by a non-profit-making company: Writers & Scholars International Ltd, Lancaster House, 33 Islington High Street, London N1 9LH. *Index on Censorship* is associated with Writers & Scholars Educational Trust, registered charity number 325003 **Periodicals postage:** (US subscribers only) paid at Newark, New Jersey. Postmaster: send US address changes to *Index on Censorship* c/o Mercury Airfreight International Ltd Inc., 365 Blair Road, Avenel, NJ 07001, USA

 • ISBN 0-904286-89-4